OVERACHIEVEMENT

OVERACHIEVEMENT

The New Model for Exceptional Performance

John Eliot, Ph.D.

PORTFOLIO

PORTFOLIO
Published by the Penguin Group
Penguin Group (USA) Inc., 375 Hudson Street, New York, NY 10014, U.S.A.
Penguin Group (Canada), 10 Alcorn Avenue, Toronto, Ontario, Canada M4V 3B2
(a division of Pearson Penguin Canada Inc.)
Penguin Books Ltd, 80 Strand, London WC2 0RL, England
Penguin Ireland, 25 St Stephen's Green, Dublin 2, Ireland
(a division of Penguin Books Ltd)
Penguin Group (Australia), 250 Camberwell Road, Camberwell, Victoria 3124, Australia
(a division of Pearson Australia Group Pty Ltd)
Penguin Books India Pvt Ltd, 11 Community Centre, Panchsheel Park,
New Delhi – 110 017, India
Penguin Group (NZ), cnr Airbone and Rosedale Roads, Albany, Auckland,
New Zealand (a division of Pearson New Zealand Ltd)
Penguin Books (South Africa) (Pty) Ltd, 24 Sturdee Avenue, Rosebank, Johannesberg
2196, South Africa

Penguin Books Ltd, Registered Offices: 80 Strand, London WC2R 0RL, England

First published in 2004 by Portfolio, a member of Penguin Group (USA) Inc.

1   3   5   7   9   10   8   6   4   2

LIBRARY OF CONGRESS CATALOGING IN PUBLICATION DATA
Eliot, John, 1971–
    Overachievement / John Eliot.
        p.   cm.
    Includes index.
    ISBN 1-59184-055-4
        1. Success—Psychological aspects.   2. Overachievement.   I. Title.
    BF637.S8E3845 2004
    650.1—dc22   2004051959

This book is printed on acid-free paper. ∞

Printed in the United States of America

In Memory of John Sackett and Dr. Tim Simpson,
world champions and exceptional thinkers, both

Acknowledgments

When it comes to support systems, I would wager that there is no greater overachiever than me. Twists of fortune and adventure have blessed me with a truly remarkable collection of fascinating, brilliant, visionary, kindhearted, character-rich compadres. I owe unquantifiable thanks to all of them, to those I have learned from and taught, been pushed by and offered encouragement from, played alongside and battled against.

My sincerest thanks to the exceptional team behind this book:

To the exceptional thinkers who serve as vivid illustrations and lessons throughout this text. To all the coaches, executives, doctors, and performers I've worked with. To Willis Wilson. To my students at Rice.

To renaissance man Edward Tivnan. Without Ed on board early, this project would never have gotten off the ground. His dedication to helping people through great writing is unmatched; his collaboration is indeed priceless.

To the entire all-star squad at Penguin Portfolio. To Adrian Zackheim and Will Weisser for being great thinkers and right on the cutting edge with me. To my editor, Stephanie Land, whose insight helped shape the look and feel of *Overachievement*, and to my assistant editor, Megan Casey.

To my incredible agent, Stephanie Kip Rostan, and everyone at the Levine-Greenberg Agency for their expertise and thoughtfulness, and for helping make this project really sing, all the way from conception to bookstore displays. To office-putting champion Jim Levine.

And finally, my profound thanks:

To my publicist David Hahn, Rick Frischman, and the out-of-the-box team at Planned Television Arts.

To Tony Apollaro and his whole peak-performing family. To John Goff, John Katen, Terry Davison. To the inspirational team at Texas Childrens'. To Martyn Howgill, Dr. Kathryn Stream, Dr. Richard Wainderdi, and Dr. Rick Stasney. To Fayyadh Yusuf, LA, Chip Hay, Shaheen Ladhani, the Simon brothers, the docs from Brown (Dr. Ravi?!), the St. Kitts crew, and Doug Paige for their wit, wisdom, and impact on the world. To the Dartmouth Family and all of its far-reaching branches. To Dr. John Corson.

To Drs. Matt and Kim Combs, Paul Thomas, Fred Paine, the rest of the Blues, and of course Ernie Baker, for writing a few pages of baseball history, for the hours of BP (particularly the Scooby Snacks), and for allowing me a deep connection with the true spirit of human competition. To Kevin Costner and Roy Hobbs.

To Bob and Darlene Rotella.

To my family.

Contents

Part I. Inside the Minds of Overachievers
CHAPTER

Part II. Becoming an Overachiever

Foreword

Dr. Jane has been professor and chairman of the neurosurgery depart-ment at the University of Virginia since 1969, and has won the Cushing Medal, the highest honor granted by the American Association of Neu-rological Surgeons. An international figure in the field, Dr. Jane was the neurosurgeon who treated Christopher Reeve after the tragic 1995 horseback riding accident that left the actor a quadriplegic.

A decade ago, I was invited to sit on a panel at a conference on med-ical education. There was a large audience, perhaps a thousand peo-ple in the room. One of the big controversies of the day in medicine was on the table—the long hours and stress that young interns and residents had to endure. The moderator asked each of us how we ad-dressed the issue of stress in our training programs. My answer was: "I try to raise the stress on my residents to the highest possible level, and if they can't take it, I fire them."

The audience was stunned. Some people began clapping, but many in the room also booed. I was not surprised. Stress and single-minded commitment to work have been demonized not just in medi-cine but throughout the culture. And the antistress forces seem to have won, at least in medical education. Residents are now prohibited by law from working more than eighty hours, though a hospital can petition to extend the work week another eight hours. I wish John Eliot's book had been available during that conference and the subsequent wrangles over "overwork" among young doctors. This book is a welcome antidote to the conventional wisdom among mainstream psychologists that to perform well we must be "relaxed." The good surgeon will be keyed up and full of the kind of nervous energy that is absolutely necessary to spend the hours required to focus on a complicated surgery—and to deal with every possible contingency.

John Eliot knows this. As a psychology academic and college teacher, he is familiar with the extraordinary progress that's been made in the field of neuroscience. Much of his own field research on "high performers" was done watching surgeons work and talking to them about how they thought under pressure (including me, I might add, in the interest of full disclosure). He also spends considerable time these days advising athletes, musicians, and businesspeople on how to transform their talent and training into great work. Dr. Eliot understands why stress is a good thing. He also understands that to be good at surgery—and just about every other complicated career and task under the sun—requires not just training in various techniques but also training in how to use the mind. I agree. My job as a professor of neurosurgery is to teach accomplished and supremely talented young doctors how to think under the gun and in the face of extreme adversity. I do so by creating as tough an environment as possible. If you're training top gun pilots, you don't make things easy for them.

The best in my business also have high levels of what Dr. Eliot calls "overconfidence." I remember starting out, wanting to be a great neurosurgeon. I expect that same dream to be the number one priority in my students' lives, too.

Such single-minded commitment doesn't often sit well with friends, family, or even colleagues. I can now recommend that the naysayers read the chapter in this book on how top performers across the board are inclined to "put all of their eggs in one basket." It's a prime ingredient in becoming the best at what you do. And, as Dr. Eliot explains using anecdotes from business, sports, entertainment, as well as medicine, when you are committed to what you do, when you love it, those eighty-eight-hour work weeks fly right by. One of the hardest parts of my job is to inform my residents who've worked through the night and are bumping up against their weekly time limit that they have to go home. "And miss tomorrow's cases?" they ask. They may be tired, but they do not want to pass up any opportunity to increase their odds of becoming a great neurosurgeon.

To be sure, it's not the way "normal" people go at things. But—and this is central to Dr. Eliot's view of high performance—how do you become extraordinary at what you do by settling for what's normal? If normalcy is your aim in life, then *Overachievement* is not the book for you.

I have been fortunate to work with some very talented people, and there has been nothing normal about them. Some have been my patients. When the actor Christopher Reeve was thrown from his horse at his Virginia farm, he was rushed to my hospital, where I led a team through the critical stabilization procedure. At the time, some did not think that we had done Reeve a favor, including Reeve himself during his darkest moments. But then, against all the scientific evidence to the contrary, he decided that he would devote himself to regaining the ability to walk. That became his all-consuming dream, and Christopher Reeve's dream has revolutionized spinal cord research. His mature realization of his own situation and his empathy for the suffering of everyone else with spinal cord injuries has provoked and inspired a national and international initiative to find a cure.

Reeve's overachievements remind me of a quotation from George Bernard Shaw that my partner, Dr. Neal Kassell, has on his office wall. It's so on the mark for John Eliot's view of performance that I'm surprised he missed it. Let it be my way of making a good book even better:

> *The reasonable man adapts himself to the world. The unreasonable one persists in trying to adapt the world to himself. All progress depends on the unreasonable man.*

If you aspire to push things forward or be the best at your business, if you're wondering how you can maximize your talent, if you're eager for some insight into how the human mind works and why we have now entered what science has dubbed "The Millennium of the Brain," and if you have no problem in being perceived as a bit "unreasonable" or "abnormal," then keep reading.

Dr. John A. Jane, Sr.

Introduction:
The Myths of High Performance

Whose life do you admire the most? Whose phenomenal success do you wish you could call your own? Have you ever wondered what they know that you don't about the path to success? Bill Gates started "fooling around" with computer software when he was a kid just because he loved it; that youthful passion has made him the richest man in the world. Michael Dell dropped out of college, convinced that his one-boy computer company would someday beat IBM, and fifteen years later Dell Computer was the number-one seller of PCs in the world. Against all odds, Carly Fiorina became the first woman to run a Fortune 20 company and then merged it with Compaq, a deal that many said could never work. The super-sized Hewlett-Packard is doing well, and Fiorina is now trying to surpass Dell. When J. Craig Venter, a surfer/Vietnam Vet-turned-scientist, announced in 1998 that he was starting a company to complete the mapping of the human genome in the next three years—and thus faster and more economically than a government-funded consortium of scientists—the biogenetic establishment attacked him as a "publicity machine" that could never deliver. A top biogeneticist warned Congress that the Venter strategy "will encounter catastrophic problems." In February 2001, well ahead of schedule, Venter announced that his Celera Genomics Group had delivered on his promise, opening a treasure trove of knowledge about human physiology and disease. Tiger Woods turned pro at twenty-one and proceeded to win the Masters in his first year by twelve strokes—and then went on to win two more Masters titles and a total of forty championships by the time he was twenty-nine.

What would your career be like if you could handle pressure like Tiger or get rich off one of your passions like Gates? Imagine what you could pull off with Dell's kind of confidence or Fiorina's steely commitment. How great would it be to pursue your wildest dreams like J. Craig Venter and show up all the naysayers in the process, not to mention earning hundreds of millions of dollars that would allow you to pursue your work unimpeded by the conventional wisdom of your field? Or maybe there's someone in your company or line of work who never ceases to impress you—your boss, a colleague, even the competition. Or maybe it's an old friend or family member who, no matter what job or challenge he or she takes on, always seems to come out on top without even breaking a sweat.

This book can help you be one of them, and boost you into the ranks of great overachievers.

Simply put, all of the above may perform like Superman, but they are not genetic freaks; they represent what we all *could* be. As smart as Bill Gates and Michael Dell might be about the personal computer business, they'd be the first to concede they have people working for them who know a lot more about computers than they do. Carly Fiorina may run one of the world's most prestigious technology companies, but by her own account she is "not a technologist," never mind a talented one; Fiorina majored in philosophy and medieval studies in college. When Venter founded Celera, scientists from the nation's best universities—with $3 billion in federal backing—had already logged years of research to decipher only three percent of the sixty thousand or so genes of human DNA. And yes, Tiger Woods is a divinely gifted golfer, but in every state in the nation there is some big strong guy who can hit a golf ball farther and a teenage girl who is a better putter. Natural talent and intelligence can certainly make life a lot easier. But neither is the measure of most major careers. Nor is luck. Whoever it is that you admire most is, in fact, a lot more like you than you might expect.

Except for one thing: They *think* differently. When the whistle blows, when the chips are down, when the deal is on the table, when they step into the limelight, they are in a special mindset. What turns ordinary people into overachievers is the way they use their minds when they are called upon to perform. And in case you think that only athletes, musicians, actors, and other entertainers "perform," you should know that any time you engage in your work, you are performing; any time you are not alone or talking to yourself, regardless of your profession, you are performing in public. To be as successful as you can be as a performer, you will need a performer's head. That is what this book is for—not to show you how to act but to teach you how to *think*.

This book is to help you regear your mind so that you can perform at your absolute best, take your game to the *next* level, and become better at what you do. But I will not be giving my intuitions or hunches about high performance; this book is not a write-up of what works for me or my list of favorite psychological tips. Everything that follows is based on scientific research that can help you improve your game no matter what you do, just as it has helped the hundreds of students and clients I've worked with over the past decade.

Overachievement is within the reach of every man, woman, and child. But not overnight. I can't wave my magic wand and instantly turn you into Tiger Woods or Bill Gates. You might be able to get a pill to decrease your weight, another to improve your sexual performance, and a third to wash away depression. But I cannot hand you a pill that will suddenly endow you with the mind of an overachiever. It doesn't work that way. There are no true "giant steps" or "seven steps" to success; I do not have a surefire, sixty-second recipe for achievement. Frankly, I believe that such prepackaged goal setting can be an *obstacle* to high performance, along with a lot of the other conventional formulae and techniques found in popular books, audiotapes, and videos about what psychologists call "peak performance." I want to show you why you should avoid that stuff; I want to show you how overachievement really happens and arm you to get there yourself—free of the psychological hocus pocus—to become, at last, the consistent overachiever you always knew you could be.

One of the most ragged clichés in sports is the importance of "the mental game"; that players who are psychologically prepared will have an edge on competitors who might be more physically gifted. Like most clichés, it's absolutely true. So, over the past twenty years, clinical psychologists have jumped into the sports arena, offering to help people work on their mental games by teaching techniques of "stress management," "goal setting," "visualization," and "self-talk." Olympic and professional athletes who have actually experienced performing at their peak, or who realized they were stuck on the second string, were quick to consult with these clinicians about how they might enhance their games. Professional sports teams added psychologists to their payrolls. And since sports is such an irresistible metaphor among business executives, many of them former high school or college athletes, Fortune 500 companies began hiring psychologists to teach their top executives the mental fitness tricks of great athletes. Articles were written and a shelf-load of books was published by self-proclaimed "world authorities" promising to teach everyone the same techniques that the pros were using to get the "psychological edge" or to have "mental toughness." Millions of Americans have bought these books, and keep buying them. You may be among them.

So why isn't everyone walking around in the Zone?

Armed with their quick-fix potions, psychologists and "performance coaches" have been propagating what I call *The Myths of High Performance*:

1. Use Your Head
2. Relax
3. Know Your Limits
4. Set Goals
5. Work Hard
6. Don't Put All Your Eggs in One Basket
7. Don't Be Overconfident
8. Be a Team Player
9. Learn from Your Mistakes
10. Minimize Your Risks

To each of these reasonable, sensible, rational pieces of advice, I say, "Absolute horse hockey." Such self-improvement balderdash will do nothing but relegate you to a career in mediocrity. Overachievers don't think reasonably, sensibly, or rationally. If your wish in life is to fit in with the crowd, then this is not the book for you.

Overachievement is aimed at people who want to maximize their potential. And to do that, I insist that you throw caution to the wind, ignore the pleas of parents, coaches, spouses, and bosses to be "realistic." Realistic people do not accomplish extraordinary things because the odds against success stymie them. The best performers ignore the odds. I will show that instead of limiting themselves to what's probable, the best will pursue the heart-pounding, exciting, really big, difference-making dreams—so long as catching them might be *possible*.

If you're really serious about being an overachiever, bag the bromides and listen up . . .

Using your head is stupid. In high-stakes performance, the real genius is someone like Yogi Berra. On his way to ten World Series rings and a place in the baseball Hall of Fame, Yogi was thinking about *nothing*.

The best embrace stress—and get juiced. Classic breathing and relaxation techniques tend to undermine most performances, eliminating the possibility of setting records. Stress is the high-level performer's PowerBar.

There are no limits. If you really want to find out what you're capable of, you cannot put limits on yourself, and you definitely cannot be cautious.

Setting goals is for couch potatoes. The long-standing practice of goal setting is actually a major obstacle to sustained, vigorous motivation—and to being great.

Hard work is overrated. Superstars know when to stop working at their job and start playing at it. In my research and work with clients, I have discovered that too much practice will turn you into a classic case of the "over-motivated *under*achiever."

All those eggs belong in one basket. Unlikely accomplishments are borne out of single-minded purposefulness. Future superstars don't get there by keeping part of their heart in reserve.

Arrogant S.O.B.s run the world. A performer can never have too much self-assurance. The best in every field are likely to strike most people as irrationally confident, but that's how they got to the top.

Being a team player may get you a gold star on your annual review, but it won't get you into the corner office. By definition, striving to be exceptional puts you outside the team. If you're a maverick CEO, you're a colorful genius. But if you're a young rogue exec, you're gone. ("Not a team player," reads your evaluation.) The best performers not only think exceptionally, they teach their colleagues to think differently, too.

Legends never say they're sorry. Having a long or frequent memory for mistakes and a short or infrequent memory for successes is a guaranteed way to develop fear of failure. High achievers dwell on what they do well and spend very little time evaluating themselves and their performances.

Risk-reward analysis is for wimps. For exceptional people, risks *equal* rewards. The challenge of uncertainty is the fun of high performance and where overachievement lies.

My counterprescriptions for high performance make some people uncomfortable; they certainly go against the grain. But top performers do not generate fame and fortune—or fervent happiness, for that matter—by following the conventional wisdom or striving to be "normal." They certainly have not reached their heights by reading pop psychology books or going to "personal power" rallies. Can you picture Muhammad Ali or Joe Namath taking notes at a Tony Robbins seminar? Or Warren Buffet or George Soros, never mind such buccaneer entrepreneurs as Ted Turner or Richard Branson?

In fact, most sport psychologists and performance coaches do not know what to make of such strange characters; their ability to succeed stands outside the understanding of mainstream psychology. Largely based on the medical model, the field of psychology has focused its research on health—being well adjusted, normal, mainstream.* Clinicians are schooled in diagnosing psychological "problems." Their training and careers are spent searching for abnormality and removing it. Not surprisingly, they view performance through the same lens. But great performers are, by definition, *abnormal*; they strive throughout their entire careers to separate themselves from the pack. What this means is that traditional "health" psychology has actually been pushing performers in the wrong direction!

My aim is to push you in the right direction to help you achieve your full potential. Of course, I am not the first person to make such a promise. But I intend to be the first to actually deliver the only book on "peak performance" you will ever need. I know that may strike some as a brash claim. But I also know from years of scientific research, university teaching, and working with top athletes—and heart surgeons, musicians, salesmen, financial experts, business executives of all stripes, even astronauts—that to perform at the top, to be consistently good at what you do when the stakes are high, then get even better over time, requires not a set of psychological techniques or exercises to "fix" your head but a mindset that would strike most people as absolutely certifiable. So count me as "overconfident" and "crazy," and then understand that in this book, I will teach you to be quite abnormal, too.

* * *

*Until just recently. In a landmark 1998 address, Martin Seligman, a University of Pennsylvania psychologist who is a former president of the American Psychological Association, criticized the field for being "too preoccupied with repairing damage when our focus should be on building strength and resilience, especially in children." Innovative programs to study positive and performance psychology are starting to spring up at leading universities, although they are still in their infancy.

I have been fascinated by human performance since I was a little kid mad for sports. My father, Rick Eliot, a coach for the U.S. Olympic Ski team in Squaw Valley in 1960, was a human performance pioneer, always looking for new physical, technical, and psychological ways to make his skiers go faster. An avid competitive cross-country skier and ski jumper, I was an eager guinea pig. At Dartmouth, I played baseball and rugby and spent a lot of time trying out new techniques promoted by "sport psychologists" to improve my performance on the field. The results I got were not so impressive, but I did receive plenty of joking from my college roommate, John Goff, who had a top-notch mental game that contributed to his excellence on the field and court. In my senior year, I began my own research into the psychology of human performance, conducting laboratory and field tests on awareness, concentration, and motor tasks under stressful circumstances. I soon realized that many popular techniques promoted by mainstream psychologists not only failed to give the performance edge they promised, in many cases they actually *hindered* performance.

I decided to continue my research at the University of Virginia for a doctorate in human performance under Dr. Bob Rotella, one of the few psychologists whose work was cutting against the conventional wisdom. Rotella had been working for years with professional golfers to increase their confidence and concentration under pressure, his success based on his athletic instincts that high-pressure performers should learn how to "trust their swing"—the extraordinary ability that made them champions in the first place.

It was the early 1990s and the buzz in the field was over a widely acclaimed new take on optimal experience that one eminent psychologist had branded "flow"—"a mental state in which nothing seems to matter," where time and space seem to disappear. This sounded like the fabled "Zone" that athletes talked about. Curious to see how this squared with Rotella's practical success and my own research on how far from the psychological norm top performers seemed to be, I decided to go back into the lab and the field to examine the concept of flow as it applied to elite performance in medicine, business, Olympic competition, and other pursuits as diverse as composing music and training astronauts. My results were surprising: This latest theory of high performance did not square any better with how the very best in every business operated under pressure than any of the previous popular explanations I had tested.

For the next four years, while teaching at Virginia and working with elite athletes, surgeons, and executives, I watched in dismay as self-proclaimed "world's leading experts" continued to promote the same techniques and prescriptions I knew didn't hold up in demanding performance settings. They were wearing people out with demands to complete forms describing their psychological states and evaluating their performances.

As I did more consulting, I began to notice that performers with the best natural instincts for consistently succeeding under pressure—Dallas Cowboy legend Emmitt Smith and Merrill Lynch V.P. Dean Trindle, to cite two different examples—were inclined to find any excuse they could to be absent the day the psychologist came to speak. When I asked them why, their answer was essentially the same: Whenever they listened to psychologists in the past, they ended up performing worse, not better. I find that many of my new clients seek me out to undo the effects of traditional psychological techniques or self-help books. To improve, they know they need something different.

I teach them to think exceptionally—to be quite abnormal by most standards of performance, and to love being so *exception*-al. Becoming an exceptional thinker is not easy. A few lucky performers seem to switch on exceptional thinking at will. The rest of us have to learn how to do it, though a 12-step program or a series of introspective pencil-and-paper psychological exercises will not do the trick. Most of what passes as "self-improvement" proposes to hand over exactly what you need: one size fits all, a cure. But no one else's roadmap to success will get you there; the myths of high performance will only get in your way.

As an experienced performance psychologist, I can educate you about the ways that top performers use their minds; I can bring you up to date on what science knows about how the brain operates under pressure. But I cannot flip a switch for you that will change how your mind works when you're under the gun. And while I know that to be a top performer you have to be passionately committed to what you're doing and insanely confident about your ability to pull it off, I cannot make you a personal gift of commitment or self-confidence. All the great performers I have worked with are fueled by a personal dream, but how can I give you the kind of feeling that launches you out of bed every morning, incredibly fired up to get to work? No amount of book learning or lectures or even the best graduate education on the planet will make you a great surgeon, business executive, or athlete. We all have to take what we have learned and personally put it to use—formulate it for *our* solutions, for the direction *we* want to go.

What I can give you is a *model* for high performance and the direction to adapt the model in a way that works for you. This book describes how the minds of top performers actually work under pressure and explains the science of the performer's mindset. I will help you learn high-performance thinking and then help you to ingrain it so that when you step into the spotlight, your performer's mindset will always drive the results. That's what this book is for—to provide you with ideas and methods that will allow *you* to remake your mind to improve your game, no matter what you do. *Overachievement* is my effort to put the *self* back into *self-improvement*.

Underlying my approach are a couple of psychological givens:

- Thinking is a habit, and like any other habit, it can be changed; it just takes effort and repetition.
- Everyone is born with the ability to develop an *exceptional* mind. You just need to decide to think differently and not care that people will say you're crazy—that is, until they realize that when the game is on the line, you are the one who always delivers.

Before we go any further, you should know that I will never claim to be a guru or "world's leading" anything, and I strongly advise you to stay away from anyone who promises perfection or claims they have "the answer." In fact, in my first lecture every year for my "Psychology of Performance" class at Rice, I put up a slide featuring my academic and professional credentials. I make it absurdly clear to the class that their teacher is someone with an impressive pedigree who knows his stuff. After all, isn't that why they've signed up for my course? Then (in a manner I learned from Bob Rotella), I go around the room, indiscriminately pointing to students: "You there, in the first row—you've got it! You're going to succeed, big time. You over there, you don't have it. You don't either," I say, picking someone else at random. "I know talent, and you don't have it." I point at someone else: "You ought to drop out of school. You ought to think about a different career, maybe even switch majors . . ." As I anoint certain students for fame and fortune and banish others to the bush leagues or a life of boring mediocrity, my students look at me with a combination of amusement and horror. "Look," I point out, "I have made a career of knowing what success looks like, right?"

After I ratchet up the shock significantly, I explain that anyone in the room who thinks I can predict their future has already broken the first rule of my class: Do not look at me as an expert. And that goes for you, too. Why? Because I do not know your specific situation. I certainly do not know anything about your dreams or your motivation, how big your heart is or how tough your fortitude. I can't tell that by looking at you, or even by reading your "file." I don't have a clue how you think under pressure. I have no idea how you handle either success or failure. And while many so-called experts act as if there were some kind of objective psychological profile for success—tall, good-looking extrovert with an Ivy League degree, etc.—no such measure exists. Proof: Look around at the hordes of Ivy League alumni populating middle management throughout corporate America. Then count the college dropouts who have invented the world's most creative projects or are running the most innovative companies.

What I do is a more inductive kind of thing. The extent of my expertise comes from the experience I have in seeing how people deal with pressure, success, and failure, noting how the most successful and enduring performers operate, and then factoring this information into what psychology knows about how the mind works under pressure. When clients come to me and ask, "What should I do to improve?" my answer is always, "I have no idea." I try to startle them to illustrate that the kind of guidance I provide varies depending on the kind of person they might be, how they work, what they want to achieve, and how much they want it. My job is to assess their current modes of thinking—motivation, confidence, focus, response to pressure and adversity, and so forth—compared to how they used to operate, and then help them either (a) get back to their old, high-performing selves or (b) develop ways to think more successfully than they have in the past.

This book will help you make the same assessment and then help you shift your thinking toward consistent overachievement. In Part I, I will take you inside the minds of great performers to see how they think and operate—how they manage to thrive on pressure and confound the critics with their ability not just to talk a great game, but to play it as well. Included in this story are the basic biology and chemistry underlying high performance. We are learning more about the neuroscience of human performance every day. I offer this science not to impress or confuse you but to *encourage* you. Virtually every self-improvement "guru" out there is offering advice that has no scientific backing. To be sure, Tony Robbins and infomercial hound Brian Tracy, who peddles hundreds of self-help products and books late at night—from *21 Secrets to Success* to *The Psychology of Selling* and *Million Dollar Habits*—have gotten rich telling people how to get rich. But it is *personal* advice based only on their experience (or worse, simply an analysis of what people will buy). If it doesn't work for you, you will have no way of knowing why because it has no basis in science. I am offering ways to change how you think and perform that are easy to learn and practice, that are scientifically sustainable, and that will have a measurable impact on how you live and work, because they are based on what we now know about how the human mind fundamentally operates under pressure.

Learning some neuroscience also has a psychological advantage: It's too easy to look at a superstar in your field and conclude that natural-born talents are the only measure of a person's success. But ordinary people accomplish extraordinary things all the time, in every field, just by learning how to exploit the potential of the human mind. Every one of us is wired to succeed to the best of our ability; we humans, for example, are designed not just to cope with pressure but to thrive on it, using it as a psychological energy bar that fuels our daily performances to greater heights. I will show you how and why in Part I.

In Part II, I will offer some tools to help you learn and, more importantly, practice how to access the overachiever's mindset. I will show you how you, too, can consistently achieve the kind of intense focus that marks all the best performers in every field. I will show you how to reshape your thinking so you will be able to trust your skills and experiences and then let 'em rip—to perform so freely and intensely that you will become not just good at what you do, but something of an artist at it.

The practical result is the prospect of finding what you really want to do in life and achieving the kind of commitment and confidence to take on the challenge and make it happen. The only remaining assessment is this: Do you *want* to be an exceptional performer, an overachiever? Are you willing to make some changes to the way you think? If you are, read on. Take notes in the margins about how each story, illustration, and element of science applies to you and your particular situation. Then put the application into practice. You'll be well on your way to a new level of talent and you'll have a blast getting there, breaking out of old, ineffective habits and tendencies that have been holding you back.

PART I

Inside the Minds of Overachievers

CHAPTER 1

"The Trusting Mindset"
(Or How to Think Like a Squirrel)

In the 1976 Winter Olympics at Innsbruck, Austrian Alpine skier Franz Klammer took home gold with a final run that skiers still talk about with awe. No competitor had yet been able to catch the leader and defending Olympic champion, Bernhard Russi of Switzerland; numerous times, officials had to halt the skiing due to dangerous, icy conditions on the course, and even though the final event had the green light, the course still seemed too slick to permit the kind of double-poling usually required for a fast start. Klammer, however, skated hard out of the gate, double-poling wildly. The ice didn't give way, throwing his weight to one ski. To regain his balance, he tried to shift to the other ski. He lost his balance in the *other* direction.

The key to winning in Alpine is to run the straightest line from start to finish, staying in a low, aerodynamic tuck while keeping your skis gliding flat, almost frictionless over the hill. Klammer was anything but aerodynamic. He whipped around the sheered corners first on one leg then on the other, clipping gates, just missing the out-of-bounds fences, his arms and feet flailing, his skis slipping and clattering as he hurtled down the mountain.

Most ski fans were praying for Klammer not to get killed. His own coach, Toni Sailer, later commented, "I closed my eyes and thought this was the end of the gold medal. I only dared reopen them when I didn't hear the sound of a crash."

Somehow defying physics, Klammer barreled over the finish line, careening to a stop, snow flying. He barely avoided piling into the crowd of fifty thousand who all seemed to be waving red and white Austrian flags. Klammer looked for the scoreboard: Russi 1:46.06. Klammer 1:45.73—the fastest time of the day and the gold medal!

The press was all over him. ABC's *Wide World of Sports*, famous for dramatizing spectacles such as the "Agony of Defeat," wanted to know:

"How in the world did you do that?"

"What?" said the gold medal winner, a battery of microphones stuck in his face.

"WIN!"

"Well, I'm a pretty good skier, you know," replied the charismatic Austrian with a wink.

"No, how did you clock such a fast time with such a terrible run?"

"What do you mean *terrible?* I think gold's a pretty good color."

One journalist pointed out that he was clearly off balance, his arms wind-milling, catching too much air yet somehow managing to ski faster than competitors who turned in nearly perfect runs. Then came the classic reporter's question: "What was going through your mind?"

"What was going through my mind?" Klammer repeated, as if trying to understand what the guy was getting at. "Nothing. I was just trying to get there [pointing to the finish line]. Fast!" Evidently Klammer was not thinking about the correct line down the course or the proper technique to maintain flat skis. He wasn't thinking about gold medals, either. Franz Klammer was just racing. Where? To the finish line.

But how did he do that?

How did he manage to keep skiing without thinking the same things that all the "average" performers (and reporters) in the audience were thinking—that he would break a leg or eat a gate or surely lose his number-one World Cup ranking? How did he keep from thinking about crashing? Those are the kind of questions I would have asked Franz Klammer at Innsbruck because the answers provide the secret of high-stakes performance not only in sports but also for actors, musicians, business executives, doctors, and performers in every other field that requires someone to step into the limelight and excel under pressure. How do they *not* think about all the distractions and possible outcomes and the details of a given performance when they're under the gun?

Fortunately, over the past decade as a student and teacher of performance psychology, and now also as a professional adviser to performers in many different fields, I have been able ask hundreds of other talented men and women how their minds work under pressure. I have found that the top players in every field think differently when all the marbles are on the line. Great performers focus on what they are doing, and nothing else. When Tiger Woods or Muhammad Ali cannot seem to make a false move, when Warren Buffet or Bill Gates is in the middle of a deal, when Yitzhak Perlman or Al Pacino blows the critics away with a performance, they are not thinking about their technique, what their teachers told them, what their attorneys or accountants advised. They are able to engage in a task so completely that there is no room left for self-criticism, judgment, or doubt; to stay loose and supremely, even irrationally, self-confident; to just step up and do what they're good at, concentrating only on the simplest nature of their performance. Superstars perform so naturally and so instinctively that they seem to be able to enter a pressure-packed situation that would terrify or freeze most people as if nothing matters. They let it happen, let it go. They couldn't care less about the results.

As we say in performance psychology, "They play with their eyes." They just look at the target and shoot. And the ball goes in, the deals get closed, the stage performance is thrilling. Often, in my opinion, the results are works of art. Asking Franz Klammer to re-create that gold medal run would be like begging Leonardo to paint another *Mona Lisa*. It just doesn't work that way.

The good news: Research and experimentation have proven that this kind of exceptional thinking is within everyone's reach. But before you can master this superstar's mindset, you first must understand why, when people ask great performers like Franz Klammer, "What was going on in your mind?" they are inclined to answer, "Nothing."

Journalists and fans tend to take such responses as displays of arrogance or coyness, or as rehearsed sound bites. But the neurobiology of high performance actually confirms Klammer's answer: What he was thinking at a cognitive level was truly "nothing."

To be sure, great performers are well trained, experienced, smart, and, in some cases, divinely talented. But the way their brains work during a performance is a lot more like a squirrel's than like Einstein's. Like squirrels, the best in every business do what they have learned to do without questioning their abilities—they flat out trust their skills, which is why we call this high-performance state of mind the "Trusting Mindset." Routine access to the Trusting Mindset is what separates great performers from the rest of the pack. By all accounts, being free to turn your skills loose under the gun is an intoxicating feeling. The source of that sensation, however, and the ability to do it, is hardwired in every one of us. In fact, you've probably already experienced the Trusting Mindset, without even knowing it.

"As If It Doesn't Matter . . ."

If I were in the room with you right now—about six feet away—I'd ask you to toss your car keys to me. You'd be able to handle that, right? In fact, I bet that if I asked you to do it six times in a row without any other instruction, you'd toss those keys right at me, chest-high, every time. I'm pretty sure about the result because I perform this experiment every year in my class by tossing my car keys to students, and having them return the toss. Sometimes I use a whiteboard marker or an eraser (if I don't want them running off for a joyride). But whatever the instrument, they toss it back perfectly every single time. If you're like my students, you'll be thinking: "What's so amazing about throwing a set of keys to someone six feet away? That's not hard."

You're right. Key-tossing is a skill that we all seem to have. I bet you could do it sidearm, left-handed or right, even behind your back. Tossing an object a few feet is so easy that, as the saying goes, *we don't even think about it.* To perform exceptionally—whether it's hitting a golf ball pure, closing a critical deal, pulling off a big sale, moving an audience with a violin concerto, or even transplanting a heart—requires you to be in that same state of mind, empty of all doubt, without any thought about the mechanics of what you're doing. You cannot pull up all those years of education, training, and experience in your memory as you perform—that's the "Training" Mindset. In the Trusting Mindset, you have to *let* all that expertise be there instinctively. Our ability is maximized when we let our skills do the work, not our heads. As professional golfers like to say, you have to trust your swing. You just have to toss the keys—pure Trusting Mindset.

The results of putting the Trusting Mindset into play are never disappointing. Anyone who has experienced its astonishing benefits is eager to figure out how to tap back into it, making it the Holy Grail of high-stakes performance. Unfortunately, people tend to devote too much time to thinking critically and evaluating themselves. In my teaching and consulting, I have found that people get it better once they understand more about how their brains actually work under different circumstances.

The Neurobiology of High Performance

You can break down the Training and Trusting Mindsets into an almost bipolar set of descriptors. Take a look at the following chart:

THE TRAINING MINDSET	THE TRUSTING MINDSET
Active Mind	Empty Mind
Judgmental	Accepting
Analytical	Instinctive
Scientific	Artistic
Wanting It Now	Patient
Calculating	Reacting
Effortful	Playful
Critical	Quiet
Intentional	Rhythmic
Controlling	Letting It Happen

These contrasting qualities of thinking, which produce different performances, also depend on a different neurobiology—as different, in fact, as you and a squirrel running across a telephone wire! When you stand fifty feet in the air at the top of a telephone pole and look at the infinitesimally thin wire you're trying to cross, a million thoughts are likely to race through your head: I'll never make it; it's too far; it's too high; the wire's too small, too unsteady; I can't balance on this thing; I'll kill myself; this is crazy; it has nothing to do with "real courage"; and so on. The squirrel, on the other hand, just scurries across the wire without thinking. Of course, that's because squirrels cannot think. Their sensory system receives sights, sounds, tastes, smells, and touches. Their brains are able to process this information, act accordingly, and execute skillful patterns of behavior. The human brain can do all of this, but it can also complicate matters: We can evaluate the sensory information and the situation, analyzing all the angles, and then intentionally train ourselves to improve our performance—all qualities of the Training Mindset. This ability to reason, evaluate, and make rational calculations is what separates us from other animals, and surely such rationality is a blessing in life—except when you are performing under pressure. Then you want to put aside the Training Mindset and respond to the stimuli bombarding you as much like a squirrel as is humanly possible. Squirrels are natural masters of the Trusting Mindset.

I want to help you find your inner squirrel. Consider that moment in a physical examination when the doctor taps your knee with his reflex hammer and your foot kicks straight out, reflexively (i.e., without a thought). It's called a "myotatic" or "flexor reflex," and the neurobiology goes like this: The blow of the hammer compresses a sensory nerve in the knee, altering its chemical structure, which, in a chain reaction, sends an electrical signal along the nerve up to the lumbar section of the spinal cord. This ascending nerve connects to a parallel descending *motor* nerve that dispatches the electrical signal down to the muscle group that causes the leg to extend. If you're sitting on the examination table and the doctor taps your knee without warning, your foot will actually kick out even before your brain gets the signal that the doctor is armed with a hammer. Neuroscientists call this chemical-electrical response "closed loop information processing." (Mention that to your doctor during your next physical—he'll be impressed.)

The classic flexor reflex is a human response that is far less complex than the neurobiology of a squirrel scurrying across a telephone wire. There are actually four types of closed loop processes:

1. Monosynaptic Reflexes (the flexor reflex), which are the shortest and quickest, involving the fewest neurons
2. Multisynaptic Reflexes, organized through spinal cord interneurons (e.g., responding to stepping on a piece of glass accidentally, or picking up a scalding cup of coffee)
3. Brainstem Regulatory Functions (such as controlling the heart and lungs)
4. Patterned Intentional Behavior, organized in the thalamus (the same kind of processing the squirrel is using)

With each progressively more complicated function, more neurons and more neural junctions are involved. Of the human body's roughly 100 billion nerve cells, the flexor reflex needs only *two* to function properly. Higher level closed processes, such as those at the brain stem or thalamus, might use a couple hundred thousand. The cerebral cortex, however—home of conscious thought, judgment, reason, and calculation—needs billions of nerves to do its thing. Information processing that occurs on that level, the Training Mindset, is called *"open* loop"—open, literally, to interpretation. Once the cerebral cortex gets involved, the transfer from incoming sensory data to outgoing action is influenced by any number of brain areas adding input, thus slowing down the system, impeding behavior efficiency, and increasing the chance of error.*

The squirrel essentially has no cerebral cortex. But the animal does have a thalamus, a bunch of clusters of neurons in the brain, or ganglia, called pattern generators. These produce programmed activity in response to stimuli. It's the highest level closed loop processing available to the brain. The squirrel runs across the wire or finds food by executing ingrained instincts—trusting them, so to speak. The signal comes in, gets turned into a pattern in the thalamus, and a response is sent out. If the wind is blowing the wire to and fro, that sensory stimulus is sent to the squirrel's thalamus, which modifies the motor pattern sent out to allow the squirrel to react to the change and stay balanced on the wire. With no influence from the cerebral cortex, the squirrel is not distracted by any complex assessment of information, and thus sticks with a closed loop process—with virtually no misplaced steps, loss of balance, or fatal falls.

We humans can assure a similar kind of closed processing by taking our cerebral cortex out of the game, as it were, and allowing ourselves to react to sensory stimuli with motor responses we have already stored. The star basketball player looks at the rim and shoots. No evaluating the distance, no decisions about how high to extend the shooting arm over a defender, how much to flick the wrist for per-

---

*The Bliss-Bodder theorem in neuroscience teaches us that there is a positive correlation between the number of neurons involved in performing and the potential for mistakes.

fect rotation, or what the consequence might be if the shot misses. No thinking period. Neurologically, the sensory information shoots up the spine to the thalamus into a central pattern generator—the "superior colliculous" is the one in charge of the kind of motor skills used in basketball—where it is organized, transferred to descending neurons, and sent back to cause the arms and hands to do what a basketball player has trained his arms and hands to do. In other words, *look and shoot*. For the star basketball player, it's as instinctive as it is for a squirrel, executed the same way as tossing a set of keys.

Unless you are distracted by external sensations or your inner critic, conscious thought will convert these to open loop operations. Once the cerebral cortex is activated, the system begins to look a lot like a California freeway at rush hour (particularly like intersections referred to as "spaghetti junctions")—millions of neurons releasing multiple kinds of neurotransmitters into hundreds of synaptic junctions all at the same time and converging at the same pattern generator (or worse, simultaneously at conflicting pattern generators). It is up to the brain to figure out where all the signals should go. When the cerebral cortex gets very active—all that reasoning and evaluating that goes with the Training Mindset—the brain's pattern generators get overloaded and thus the system gets bogged down, producing less efficient, less successful action, with a greater number of mistakes. In short, you don't perform with your "A game."

But you are still capable of being a skilled "truster." As the experiment showed, we are born key-tossers. Tossing a set of keys seems to require no thought; it's very squirrel-like. The consequences are minimal, so we don't bother to use our cerebral cortex. We just act, and thus the thalamus produces whatever pattern it has stored via a closed loop. But if I told a large group to come back next week for one chance to toss that same set of keys into my hand, chest-high—this time for a $1 million prize to the most accurate tosser—enter open loop processing. Things would likely turn scientific; people would start practicing. A few contestants would surely find a way to sneak into the room at night to get in some repetitions on the "game field." They'd set up video cameras to help them work on their key-tossing techniques. "Did I keep my wrist square with the target? Was my elbow aligned for the optimum toss?" I wouldn't be surprised if people started going to the gym to get into shape.

What was a simple, "minimal synaptic" task, not to mention a fun game, is now difficult and filled with potential for anxiety. Once the pressure is on, people try to toss a set of keys across a room and end up choking. Imagine if we turned key-tossing into a college sport with full-ride scholarships. Summer key-tossing camps for kids would appear. Coaches would pop up around the country, charging sixty-five dollars an hour for private lessons. How-to books would hit the display shelves at Barnes & Noble. Before you knew it, Fox Sports would sign an exclusive TV contract; Nike would buy rights to print their logo on the keys; and depending on the genius of the promoters and advertisers, we'd be on the way to forty million people watching the "World Series" of key-tossing.

If you think that's crazy, remember that the multibillion dollar professional sports industry evolved from games invented by kids in backyards and sandlots. And then consider the rapidly increasing popularity of the X Games (professional skateboarding, sky diving, and street luge). And there are those lumberjack championships on ESPN, in which men and women compete against each other, sawing massive logs. I recently read of people training for an annual hot-dog eating contest in New York City, featuring a point spread, performance enhancing drug accusations, instant replay review, and a two-time champion who has turned his wins into more than $150,000. But it's still just eating hot dogs—or skateboarding, or chopping down trees. What has changed is the mindset. That instinctive, free-wheeling, "What's the big deal?" *trusting* attitude has been replaced by an analytical, critical, evaluative, "there's a fortune hanging on this toss so I better make sure I've got it right" *training* approach to performance.

Superstars do not think that way. When it's go time, when it really counts, technique is not on their minds. Like a child playing tag or kicking a soccer ball against a backboard, they give their skills free reign and do not focus on anything but the target of that particular moment. Or in the words of the three-time defending hot-dog eating champion

Takeru "The Tsunami" Kobayashi, weighing in at a mere 145 pounds: "I was standing right next to him [6 feet, 5 inch, four-hundred pound foe Eric "Badlands" Booker], but I was too focused on my game. I didn't want to suffer the mistakes I had made in the past, where I was looking around to see what everyone was doing. It was just me and the dogs."

That is the Trusting Mindset at work, albeit for the curious honor of eating a "world record" fifty and one-half hot dogs in twelve minutes. ("The Tsunami" won his third title in a row in 2004, beating Booker again—and two other four hundred pounders.)

When the job is on the line, great thinkers resist the urge to be smart, cautious, or scientific. They manage to keep their cerebral cortex off the playing field or out of the boardroom. For them, performance is simply "child's play," which suggests a useful definition of the superstar's edge:

The Trusting Mindset is what you were in before you knew any better.

The Feel of It

Athletes who've actually been in the Trusting Mindset are notoriously inarticulate about what happened. Franz Klammer could not get much beyond the description that "nothing" was going on in his mind. Most athletes tend to stress how little control they try to exert—"I was playing out of my mind" is a common description—while they let their skills simply take over. Similarly, astronauts, pilots, and well-trained soldiers who have performed superhuman feats with their lives on the line talk about being a little concerned at first—"and then my skills kicked in." Actors and musicians tend to talk about it in spiritual terms: "I was in the present." "I stayed in the moment." Some performers have described an almost out-of-body experience in which playing the role or the music comes so easily that they have the feeling of hovering over their own performance, feeding off the audience's response, watching themselves like an external observer.

And while the press has not quite gotten to asking wizard entrepreneurs, CEOs, heart surgeons, or other highly successful business executives what it felt like to score big under pressure, I have, and their answers are pretty much the same as what I have heard from the many athletes and musicians I have worked with or interviewed: They were so totally involved in what they were doing that they can remember only the feel of the performance; they weren't cautiously thinking through their steps or evaluating themselves.

I think you know the feeling. Go back to key-tossing, to that sense of doing something that doesn't really count, the freedom of performing like a kid at play. Nothing is riding on throwing the keys, so you just let them go, and perfectly every time. Here's another example I like. It's one that former college football coach and NFL Super Bowl champion Jimmy Johnson used to help his players play with more abandon, and which I now use in my class:

> *Put a two-by-four board on the floor*
> *and walk from one end to the other.*

It is not hard. Not one of my students has ever fallen off the board. If you videotape yourself doing this exercise, you will see that your foot hits the middle of the board every step of the way, as if you were walking down the street. Your eyes just look past the board at the far end, to where you're going, and your feet just move.

> *Now suspend that board thirty feet in the air*
> *and walk from one end to the other.*

It's a lot harder. I suspect that your form would change: You'd inch along, maybe extend your arms for balance, look down at the board or the ground below. Or maybe you'd stand at one end and say, "No way!"

Yet the process it takes to walk across that board—on the ground or thirty feet in the air—is exactly the same. Even for the midair walk, all you have to do is look at the other end and go, as if you were walking down the street (or walking along the board as if it were on the ground). Theoretically. Practically, it's a different matter. And this, I believe, illustrates the *feeling* that accompanies the Trusting Mindset perfectly. A tightrope walker is in a Trusting Mindset in an environment where everything screams: "Watch out! Be careful, gauge every step, get back in the *Training* Mindset!"

The difference between circus performers and the rest of us is that they have trained themselves to perform just like squirrels and step onto a sky-high, swaying wire, effortlessly and simply, as if out on an afternoon stroll.

Speeding Toward the Bottom Line

It is easy to see how this kind of trusting mentality might work for an actor or musician caught up in the moment of performance. Like a downhill skier, they are in no position to stop and evaluate what they're doing. They, too, have to adjust on the fly. But what about the business world, where rationality and evaluation rule, where success is determined by profit and losses? Every quarter, financial officers are checking the balance sheets. In business, the definition of a successful performer is "making your numbers." Surely, that requires depending on the higher processing of the cerebrum.

But legendary business performers don't think this way. Like legendary athletes, they divide their time between working on their game and playing it, between training and trusting. And while in business verbal skills are likely to be more important than motor skills, business superstars practice accessing their inner squirrel in order to perform their best in high-stakes situations.

Consider sales. The salesman on a call has to give a spiel about a product and must be prepared to answer questions on the spot. For the experienced salesperson, the closed loop processing of information will occur just as it does for the key-tosser or basketball player (though using different neurological networks). Sensory stimuli will be sent to the parts of the brain that specialize in cue recognition and language production (Wernike's and Broca's areas, named after the scientists who discovered them). Depending on a customer's questions and reactions, a skilled seller will generate a pattern of explanations, facts, or illustrations. Just as the athlete relies on the right motor patterns ingrained from years of practice, sales pros—or any top business executive, for that matter—will trust the visual, spatial, and verbal patterns stored during their education and work experiences to be at their side during an important deal. They, too, just let it happen.

When you talk to great salesmen, they tell you stories of pulling off an amazing close. Typically, the result was unanticipated. They went into a meeting, began talking to the guy on the other side of the desk, whom they didn't expect to be in a buying mood. They break the ice by talking about the football game on Sunday, marveling at how Emmitt Smith took over Walter Payton's all-time NFL rushing mark at thirty-three years old in his final opportunity to break that record in front of his family and home crowd. Suddenly, they realize that they were both at the same game, sitting only two rows away from each other! The experienced salesman reacts to that coincidence by building on it, keeping the conversation flowing, looking for more connections that might create the kind of bond with his client that will clinch a sale. They proceed to discover other things in common: friends, colleagues, interests. Before they know it, two hours have passed and, better still, the meeting ends with a handshake worth six figures.

Neither the genuine pleasure of those two hours of work nor the sale that resulted was planned. No formula exists for pure salesmanship any more than for an astonishing round of golf or a great night on stage. Yet many companies give thousands of copies of books on "ten proven strategies to sell anything" to all of their employees, or actually have their own hundred-plus page sales manuals instructing 1) You dial the number; 2) You say, "hello"; 3) You begin by talking about . . . ; 4) You raise the problem, and then say ____. It's as if the work could be successfully completed by a well-designed computer program. But when you are *thinking* about how to sell, step by step, the kind of easy personal and emotional connection that increases your odds for selling disappears. The big sale is a lot less likely to happen if you are counting up the number of widgets you're selling, translating that total into gross and net profits, or keeping a watchful eye on your approach and delivery, instead of engaging your customer. Such self-consciousness only fires up your cerebral cortex, putting those billions of neurons to work, and in such an overloaded mental state, mistakes get made: You fail to pick up subtle but important cues from a sales prospect. You stumble over your notes in a presentation to the board, and when questioned, you give poor answers or explanations. After it's over you say, "Oh, I should've . . ."

Selling is very different from trying to be a salesman. Getting an A in "Sales and Marketing" at Harvard Business School is not the same as being what the celebrated General Electric CEO Jack Welch used to call an "A player" in the sales department at GE. One, in fact, is a classic example of the Training Mindset, while the other is a result of the Trusting Mindset.

That is not to say that great salesmen can ignore training. Far from it. Hundreds of hours of practice and sacrificed weekends spent at training programs are necessary to develop your talent. But there is a time to evaluate how you did and what you must do in the future to improve, and there is a time to perform. When sales count, when the company's bottom line is in your hands, it's time to enter the Trusting Mindset. The best executives go there all the time; they've purposefully devoted so much time to practicing thinking that way that they can switch it on at will. And so do the best entrepreneurs, surgeons, diplomats, politicians, and other best-in-the-business performers.

"When I concentrate on the target, I forget everything else," says Hisashi Yamada, a top engineer for the Toshiba Corporation in Tokyo. He's actually talking about his accomplishments as a champion archer. But Yamada switches on that same kind of trusting focus at work, where he is leading a joint team of Toshiba and NEC engineers in a tense race against Sony and Matsushita to develop the next generation of high-definition DVDs. From his years of competitive archery, Yamada knows that when he "forgets about everything else," he is likely to be more successful at whatever he does.

In fact, business people have to switch into the trusting mode more often and more quickly than athletes or even tightrope artists. Performing on the high wire, like most sports, is a programmed affair: The show is at 7 P.M., and so at 6:45 you are ready to go. In business, however, the phone will ring and suddenly you're talking to a client who has just announced that he's pulling a million-dollar account from your company. You are not only already out on the high wire, you are in the middle of a step. Only someone who's conditioned her instincts to be in the Trusting Mindset can keep from falling, from losing that million-dollar account.

How do great performers in every field switch on the trusting mode at will? Some do it intuitively, and that is why we call them "natural talents." Others, however, have learned to trust their abilities and their experience by gradually spending more and more time at work in the Trusting Mindset. You can learn it, too, but you have to be willing to be uncomfortable at first. If you're skilled at using your Training Mindset, just letting yourself trust will feel quite foreign.

Often when I describe the Trusting Mindset to my clients, they immediately ask, "What do I have to do to make it happen?" I tell them to *do* nothing—and then repeat it again and again. They look at me as if I'm crazy. But that's exactly how the best perform; they practice thinking of nothing when the pressure is on. To win medals at downhill skiing like Franz Klammer, you have to practice careening down icy cliffs at 100 m.p.h. No one else—or any 12-step program— will do it for you. Success depends on emptying your head rather than filling it. You can do that, too—if you're willing to retrain your mind. It will take some work. To join the ranks of overachievers will require you to make some perhaps uncomfortable and often misunderstood choices about how you think when you're performing. You must, for example, start putting more pressure on yourself rather than less.

CHAPTER 2

Butterflies Are a Good Thing

For decades, in surveys of what Americans fear most, the runaway number-one answer is public speaking. People are actually more afraid of performing in front of others than they are of dying. Who hasn't been there? You step into the spotlight. Your heart is pumping as if you're running a marathon. Your mouth has turned to cotton. Butterflies are using your stomach as their exercise room. Your armpits are faucets. Your hands or knees are dancing to an unknown drummer. Even if you succeed, the prospect of going through such an experience again causes even veteran performers to have "performance anxiety" (a.k.a. "stage fright"). I don't care how huge a sports or drama fan you are, you don't want to be anywhere near a dressing room latrine before the big game or show. Actor Anthony Hopkins throws up before almost every appearance on stage. After a brief stint in a Broadway play, Jane Fonda announced she was quitting acting for good. She had become so anxious before each performance that as she walked to the theater each night, "I was praying I would get hit by a car." Little wonder that psychologists have devised all sorts of techniques to "manage stress."

Avoid them like the plague! Working on techniques to manage stress is a bit like trying to win the Indy 500 by putting a governor on the engine of your race car or swapping out a powerful V-12 for a V-4 because it offers a "quieter ride." You wouldn't do that. Not if you were after the checkered flag. Not if you were racing star Jeff Gordon. No superstar is about to give his opponents an edge. Nor should you by trying to relax when the pressure's on.

Great performers welcome pressure. They thrive on it. Instead of trying to control or erase pressure, they use it as a kind of energy bar. The best players in any high-stakes field—business, entertainment, law, surgery, as well as sport—recognize that pressure occurs at the moments when meaningful accomplishment is possible. In fact, that is the reason why performers perform: for the opportunity to tackle challenges head on, to do something significant, to demonstrate what their talent and hard work can produce. Those who perform well consistently—the superstars—are always looking for the opportunity to take their game to the next level.

This partnership with pressure is also the reason superstars tend to find an excuse to be absent when a psychologist visits. They know that their ability to perform consistently well has nothing to do with imagining themselves on a peaceful island, reminding themselves to be cool-headed, or relaxing. They don't want to relax. For them, pressure is a doorway to success. To an exceptional performer, the term *stress management* is really an oxymoron. Show them someone lying on the floor with their eyes closed, trying to make the nerves go away, and they'll show you someone who is easy to beat.

I was trained to help people perform well in anxiety-provoking situations. But I won't be giving you any tips on how to relax. Too often, the techniques designed to allay stress become an obstacle to getting better; what is supposed to be a means to an end becomes an end in itself and a good explanation for why a lot of teams that have hired psychologists still produce losing records. What I do is completely different from stress management. I see my job as improving a client's performance, and the challenge is pretty much the same whatever the venue, whether it's the operating room, the concert stage, a sales call, the boardroom, or the playing fields. Over the years, I have discovered that I cannot enhance anybody's performance without getting them not only to live with the butterflies that come with high-pressure jobs but to embrace that kind of physical response, enjoy it, get into it. That's the first real ticket to being a performer who thinks exceptionally.

Let me tell you a story about:

How Bill Russell Found That Throwing Up Before a Game Was an Asset

Bill Russell is one of the great names in basketball, an All-American from the University of San Francisco and the only athlete to ever win an NCAA Championship, an Olympic Gold Medal, and a professional championship all in the same year—1956. During the 1950s and '60s, Russell was the leader of a Boston Celtics dynasty that won eleven NBA championships in thirteen years and was named by *Sports Illustrated* the "greatest team of the century." Bill is regarded as the finest team player of all time. Few in the history of the game were as good at both offense and defense, few were as intelligent, and no one could match his infectious laugh. But Bill Russell had this one problem: He threw up before every game. Russell got so nervous in the locker room that he couldn't start a game without running to the closest stall to barf his guts out. The Celtics brought in a doctor to make sure that he would not be dehydrated, and his fellow players enjoyed ribbing him about having to give up lunch before every contest. After all, they played in the NBA, too, and they didn't have to boot each night.

But one evening late in the 1963–64 season, as Russell tells the story in his autobiography, *Second Wind: The Memoirs of an Opinionated Man*, he walked into the Celtics locker room and realized that for the first time in his career, he felt fine. He got ready for the game, and the other players looked at him with amazement. What about the vomiting ritual? "Not today," said Russell. The clubhouse erupted with applause, commending the veteran center for achieving one more career milestone: not stinking up the place before tip off. Russell collected his high fives and headed out onto the floor of the

Boston Garden—and played the worst game of his career. He was flat, slow on defense, lethargic. Bill Russell was, well, not Bill Russell.

The pattern continued as the season wore down. He'd show up at the Garden, feel fine, relaxed, no need to vomit, and then go out and play poorly. The Boston press hammered him: "Russell's Slump Causes Celtics Another Loss," "The Legend Finally Loses his Touch," screamed the headlines. The notoriously ungenerous Boston sports fans wondered: Is Russell's career over? Russell began to wonder if they were right. The Celtics of those days also featured such other future Hall of Famers as Bob Cousy and Tommy Heinsohn, not to mention John Havlicek, Frank Ramsey, and K. C. Jones, so the team coasted into the postseason. But with the seeming lull in performance after seven NBA Championships in a row, the press was grinding its teeth: "Can the Celtics Repeat without Russell?"

Game 1 arrived. Russell showed up three hours before the 7:00 P.M. start time, hoping to avoid the fans and the media, only to find a line of boisterous Celtics fans already snaking around the arena. The place was electric. It was as exciting as his first NBA Championship when he was a rookie making history. Ducking into the Garden, he remembered what it felt like seven years before, when the team first pulled together to win it all. Suddenly, Russell felt the pressure. His nerves were jumping. As soon as he entered the locker room, he ran for the toilet and yakked up dinner, just like old times. Then he busted down the stall door and charged back into the locker room, shouting to his teammates, "We're going to win, guys! We're going to win!" Bill Russell had finally made the connection between feeling pressure and success. To play well, he not only needed his nerves but fed off of them to fuel his passion for the game, his love of competition, his focus on the task at hand. The Celtics won their eighth straight title.

Great performers do something so special that most of them don't even know they're doing it. It's a frame of mind, a kind of exceptional thinking during a performance that involves no thinking. Many Hall of Famers have no idea that they're exceptional thinkers. Russell, like the best old-school athletes and their equivalents in every other field, just did what came naturally. Studying the science of "performance enhancement," though, allows us to understand what Russell did intuitively over most of his career and apply it to improve performance intentionally. We can now teach his kind of thinking to everyone.

No, I'm not talking about learning how to be sick to your stomach. I mean learning how to use your biology in your favor. When someone comes to see me about performing better under pressure, I don't prescribe stress management. There are a lot of psychologists who make a good living teaching stress management, and there are a lot of people who need that kind of counsel. But at high levels of business, medicine, entertainment, and sport, learning how to relax when the pressure is on will not improve performance. In many cases, it will cause slumps just like Bill Russell's. If Bill had come to visit me, I would have coached him to get nervous.

Being a clutch player means thriving under pressure—welcoming it, enjoying it, making it work to your advantage. I can teach you how to do this, but first you will have to retrain some instincts, and that will require understanding two things:

1. Everything that your body does to you when the pressure is on is good for performance.
2. Pressure is different from anxiety; nervousness is different from worry.

Butterflies Are Normal

What is really happening to the body? Like almost every animal, humans have bimodal sympathetic and parasympathetic nervous systems that have evolved over thousands of years. One stimulates the heart, lungs, eyes, and muscles; the other suppresses them. One prompts basic bodily functions such as digestion and processing water and waste; the other shuts these systems off. They work in tandem. The sympathetic system is crucial for finding food, being on the lookout for dangerous predators, and defending against enemies, while the parasympathetic system keeps the body fueled, warm, working efficiently, and prepared for reproduction. When one turns up, the other turns down, and vice versa.

Under pressure, the brain switches the body to red alert. This activates the sympathetic nervous system, and energy is redistributed from parasympathetic tasks to maximize sympathetic tasks:

- The mouth goes dry, sometimes called "cotton mouth" because the body is channeling effort into tasks more important than producing saliva. We don't need extra spit to sink a free throw at the buzzer.
- The sensation of "butterflies" occurs in the stomach, resulting from excess stomach acid because the digestive system is shutting down. During a major presentation to the board, who's eating lunch?
- The stomach cramps because the stomach lining is shrinking. The body has stopped producing bile and is trying to get rid of any remaining food. Bill Russell was a textbook case.
- Sweat flows, a safety mechanism to prevent the body from overheating. Even an audition for the New York Philharmonic is not worth boiling vital organs.
- Hands, feet, or knees begin shaking. That's the body sending faster motor signals from the cortex through the motor neurons out to the extremities, which will be running, throwing, illustrating, acting, keyboarding.
- The heart beats faster to get more blood through the arteries, carrying nutrients and oxygen to the working muscles and brain cells so they can perform at a higher level.
- The eyes dilate, and vision becomes more acute.
- The mind races, processing a greater amount of information in a shorter amount of time.

All of these adaptations are the body's way of making us perform more efficiently when we're under the gun. When humans face stress, we are hardwired to respond favorably. Our bodies know just what to do. Quicker hands and feet, more oxygen and fuel to our muscles, greater visual acuity, increased mental capacity—sounds like a pretty good formula for coming out on top, doesn't it? So whether you are running the hundred-yard dash in the Olympics, trying to get one hundred stitches into a patient's heart within a minute, getting your fingers to play the allegro in a Mozart violin concerto, or pulling off the biggest sale of your career, why would you want to be more relaxed?

Relaxation teaches your muscles to lose tone, your brain to be passive. You cannot win gold medals without muscle tone, nor can you perform at your utmost with other parts of your sympathetic nervous system switched to "slow." Most people experience fight-or-flight symptoms and *bam!*—their performance is overwhelmed by feelings of anxiety. But arousal and anxiety are not the same thing. You simply have been conditioned or taught to treat them as equals. They're not.

Loving the Uncertainty and Eliminating the Anxiety

- The physical symptoms of fight-or-flight are what the human body has learned over thousands of years to operate more efficiently and at the highest level.
- Anxiety is a cognitive *interpretation* of that physical response.

Most people have come to believe that anxiety and stress go hand in hand. That assumption, however, is dead wrong. Stress need not produce anxiety. Once Bill Russell figured out the connection between his body's physiological preparation and his performance, he actually was relieved to be throwing up before the big game because he recognized it as evidence that he was ready to play his best. Butterflies, cotton mouth, and a pounding heart make the finest performers smile—the smile of a person with an ace up their sleeve. Fight-or-flight symptoms comprise the extra juice they'll need to go up against the best, so they welcome it. Many CEOs have confided to me that what they love most about their jobs are the aspects that make them the most nervous. They definitely would agree with Tiger Woods, who has often said, "The day I'm not nervous stepping onto the first tee—that's the day I quit."

All the great athletes, musicians, actors, doctors, and business executives I've talked to seem to think the same way. So why does everyone else identify the body's sympathetic response to high-stakes situations with fear of failure? The confusion tends to stem from childhood, almost as an accident. Here's what happens: It is the first time you have to deliver in public. You are eight years old, playing in your first Little League game, giving your first recital, appearing in your first play, or delivering that debut book report from memory before the class. Your body goes nuts, registering all the classic fight-or-flight symptoms. On some level (and it's usually not a higher cerebral level because, hey, you're eight and you don't process things that way yet) you are wondering, "What is happening to me?" Then you proceed to perform poorly. You strike out three times and let the ball roll right between your legs, you blow your lines, you forget the next note, you blank on what the book was about. The next time you are called upon to perform in public, your body still reacts to the pressure, but you think, "The last time I felt this way, I was so awful that the other kids laughed at me." Before you know it, you have attributed poor performance to the body's natural response under pressure. You essentially instructed yourself that the root of the problem was your body's effort to help you perform to your utmost. Trouble was, you didn't really have any "utmost." You performed badly because you simply were not yet very skilled. You were only eight years old! Your teacher probably didn't teach you how to prepare your speech; you hadn't practiced enough with your instrument. Some of the greatest athletes in history were lousy at age eight—or much older. (Remember: Michael Jordan got cut from his high school team sophomore year.)

Thus begins of a vicious cycle between physical reactions to pressure and high anxiety. For the rest of your school days and then on the job, whenever you are asked to perform in public and the symptoms of arousal appear, you fill your head with negative thoughts. That is why amateur golfers with decades of experience still dread standing on the first tee, or why fifty-year-old executives live in terror of every presentation or big meeting with the board. Performing poorly becomes identified with the body's natural invigoration mechanisms. The anxiety gets worse until you finally tell yourself, "I have to learn how to relax."

The mistaken identity between stress and anxiety is so ingrained that when I ask new clients to tell me about their experiences performing under pressure, they often respond with a soliloquy on fear. I want to hear about breakthrough moments, the good stuff, but they tell me about choking, doubt, and ducking every opportunity that might activate such awful feelings. No wonder in our culture few words carry a more negative connotation than "pressure" and "stress." Stress gets blamed for everything that doesn't have an otherwise clear diagnosis. Going gray or losing your hair? Must be stress. Unidentified pains or headaches? You guessed it. But stress is not the cause; it's how you interpret stress that causes psychosomatic illness.

In performance arenas, psychologists call this "self-intimidation." You feed your mind with thoughts and instructions that your body is doing something wrong. You tell yourself that you're not going to perform well because of your own natural instincts. You use emotionally exaggerated language such as "my heart is jumping clear out of my chest; my stomach's so twisted upside down, the knots will never come out." Often you say, "If only I could just relax, I'd do so much better." You undermine your confidence by creating an irrational fear of yourself. Athletes like Dennis Rodman and John Rocker make a multimillion dollar living out of intimidating opponents. Most people already are intimidating themselves—for free.

A Case in Point—and the Remedy

In the spring of 2000, a student finishing his master's degree at Rice University's Shepherd School of Music came to me for advice. Jamie Kent was a talented trumpet player preparing to sit for a round of extremely competitive auditions that would determine his future as a professional musician. Jamie's teachers at Shepherd, which was recently ranked above the renowned Juilliard School in New York as the nation's number-one music school, thought highly of his skills and had helped him line up an impressive array of interview performances, from the New York Philharmonic to the Texas Brass. Jamie dove right in.

But he didn't land a job. At the very moments when his future depended on performing at his finest, Jamie racked up a series of subpar performances. When he came to me, we immediately began discussing pressure. Jamie filled me in on the brutal realities of breaking into the world of classical music. Turnover in symphony orchestras is low, competition is high—particularly in the trumpet section, one of the smallest in most orchestras. He reported how nervous he felt prior to going on stage, how difficult it was to warm up for a big audition with a dozen other aspiring and equally anxious trumpet players awaiting their calls. He told startling stories of the kind of cutthroat antics that you might expect in tryout camp for a professional football team, but not for a symphony orchestra. Ambitious trumpet players went to diabolical lengths to psych each other out with a combination of fancy playing in the rehearsal room and intimidating stories about musicians whose failed auditions with one orchestra got them blacklisted with every orchestra in the country. They pointed out flaws to "be helpful." They built up the competition to increase anxiety: "Did you know that *he's* related to Duke Ellington?" they'd say about one talented candidate. About another: "I heard they even bought him a first-class plane ticket." And so it went, according to Jamie. The musicians' head games stopped only when it was his turn to audition, but by then his mind was so shaken that the odds of success decreased with every gasp of breath he sucked in to try to calm his nerves.

As we talked about how he handled the pressure of auditioning, it became clear that Jamie had developed a classic case of self-intimidation. He had started rehearsing less and worrying more. He tried to find ways to banish pressure from his mind. At auditions, he stayed away from the warm-up room until the last moment, avoiding the psych-out sessions among the other trumpeters preparing for their turns. He took time off from auditioning. He even canceled some auditions for orchestras that he would have loved to be part of because he told himself he wasn't "ready." Jamie was mired in the kind of avoidance routines that professionals in many fields fall into when they encounter pressure: Marketers anxiously joke with each other about an impending advertising pitch, creating excuses ahead of time; executives sneak off for a drink before heading into a presentation to the company's stockholders; attorneys stay up all night going over needless details for the next day's closing arguments. In each case, arousal is viewed negatively and thus avoided or buried by overwork. Such relief, however, is temporary. When the task resumes, less time is available for last-minute preparation, which only increases the anxiety about the performance.

To get Jamie's career back on track, I taught him the same things I've often taught salespeople, attorneys, and executives whose very success is bound to increase the pressure they're under: to view nervousness not as an obstacle but as a welcome friend, and to practice the fight-or-flight response in order to learn how to feed off the added emotion.

Practicing Pressure

How do you know if you're a victim of self-intimidation? I advise my clients to examine a list of their performance choices. Typically, people bothered by "butterflies" will start avoiding any situation that might stir up their nerves. Jamie Kent didn't like the thought of scheduling auditions, so he limited them. He turned down opportunities in favor of staying home to practice. An attorney will turn down a big case, or file for a continuation; a salesman will let a colleague make the call on a client with a reputation for being an especially hard sell; a reporter will avoid investigative assignments that will require cornering people who would rather not be interviewed; an executive will delegate presentations to underlings or turn down public speaking invitations. How many people do you know who have gotten bogged down in a low-level job because they can't take the stress that comes with more responsibility or with going on interviews? If you find a pattern where the fear of nerves is lording over what you decide to do in life or work, you probably have fallen into the trap of intimidating yourself.

The remedy I prescribe for self-intimidation is to unlink arousal from anxiety. When your body is in a charged state, you must first recognize that anxiety is the result of a psychological misinterpretation of that arousal and then practice choosing the correct interpretation. Sometimes just explaining the distinction does the trick. As I was writing this chapter, a friend who has been a professional speaker for years told me that she suddenly had gotten a bit shaky at the podium. A couple of weeks before, she actually had fainted a few minutes into a speech, probably the result of jet lag. The next time she took the podium, her ordinary performance anxiety had increased markedly, and it was not one of her best performances. The following week she was scheduled to deliver a keynote speech in Europe at the annual meeting of top executives of a major international firm—for the biggest fee she had ever received. If that wasn't pressure enough, she conceded that she couldn't shake that fainting episode from her mind; she was getting more anxious about the speech by the day. I no sooner remarked on the coincidence—that I had been writing earlier about how so many people identify the physical symptoms of stress with the psychology of anxiety—when she said, "That's it! That's my problem." Evidently, no longer—a few weeks later, she called to tell me that she had been in top form for her big speech, better than ever.

If you know what you're doing, if you're good at your job, the "nerves" actually can make you perform better. You have educated yourself or worked for countless hours perfecting the skills that make for good performance in your field. You now have to start training yourself to accept that arousal is a good thing. How? You learn to love pressure by performing under pressure. You must put yourself into pressure situations in which you get nervous and then practice assessing what the pressure can do *for* you, as an asset, a welcome friend. Pressure often signals an opportunity to excel. You must practice understanding that by making a conscious association between the "nerves" and the potential to perform, as the Olympic Creed says, "Higher, faster, stronger."

In Jamie Kent's case, the ultimate satisfaction he got from playing music came from moving an audience, giving them a feeling to hold on to. Without being "up" himself, a performer is not likely to charge an audience. Jamie would only be playing notes on a page. But with his blood pumping, he could do what the famous jazz musician Joe Sample used to talk about: "Just let my raw emotions tell me where to go. When I let that happen I knew I was going to touch someone else." Once Jamie began to use his pre-performance time to work at *creating* arousal instead of trying to find new ways to avoid his feelings, those high-stress waiting rooms turned into Jamie's playground. While the other trumpet players focused on their anxiety or on increasing anxiety in each other, Jamie concentrated on feeling the music move him inside, then creating the inspirational emotion he could bring with him into the audition hall to help him make his trumpet sing. He had learned how to enjoy pressure, not only to see what it could do for him, but how much fun it was.

Isn't this exactly what kids do when they're practicing a sport on their own? "It's the bottom of the ninth, the final game of the World Series, two outs, a man on third, and up steps . . ." "Here he is on the eighteenth at Augusta National, the crowd silenced, a ten-foot putt for a million dollars and the Masters!" Even playing in the sandlot isn't as much fun unless there's something at stake. We adults must encourage this kind of thinking. We must urge kids at an early age to enjoy pressure, and teach them the difference between stress and anxiety. It's something that little kids actually can learn a lot faster than adults— much like the natural ease with which six-year-olds master new languages.

And to be good examples, we grown-ups have to become more mature about our own attitudes toward stress and embrace pressure as a way to enhance our performance. That is why, after all, when we're on the links we put "a few dollars" on the match—"to make it a little more interesting" (i.e., to increase the pressure). Why not also fool around with increasing the pressure in various work-related situations, starting with low stakes and working your way up? If you have a speech to give or a presentation to make, try it in front of a few good friends or family members. I guarantee it will get your blood pumping. The next time around, try it out on a few of your colleagues or your department as a trial run before you face a big audience. I am always amazed when an attorney confesses that he or she prepares an argument to be made in court by sitting in the library with a pad and paper. If you have to address an audience, even a tiny one, you had better rehearse in front of some kind of audience. A lot.

Astronauts spend months in simulators going over and over the procedures they will be required to carry out in space—not so they will be able to relax in that situation, but to train to use the inevitable physiological response to their advantage. To keep their games sharp, the best golfers in the world like to play for a lot of money even during practice rounds. During spring training, baseball pitchers Greg Maddux, John Schmoltz, and Tom Glavine have been known to put as much as ten thousand dollars on a game of golf before heading to the diamond. Is it any wonder that the Atlanta Braves' pitching staff swept almost every Cy Young Award for a decade? Campaign managers put their candidates through mock press conferences. If the president of the United States rehearses his press conferences and major addresses to Congress in front of audiences made up of top aides and other staffers, shouldn't you be putting in some time simulating pressure situations?

And once you start enjoying that kind of pressure, I advise you to ratchet things up a notch. Incorporate some distractions in your rehearsal. Encourage audience members to heckle you or ask the toughest questions they can think of. It's rarely "smooth sailing" in the simulators at NASA. The flight directors intentionally cause the computers to fail and the shuttle to start spinning out of control. Similarly, Earl Woods often has told the story of how he used to try to distract young Tiger during their rounds on the course. When his son was in the middle of a swing, Earl would yell at him, insert his shadow into the kid's line of vision, peg golf balls at him, do anything to throw off his game. He said his tricks annoyed the hell out of Tiger and often affected his swing or shot. But then one day when he tried to distract his son, Tiger looked at him, smiled, and then proceeded to hit the ball a mile. Earl Woods knew that his game of distractions was over. Tiger knew that nothing his opponents, the fans, or the press fired at him on the course could be worse than what his father had done to him.

In summary: Practice, practice, practice. I have worked with clients who have spent fifteen years intimidating themselves or avoiding pressure who expect to turn themselves around in a few days. I am pretty good at what I do, but not that good. Breaking bad habits takes time. In fact, the research on what it takes to break an old habit and learn a new one indicates that such a transition could take thousands of trials. And always remember: The only time top performers get worried is when their heart is *not* racing. Unless you learn to love pressure—to perceive stress as an advantage—you are unlikely to enter the ranks of exceptional performers.

Jamie Kent, by the way, turned it around. He is now an award-winning trumpet player in the Texas Symphony. He also has played with the American Symphony Orchestra and the Denver Philharmonic; he's even performed for the president. I just received a nice holiday card from Jamie in which he mentioned how much he now enjoys playing to a packed house, particularly with people in the audience he needs to impress. So start practicing. Learning to love pressure is essential to becoming the kind of exceptional thinker for whom overachievement is a way of life. And in the next chapter, I'll explain precisely what I mean by "exceptional thinking."

CHAPTER 3

The Wisdom of Yogi

Yogi Berra, that is. My goal is to get you to think like Yogi. I am serious. Of course, I realize that if a CEO were looking for a consultant to improve the all-around performance of his top executives, Yogi Berra would probably not be the first name on his list. The head of surgery at Harvard Medical School is not likely to think of a retired New York Yankee catcher as the perfect example for how young doctors should go about their business in the operating room. When considering how the mind contributes to one's career, most people think about the traditionally educated mind, that steel-trap, calculating machine that is always one step ahead of everyone else in the chess games of life and work. Yogi certainly doesn't fit that model: His formal schooling ended after the eighth grade, and his reading preferences seemed to begin and end with comic books. Even among the poorly educated ball players of his own post–World War II generation, Yogi was the personification of goofiness—a simple, childlike figure who happened to be able to hit a baseball extremely well, a kind of idiot savant of Yankee Stadium. His twisted logic and syntax have made him a national comedic icon: "It's déjà vu all over again." "I didn't say everything I said." "Little things are big." "If the world were perfect, it wouldn't be."

But Lawrence Peter Berra, fondly known as Yogi,* is also a member of baseball's Hall of Fame, an honor that is not doled out on the basis of how many cockeyed things a player says over a career. A man of modest size, speed, and agility, he hit a record three hundred home runs for a catcher over seventeen seasons with the New York Yankees, fourteen of them ending in the World Series—another record—with the Yankees winning ten world championships, yet another record. Yogi may have left school after the eighth grade; he may have read comic books instead of *The New York Times;* he may have taken hour naps from 2:00 to 4:00; and he may have seemed, to everyone who met him, to have a backward way of looking at the world. But the guy was a genius—a genius at performing. I would argue that his success as a performer is entailed in his realization that, in Yogi's own inimitable words:

Ninety percent of this game is half mental.

At least. One of the reasons I love Yogi as a paradigm pressure performer is that during his playing years he had a reputation for "living in his own world"—for being a bit strange, rather abnormal. But that's the point. Who wants to be normal? I suspect that the reason you have picked up this book is that you want an edge on everyone in your line of work. By definition, extraordinary performers are beyond the norm; they are exceptions to the rule, *exception*-al. Their achievements stem from the way their minds work: Abnormal demands and goals require an abnormal mindset; to be exceptional—to innovate, to break through—you need to think exceptionally.

When I tell this to my students and clients, they get it and they don't. That extraordinarily successful people are extraordinary seems so obvious that it's not even worth contemplating. For most, however,

---

*According to Berra, as a kid he liked to sit cross-legged, and a friend remarked he looked like one of those "yogis," and the nickname stuck—more appropriately than his friends could ever know, in my opinion.

"extraordinary" is translated to mean "naturally gifted," "genetically talented," or just plain "brilliant," and therefore out of reach of the ordinary, merely competent majority. That's not at all what I mean. By "exceptional thinking" I mean using the mind in ways that will be spelled out in detail in the next several chapters.

The first, and perhaps best, definition of *exceptional thinker* is someone who sees the world and his place in it differently from everyone else. Others look at them and simply shake their heads: Unconventional thinkers strike most people as strange, even a little crazy. But great performers in all fields seem immune to what outsiders think about them. Their sense of themselves never depends on the feedback—positive or negative—they get from their environment. They know that the world tilts toward the conventional, that what most governs our lives is the inertia of circumstance, and that most people, particularly those in authority (and the media that props them up), are biased toward what they know best, what they already believe, as if no one is allowed to believe otherwise. Isn't that what "traditional values" are—what everyone believes is best? History, though, shows us that the people who end up changing the world—the great political, social, scientific, technological, artistic, even sports revolutionaries—are always nuts, until they're right, and then they're geniuses. The history of science, for example, has proven over and over that a discovery attacked because it goes against the wisdom of the day is likely to be a paradigm-busting event only accepted once the scientific community has had time to grow accustomed to the new idea (cf. Copernicus, Galileo, and Newton, just for starters). A look back at the breakthroughs in the world of commerce will show the same tension between the conventional wisdom and the "Next New Thing." The invention of paper money or national currencies, not to mention credit cards, stirred up all sorts of controversy.

It used to be that companies were threatened by having too many unconventional thinkers around. Corporations saw themselves as one big family or team, and such mavericks would only cause problems. In this era of globalization, where competition is worldwide, the mavericks have come into their own. "There are no longer any boundaries for where the talent is, and where and how it can be deployed," explains American Express CEO Kenneth Chenault. "The battle at home and around the world is going to be for ideas and non-traditional thinking, and we have to look at the entire global marketplace as the playing field." Better start recruiting the Yogis of the world as consultants to teach people how to step out of the bubble of conventionality and see the world and their places in it differently. If you're interested in moving up, you'd be wise to adopt Yogi's kind of wisdom.

If you don't consider yourself a born exception-al thinker, don't worry. Thinking is a habit, and like every other habit, good or bad, exceptional thinking is something you can pick up. The essential elements are learning to stick with your own perception of yourself— living in your own world—and letting *your* reality, not the reality presented by other people or particular situations, control your performance over time.

Creating Your Own Reality—and Bringing Everyone Else Inside

Exceptional thinkers see the world through their own lens. In fact, they invent the lens. And if that lens doesn't help them see the world the way they want to see it, they invent another. As a kid, the only thing Yogi could think about was being a Major League ballplayer. He quit school in the eighth grade and went to work in a coal yard. "At three o'clock," he recalls, "I disappeared to find a ball game." His boss didn't take too kindly to Yogi skipping out early while everyone else was toiling away, so he fired him. It was the Depression, and Yogi had to help support his family. He took a job working on a Pepsi-Cola truck. But when Yogi looked in the mirror in the morning, he saw a professional baseball player, not a stock boy. So he went through the motions unloading the truck until an opportunity popped up for him to engage in his real calling. That got him fired again. Then he landed a job working in a shoe factory—"making seventeen dollars a week, the most money I'd ever seen"—but again, as soon as the job started interfering with baseball, he quit. His traditional Italian family was mystified by how he could pour so much energy into a game that wasn't paying his bills. Yogi, however, had a very clear vision of his place in the world; in fact, he was so eager and so committed to his dream of playing in the major league that he learned how to play all nine positions.

At age sixteen, he tried out for his hometown team, the St. Louis Cardinals. His dedication didn't pay off. The Cardinals' owner, Branch Rickey, considered one of the greatest eyes for talent in the history of baseball, pulled Yogi aside and told him that he would never make it as a major leaguer. He wasn't big enough; he didn't have the natural ability. Yogi was disappointed but undaunted. "I thought I was good enough to make it," he recalls. He didn't listen to Branch Rickey. He stuck with his perception of his potential as a baseball player. A year later, the Yankees signed him.

As a teenager, Yogi had already mastered an important lesson in the art of high performance: He viewed his talents through a special Yogi lens, and he managed to get the Yankees to look through that same lens and see the promising young baseball player the Cardinals could not see. I have found that the best performers in every field tend to think about themselves and their careers with the same kind of filter—a commitment to their way of seeing the world and their special place in it that friends and family consider abnormal, if not a bit loony. Whether they ended up as famous entrepreneurs or heart surgeons, super salesmen or sport phenoms, they started out inclined to believe that they would excel long before the evidence was in (or, in some cases, even before they chose a career). At an early age, they were motivated to succeed and let nothing get in the way—neither the opinions of others nor their derisive laughter, not the probabilities for failure, or even failure itself.

When Michael Dell was fifteen years old, his parents allowed him to use his savings to buy his first computer. When he got it home, he immediately took it apart. Understandably, his parents were irate. "They thought I had demolished it," Dell recalls in a recent memoir. "I just wanted to see how it worked." Over the next few years, the young

Dell haunted local computer stores and even skipped school for days at a time to drive to industry conventions. He soon realized that though stores were selling IBM PCs for about three thousand dollars, the actual components of the computer cost only six or seven hundred dollars. He began building custom computers for friends, quickly concluding that he could compete with the computer stores and still make a tidy profit to buy "all the things your typical high school kid would want."

Dell was in the computer business, and he hadn't yet graduated from high school. When he went off to college at the University of Texas, he had three computers in the backseat of his car. After class, Dell would hustle back to his dorm room to upgrade a few, which he would then sell to other students or faculty. The word got around, and soon doctors, lawyers, and businesspeople around Austin were dropping off their computers at Dell's dorm for an upgrade. He applied for a state vendor's license and immediately started underbidding Texas stores for state contracts on personal computers. Soon Dell was much too busy upgrading and selling computers to go to class.

And then he got a call from his parents.

His parents had been alerted by university authorities that their son's grades were tumbling and that he hadn't been attending class. They were at the Austin airport and on their way for a surprise visit! Dell managed to stash all the computers he was working on behind the shower curtain in his roommate's bathroom before his parents arrived. "You've got to stop this computer stuff and concentrate on school," his father announced. "Get your priorities straight. What do you want to do with your life?" Dell's answer: "I want to compete with IBM." His father didn't think that was very funny.

But young Michael Dell was serious. He knew that his fascination with computers was more than a hobby or passing phase. He saw an amazing business opportunity. He recognized that if he could get computers into the hands of every big and small business, every student, everyone, "it would become the most important device of this century." Right then, at the age of eighteen, Dell knew the answer to his father's question: He wanted to devote his life to building better computers than IBM, selling them directly to consumers, and becoming "number one in the industry." He decided not to divulge that dream to anyone "because they probably would have thought I was crazy. But, to me, the opportunity was clear."

After just five years, Michael Dell, a college dropout, raised $35 million in an initial public offering of stock, bringing the market capitalization of Dell Computers to $85 million. Ten years later, in 1999, the company Dell had started with a thousand dollars from a summer job became the largest seller of personal-computers in the United States, racking up sales of more than $35 million a day—and thumping IBM. Today, Dell's company still dominates the personal-computer market, ahead of Hewlett-Packard and IBM, and in 2003 Michael Dell announced that he was going after Sony's and HP's market share in the consumer electronics business—flat-screen TVs, MP3 players, and Pocket PCs—all sold exclusively online, as Dell does with its computers.

Michael Dell, now thirty-eight, is one of those lucky people, like Yogi, who seem to spring from the womb as exceptional thinkers and are able to get the rest of us to see the world through their eyes. But anyone can learn to think like that—provided they're willing to be considered "weird." By his own measure, Dell was one weird kid. "When I was in the third grade," he writes, "I sent away for a high school diploma." He had seen an ad: "Earn your high school diploma by passing one simple test." For the young and restless Dell, "trading nine years of school for 'one simple test' seemed like a pretty good idea to me."

At about the same age, but growing up in London, Richard Branson, the irrepressible and self-described "adventure capitalist" who founded Virgin Music and Virgin Atlantic Airways, had not yet learned how to read. He was dyslexic and terrible in school; he scored in the lowest percentiles on standardized* and IQ tests, but unlike

---

*By all the classic measures of potential, Branson was an utter failure. Think about how many people, and how many organizations, rely on standardized testing for recruiting, selection, promotion, and more. What if Branson had heeded the test results? What if *you* do, or your company does?

Dell, Branson was a chip off the old block: Both his parents, not to mention assorted relatives, were independent, even eccentric souls who supported his wild entrepreneurial schemes with their own time and money. "Irreverence ran on both sides of my family," Branson has written. "My parents brought me up to think that we could all change the world." From an early age, he believed them; he adopted their lens. Upon graduating from high school, where he struggled academically but was launching what became a hugely successful national magazine for students in Great Britain, the headmaster's parting words were: "Congratulations, Branson. I predict that you will either go to prison or become a millionaire."

Branson quickly realized that he could use his magazine, *Student Magazine*—which didn't have the kind of catchy or inspiring name that accepted business wisdom would advise for promoting and branding new products—to sell mail-order rock-and-roll records at discounted prices to his teenage readers who, according to some basic market research, spent a great deal of their money on records. Soon *Student Magazine* was floundering financially, but cash was flooding in from music fans. He'd failed at his first business and knew nothing about music, so why not? Branson decided to go into the record business. But what should he name the new company? "What about Virgin," suggested a young woman on the magazine staff. "We're complete virgins at this business."

When the mail-order music industry was threatened by a major postal strike in England, Branson and his fellow Virgins (in the record business, at least) saved the business by quickly opening a record store, even though "we had no idea about how a shop works." In 1971, Britain's record stores were dominated by two large companies and staffed by salespeople in drab brown or blue uniforms who displayed great disdain toward their longhaired customers. Branson saw a different music purchasing environment. He viewed a shop that conveyed the excitement of the rock and roll that the kids loved, and one that would make his customers feel at home. While grounded strategists were dumping on Branson's image as unprofessional, Virgin was rapidly becoming the record store of choice in London.

The more immersed he became in the music business the more business opportunities Branson saw. He had heard the recording studios were stodgy and overbooked, forcing some groups to record at breakfast time. Branson reckoned that a big old house would be a more comfortable and creative atmosphere for rock music makers. He found an old manor house outside of London, borrowed most of the price from a bank, with a supportive maiden aunt chipping in the balance, and bang! Virgin was in the recording business. By the end of 1972, Virgin had opened fourteen shops, several in London and one in every major city in England. A year later, the company produced four records, including the Mike Oldfield tune "Tubular Bells," which became the number one song in Britain and eventually sold more than thirteen million copies. Branson was twenty-three, and without a moment's thought toward his age or experience found himself in New York making a deal with Atlantic Records to distribute Virgin's music in the United States. The Virgin label signed the punk group the Sex Pistols and then Boy George, whose phenomenal success helped Virgin make an £11 million profit in 1983. Virgin was becoming one of the world's leading music conglomerates. Branson had forced even his critics (of which there were legions) to look at the music business through his lens.

Branson was not satisfied. He began publishing books, producing movies, and, in 1984, with a leased jumbo jet from Boeing, Branson and his partners launched Virgin Atlantic Airways, with 250 journalists aboard the inaugural flight to New York—most of whom had written stories making fun of a man who thought he could start an airline company with *one* plane, one he didn't even own. Nineteen years later, Branson's smiling face was on the cover of *Fortune*. Inside, the story noted that "Richard Branson is not the world's best businessman, or the most successful, or the wealthiest—he simply has the most fun." The unconventional entrepreneur had amassed a billion-dollar fortune "by doing things business strategists suggest he shouldn't." And Branson keeps expanding the Virgin brand, against all odds: Virgin Megastores; Virgin Rail; Virgin Direct, a financial services company; Virgin Mobile; and even Virgin Cola. (Branson managed to get a Virgin Cola machine placed under the Coca-Cola bill-board in New York's Times Square!) He now owns more than two hundred enterprises worldwide.

According to Branson, he has done it all by embracing change, never going with a business plan unless it was "fun," and cultivating a company that "thrives on mavericks." Not only does he surround himself with people who get into his off-center, at times loony way of looking at business and the world—in 1985 he was certain he could be the first to fly a hot air balloon around the globe—but he encourages employees at all levels of his ventures to come up with their own "realities." He'll give millions to confidently support the individual perceptions of his staff, personally encouraging every one of his five thousand employees, every month in a handwritten letter, to prioritize fun over profit. He even publicly donned a wedding dress to help a flight attendant launch her idea for Virgin Brides—a heck of a vision for a company name in and of itself.

There's nothing "normal" about Branson. Note how similar the attitudes of such brash, visionary entrepreneurs as Dell and Branson are to the athletes that the media is inclined to brand as "weird" or "arrogant." Compare Yogi or Ted Williams, another Hall of Fame baseball player who refused to tip his hat to the fans as they screamed in admiration for his talents as a hitter; or the yellow-haired, much pierced, tattooed, and derided basketball player Dennis Rodman, who managed to help Michael Jordan and the Chicago Bulls win a string of NBA championships; or even the more gentlemanly Tiger Woods. When Woods announced in 1996 that he was dropping out of Stanford to turn pro with $60 million in deals with Nike and Titleist, many tour players were publicly indignant: The twenty-year-old had yet to prove that he was worth that kind of money. The moans and groans were even louder when Woods won a tournament and claimed he had done it with "my B game." But Tiger quickly silenced his critics by firing a cool twenty-seven under at Las Vegas to win just two months after going pro, and then, in his first year as a pro, breaking Jack Nicklaus's tournament record in the Masters, winning by twelve. Other golfers and the media may have doubted Tiger's potential, but he never did. When asked if he envisioned winning so soon, he nonchalantly replied, "Yeah, I did."

Anyone who strays too far from the majority view or the conventional wisdom is bound to be labeled "arrogant," "a maverick," "a wildman," "weird," or even "crazy." Of course, in the opinion of exceptional thinkers, it is the mindset of ordinary people that is strange, not to mention counterproductive. That the world is overflowing with mind-boggling problems that must be solved (poverty and terrorism immediately come to mind) is something that everyone can agree upon. But how do such problems get solved if everyone is limited to being "normal" and doing things the way they've always been done? Even if they tried, people like Dell and Branson and Yogi would be hard pressed to see the world through the same lens as the majority of people. Somehow, they never picked up the inclination to think "ordinarily"; somehow they avoided getting caught in the net of society's conventions. Branson, in fact, delights in his efforts to "upset the applecart, to put noses out of joint in stale boardrooms around the globe."

We all give lip service to "free will," and then live our lives chained to convention, popular opinion, and trends. That's why I point to the Yogis, Dells, Bransons, and all the other blessed *enfants sauvages* who choose to live in their own worlds, deaf to their critics. We have to understand that as strange and outrageous as such people often seem to be, it is they who make us sit back and marvel at human ingenuity and talent. If you really want to break from the pack, you have to risk being perceived to be as eccentric as these people. You have to think exception-ally—a LOT.

You Believe in "Free Will," Right?

Many people tend to consider the way they think to be genetically determined, like the color of their eyes or hair. "I'm sorry," they will say. "But that's how my mind works." If you are always overanalyzing what you're doing, if you judge your behavior according to how other people view you, if you don't have the self-confidence about your potential to push the envelope even just a little—if that's the way you've told yourself your brain works—then your mindset has become a major obstacle to being a successful performer.

Happily, you can change how you think. Thinking is not predetermined like the color of your eyes. It is the difference between, as psychologists say, "traits and states." Eye color is a genetic trait. How you think is a state—a state of mind, momentary, malleable, within your control, changeable, even programmable. And while there's a great deal of talk about "how someone's mind works" and "she's been focused since birth," it's just loose talk, not to mention bad science. More often than not it's an easy excuse for not being a better thinker. That some people are born to be successes while others are born losers, and the best most of us can do is hope that our DNA has aimed us toward the front end of the line, has no basis in fact or science. Nor does success only depend upon how our parents have raised us or on education or other kinds of training. Don't get me wrong, God-given talent and proper training are valuable variables for success. Michael Dell and Yogi Berra are natural exceptional thinkers but they also *worked* at how they thought. Richard Branson definitely was lucky to be born into a family that appreciated the value of bucking conventions, but he still had to choose and execute his thoughts and ignore the legions of Britons who wanted to see him fail. I make a good living advising people on how to improve as performers, but I myself have to get busy deciding what lens I'm going to look through each day. Talent or training alone may tee up high-level performance, but they are not sufficient.

Success is due neither to nature *nor* nurture. Everyone can choose to change how they think, but there is a resistance to this idea. We believe that we are stuck with "the way our mind works" or with the education that we've been handed or with the responsibility to "think like a grown-up." But that's just conditioning. Whether you made the choice consciously or not, you still made a choice about how you think and you've been conditioning it ever since. When we practice a certain behavior—that is, doing it over and over—we actually produce new and stronger synaptic connections. Nerves pass information by releasing chemicals (dopamine, serotonin, epinephrine, acetylcholine, etc.) called neurotransmitters from their synapses into the space between neurons—the synaptic junction. The neurotransmitters either bind to receptor sites on the dendrites or body of another neuron, or are reabsorbed by the presynaptic "terminal button." In basic terms, the more a nerve cell is activated, the more neurotransmission is optimized to keep up with the "flood" of signals. The whole process is formally called "Hebbian Learning." And it works in the other direction as well. When a neuropathway is inactive, neurotransmitter volume decreases, channels are lost, and receptor sites die. The next time the corresponding motor pattern or memory or skill is required, the less strong, the less effective the brain signals will be.

Thinking patterns, therefore, are a product of repetition. What you experience as a set mindset is nothing more than a strong pattern of synaptic junctions with a lot of neurotransmitters. If you want to change the way you think, you merely weaken the synaptic junction and strengthen new ones. In other words, choose a new lens through which to see reality and start using it the majority of the time. The military and NASA purposefully train people's bodies *and* minds. The rest of us, however, do not train that way. We do not identify a thinking pattern that we want to use under pressure and then practice it, over and over. We do not put our minds through intentional repetition so that when the going gets tough, rather than freaking out we know that the training will kick in. The military, of course, are specialists in disaster. Most of us are not. We tend to coast through life and work in normal gear. On the occasions when we need to think exceptionally— for an important job interview or in closing a big deal, for example— we can only hope that our minds will rise to the occasion. And that uncertainty and lack of preparation only increase our anxiety and fear of failure.

The top guns in every field do not leave how they think to chance. And neither should you.

You're in the Driver's Seat—Not the Performance

Most people walk around with a constant conversation going on in their heads, logging literally thousands of thoughts a day. Many people treat this inner conversation as if it were a physical necessity of being human, like their heart rate or the air coming in and out of their lungs. We get so used to this inner blather that we forget it's happening. But it is not mere brain-stem activity. It is our cerebral cortex doing its rational, analytical thing. It is our superego warning us to respect the law and the values of the community. The higher brain and a value system are valuable things to have when you're strategizing important decisions and judgments that affect the lives of others. But when you are performing under pressure, the highest part of your brain is not your friend.

Simply realizing that scientific fact is the first step to gaining control over your thinking. Just imagine trying to do your job with the boss always looking over your shoulder or accompanying you on your sales calls, providing commentary as if he were a broadcast analyst breaking down your game at every moment. When you go to lunch, the boss is there, giving color to the play-by-play. When you go home, he's at your side. And at the end of the day, as you climb into bed, he's tucking you in. An absolutely horrifying and nutty idea, to be sure. But allowing the information and second-guessing buzzing around your cerebral cortex is the brain's equivalent of having your boss whispering in your ear nonstop. If you don't want your actual boss following you around with criticism, why do you let your internal boss mess with your mind? If you don't put a lid on that voice, you are walking through life with the wrong person talking to you—and that wrong person is you. To borrow from Yogi Berra again: "I can't think and hit at the same time."

Typically, most people allow events to control how they think. You make three sales calls and get three rejections, your boss discards your memo, your car breaks down on the way home. How was your day?

"Awful, miserable, a total bummer." What is your mental state? It need not be "awful, miserable, a total bummer." To be sure, you cannot control how your customers respond, what your boss thinks, or the condition of the roads, but your response to the day's setbacks is really up to you. Once you are home and the sun's still out and the flowers are blooming, you could decide to work in the garden, take a run, or head over to the golf course to play a few holes.

Why limit your pleasure in life to only the days when everything happens to go right? Often people to come me for help and lament that they wish they could be as positive-minded as other people. They will point to a cheery colleague, or maybe even famous people who have reputations for their upbeat personalities—Tom Hanks, for example, or Oprah. Psychologists call it "False God Syndrome"—assuming that successful people or role models are psychologically different from the rest of us. Wouldn't it be nice to have such a special, problem-free life? The fact is, of course, that Tom Hanks and Oprah Winfrey, and everyone else you might admire, have their bad days. They, too, have business and family problems. Tom Hanks has kids who have to get into college. Oprah has employees who are not always as happy or as competent as she might like. Everyone has to deal with persnickety colleagues or superiors. There's a lot going on in everyone's life, and if Tom Hanks or Oprah always seem to be in a good mood, it's because they have chosen to get into that mental state. When that camera switches on, they have to switch off all their other daily annoyances and focus on the business at hand, which is being good ol' Tom or congenial Oprah.* The fact that they've logged in so many hours practicing exceptional thinking is one of the primary reasons they make so much dough.

You can do the same. It's the difference between being a victim of all of the thoughts that pop into your head and assessing whether you

---

*An extraordinary case in point is Bill Cosby, whose son, a graduate student in education, was senselessly murdered after he left a Los Angeles freeway to fix a flat tire on his car. Cosby, who has created an educational foundation in his son's name, has continued to work as a comedian.

really want to think that way. It's the difference between accepting other people's perceptions of you or your own perception. It's the difference between letting your frustrations and depressing thoughts control you and taking control of what you will think. Blessed with free will, we humans can choose how we think. Your future depends on the decisions you make today, tomorrow, and the day after that.

I like to compare this difference to a speedboat towing a waterskier. When the boat turns right or left, the skier inevitably follows. If the boat goes straight ahead, the skier is in no position to go right or left. And while the skier is the performer, it is the driver of the boat who is controlling the performance. When you let your bad day control your mindset, you've put your brain on water skis. Your thinking—happiness and enjoyment included—is at the whim of what's going on. And you are not alone. Most performers in most fields allow their performance and the lens through which they see the world to be dictated by the circumstances unfolding around them: Are they winning? Are they closing deals? Are people viewing them favorably? Is everything going according to plan? When circumstance is at the wheel and your brain is tagging behind like this, you're in for a yo-yo ride. You'll be up and down and inconsistent.

The best and most steady performers make sure their heads are in the boat, not on the skis; results are out in the wake. The best performers also know that such mental control does not always happen immediately, which is why the waterskiing analogy fits so nicely. When the boat turns, the skier does not follow immediately. Hanging out there at the end of the tow rope, there will be a moment's lag time before the skier is back in line with the boat. But when the boat goes straight long enough, the skier, too, will be straight behind it. Analogously, if you think consistently, performance will follow. The alternative is to leave your thinking up to chance, and merely hope business goes well so your feelings and emotions will, too.

One other thing:

Beware of Experts

We have become a nation of "experts." Turn on the television, and there they are—experts on movies who have never made one; experts on rap who only know how to wrap; experts on celebrity who are only wannabes; experts on Major League baseball who have never watched a 95 m.p.h. fastball coming their way; experts on politics who have never run for office; even experts on war who have never been under fire. If I were limited to only one tip on how to become a better performer, it would be simply:

Ignore the experts.

They have no idea what you really want to achieve, or how bad you want it. They look at standardized tests—or scouting reports, or physical stature and looks, or worse yet, psychological "profiles"—and conclude they know all about you. They assume they can predict how successful you will be. Yeah, right . . . like Richard Branson's IQ score predicted his income or his ability to connect with people.

The best performers force the experts to see the world their way. Yogi knew that he could make it in the major league in spite of what the legend Branch Rickey thought of his tryout. When Dell Computers announced that it would be bringing its direct sales model to the UK before a press conference of twenty-two journalists, according to Michael Dell, "about twenty-one predicted that we would fail." The direct model would not work in the UK. Against all predictions, the Dell model succeeded in England, and then in Germany and even in China, although all the experts warned Dell that selling English-language computers in China was a pipe dream.

So much for expert opinion. The only true expert on you is—you. Beyond that, only people who take the time to get to know the intangibles about you are worth using as resources. Real "experts" are there to assist you in solving your problems and to facilitate and encourage your progress toward where you want to go—to help you keep thinking exceptionally in the face of obstacles to great thinking. In fact, the real expert is not really an expert at all, but a *support system*. What we all need is the kind of support that functions like a personal coach who helps us work through certain problems, has suggestions for appropriate fixes, but never tries to limit anyone. These kinds of experts teach you what they have learned from experience, particularly from dealing with other performers with problems like yours. They never make judgments about whether you are good or bad. "Do you think I will make it?" is a question that my clients usually ask me, and my answer is always: "How would I know? You tell me." The most important thing that you can do in developing your talent is to have your own sense of what your potential is. And, by definition, potential has nothing to do with your past track record. It's about your future, and my job is to help my clients get on the fast track to their futures.

Society is constantly analyzing and evaluating us and coming to conclusions about what we can do without really knowing our inner talent. Of course, every organization must pick and choose. And I certainly feel the pain of the hiring executives of major corporations, faced with the hordes of gifted graduates coming out of school every year. How do you pick? What kind of criteria should you use? To find the best candidates, the NFL, for instance, administers a battery of psychological tests, forcing the best college football players in the country to answer upwards of eight hundred pencil-and-paper questions that the experts believe will provide franchises with important information about who will make it in the NFL and who will flop. They are looking for team players; no weirdos, wildmen, or troublemakers allowed. I wonder how Yogi would have done on those tests. Or Joe Namath. Or Muhammad Ali. (What would they have learned about one of the game's most talented players, O. J. Simpson?) And for every great extrovert in sports (Namath, Ali, Deion Sanders), there is the strong, silent, even surly type who is also a superstar (Tiger Woods, Ted Williams, Barry Bonds, Larry Bird). If you're looking for a Muhammad Ali type for your team, do you cut a Tiger Woods? That's why sports teams tend to go for clearly objective, racehorse measures: size, speed, and agility, rather than potential.

In the business world, the criteria tend to be grades, degrees, and references. But for every big, fast athlete, there is a five foot, eight inch Spud Webb or David Eckstein. For every gifted young kid, there is a late bloomer like Michael Jordan or Julius Erving who was not a high school basketball phenom. For every brilliant student from a top business school, there are a bunch of "screw-ups" who will surpass the former in the business world. Is there a company in the world that would have hired the young Richard Branson? (And if someone actually hired him, how long would he have lasted?) Moreover, just because people are gifted at selling themselves in a job interview does not mean they will be equally successful at selling your product.

Those visible measures for success are never as important as the psychological ones. To assess that psychological edge, I have to interview people very carefully about how they operate under pressure and then watch them perform. But if you walked into my office today for a consultation, I would also want to know immediately: Do you have an exciting, vivid vision of the world and where you are in it? Are you extremely committed to the success of that vision? Are you so confident about your potential that other people will think you're a little too cocky for your own good, maybe even out of your mind? In my book, that's a good thing. In the world of high-level performance, it's essential. So ask yourself, do you create your own reality? How do you view yourself and events around you? What is your Yogiesque lens? How much do you believe in that lens?

CHAPTER 4

Embracing the Last Taboo—
Being as "Unrealistic" as You Can

They all laughed at Christopher Columbus when he said
the world was round;
They all laughed when Edison recorded sound.

—"They All Laughed"
Lyrics by Ira Gershwin

You would have thought that by now we would know better. People like me who study success and what makes one person a better performer than another do not know many things for certain. But one thing we do know for sure is:

You will not do incredible things without an incredible dream.

Nevertheless, when I ask my students or clients what their dream is, they squirm and blush and say such things as, "Well, I don't know if I really want to get into that," or "You're going to think I'm crazy if I tell you." When they finally spill the beans, they preface it with, "Okay, but don't laugh." People these days seem to talk about their sex lives or personal family matters like they talk about the weather, but dare not utter a word about what really stirs their souls. They are afraid to confess that they want climb the Matterhorn or play golf on the Senior Tour or conduct the Boston Pops; they are embarrassed to admit that they're writing a screenplay or would love to quit their job and make a living chartering tall ship-sailing adventures around the world. Revealing your ultimate dream has become one of the few things not fit to mention in polite company.

Talking about dreams may be the last taboo.

Recently, a student at Rice came to me for some advice. Vaughn Walwyn is one of the top college long jumpers in the nation; he is also a straight-A student who sings in the church choir. Born in the Virgin Islands, Vaughn has had multiple ambitions ever since he was a kid: to go to a great university in the United States, to set NCAA long-jumping records, to represent his country in the Olympic Games, to write and produce music that moves hundreds of thousands of people, to win Grammy Awards. And ever since he was a kid, family, friends, and teachers, concerned that such big expectations would only lead to major disappointment, have tried to calm Vaughn down, to get him to limit his dreams. What athlete sings rap music at the opening ceremonies of the Olympics as the torch is being lit? It's just not done.

But Vaughn didn't listen. He moved to Texas. He won the Texas long jump championship—in style, breaking the state record. He got accepted to Rice University, one of the top fifteen schools in the nation. He began working toward his dream of the Olympics. Right away, people started warning him about the difference between high school and Division I college track and field. They reminded him that out of all the talented long jumpers in America, only a few qualify for the Olympics. The odds of actually winning a medal? Well, Vaughn was smart enough to do the math. He really ought to temper his attitude.

Vaughn didn't listen. By his junior year, Vaughn's long-jumping ability was attracting national attention. The 2004 Olympics were suddenly a real possibility, and the track coaches were eager for him to devote more time to improving his technique. His professors, however, were annoyed when he missed class because of meets. And that business of staying up all night composing songs and converting his dorm room into a studio in hope of getting a record contract? Just about everyone thought he ought to be more "realistic" and start managing his time more sensibly. Vaughn tells me he's lost count of the people who've recommended that he "ought to start acting like a responsible adult."

Certainly such advice can come out of a genuine concern for your well-being; but I find it stems, more often than not, from most people's own fears: They don't want to fail, so they don't want you to fail. Besides, if they tell you to go for it, and you don't make it, it would be their fault, right? They certainly don't want to be responsible for your frustration and disappointment. If they have some insight or knowledge that can prevent you from being heartbroken, that's good advice. It *seems* logical. Just not to exceptional thinkers like Vaughn Walwyn. For Vaughn, going to class, training to be a world-class long jumper, and composing music all night for that first album that will surely go double platinum (as it always does in his dreams) is what keeps him fired up. Like other performers who are chasing a great dream, Vaughn doesn't waste any time trying to prevent upsets along the way. He doesn't mind the criticism. Obstacles are just part of the process. And those unpleasant feelings of failure? They can't even come close to outweighing the propelling passion of his dreams.

So it was really no surprise to me that when Vaughn actually made a connection at a major record company and needed advice on what to say in the cover letter for his demo tape, he was wary that all he would get from his friends and family would be another lecture on "being realistic." He came to me not because I have any particular talent at writing cover letters, but because of my reputation around campus for teaching classes that encourage students to have dreams even wilder than Vaughn's. I never discourage a student's dreams, and it is not because I enjoy upsetting coaches or parents. Psychological research over the past two decades has shown that an individual's dream is a crucial motivator, no matter how improbable or nutty that dream may seem to everyone else. As Ira Gershwin noted, to make history you have to be a little bit nutty. "Normal people" do not sail westward from Europe hoping to find the Far East (Columbus) or build amusement parks in a Florida swamp (Walt Disney). Normal people do not believe they can run the mile faster than scientists are "proving" the human body can go (Roger Bannister, who broke the four-minute-mile barrier in 1954) or pitch in the major league even though they have only one arm (Jim Abbott, the handicapped pitcher who played in the major league for ten years, from 1989 to 1999). Normal people do not quit practicing law to write a novel (John Grisham) or take a breather in the prime of their legendary acting career to race cars or found a popcorn/salad company that donates all its profits to help kids with serious illnesses (Paul Newman). There's nothing normal about going to bed at night dreaming about revolutionizing science, medicine, computers, the marketplace, or the world.

Exceptional people are willing to put up with the smirks, the jokes, and the laughter, to pursue happiness. Vaughn Walwyn's dreams might constantly get put down; they might never come true. But he'll always be vibrantly happy. And knowing the way he thinks, I suspect you'll see him on MTV pretty soon.

Redefining "Dream"

The kind of dream I am talking about is not some midsummer night's fantasy. Nor is it an object or a thing. A dream is not even a goal.

It is a feeling.

For years, Paul Newman was notorious in New York restaurants for insisting on making his own salad dressing. Back in the late 1970s, most of what passed for salad dressing in the United States, particularly the mass-market brands, contained artificial coloring, chemical preservatives, and sugar. Newman was so enamored of his own mix that one Christmas he dragooned his old friend A. E. Hotchner, a writer and biographer of Hemingway, to mix up a batch of his dressing in a washtub in the actor's dank cellar in Connecticut and fill up a bunch of wine bottles with the stuff. The plan was for the Newman and Hotchner families to go around the neighborhood on Christmas Eve singing carols and handing out the bottles of salad dressing as gifts. (As if having a movie star serenading you weren't enough; but Newman "was very proud of his salad dressing," according to Hotchner.) When Newman saw how much was left over, he had the bright idea that "we would bottle the rest, hustle it at some upscale local food stores, make a buck, and go fishing."

Food professionals and bottlers, however, were not encouraging. Historically, "celebrity products" (Mickey Mantle's barbecue sauce, Reggie Jackson's candy bar, Bill Blass's chocolates, Frank Sinatra's ties, etc.) had lost, by one account, upwards of $900 million in startup costs. One company actually was willing to do a test—for a mere three to four hundred thousand dollars! Newman and Hotchner decided to go it alone with forty thousand dollars of seed money from the actor and free legwork from the writer. "From the very beginning, we bucked tradition," recall the salad dressing neophytes in their amusing book about their salad days, *Shameless Exploitation in Pursuit of the Common Good*. "When the experts said that something was 'always done' in a certain way, we'd do it our way, which was sometimes the very opposite." As Newman's quest to market his own salad dressing ran into more opposition, Hotchner began to get more phone calls from the actor on location from movie sets such as *Absence of Malice* and *The Verdict*, or from racetracks at which Newman was pursuing his other passion of race car driving, or from airports between speeches on behalf of the nuclear freeze movement, another one of the actor's hobbyhorses. "The overriding purpose of these phone calls was to get his dressing into a bottle, a bottle bearing the Newman's Own name on a proper label, a bottle that would allow us to thumb our noses at the naysayers."

Newman was one of those born exceptional thinkers, and his unusually long career as an actor had only convinced him that his unconventionality had kept him at the top of his game. "It was his theory," the coauthors write, "that he had to keep things off balance or it's finito. That's why he took up racing cars when they said, 'Not when you're forty-seven years old, are you out of your mind?' That perversity also accounted for many of his risky movie roles, going where he hadn't been before."

The salad business became one more confirmation of the benefits of being unrealistic in life and work. Doubtless you've noticed that Newman's Own salad dressing made it to the supermarket shelves—along with his brand of popcorn, ice tea, and pasta sauce. What you might not know is that Newman's Own has become a major food brand—one of the great successes in the history of the American food business, with annual sales of more than $100 million and profits of $12 million. And all the profits from Newman's Own have been donated to charity and used for establishing the Hole in the Wall Gang camps for kids with serious diseases—more than $137 million since the brand got its humble, against-all-odds start in 1982. Of course, traditional business executives would advise keeping a profit margin to protect for the future or maintaining a higher cash position, "just in case." But from the start, Newman wanted to give it all away "in the pursuit of the common good"—and for the thrill of showing that there's always a different way of looking at things.

Where Does Such a Dream Come From?

A dream begins as an idea or an instinct, some notion in your gut that says, "You know what? I'm going to . . ." It can be a feeling that you've had for a long time, like Yogi's desire to play in the major league, or a new idea in your head that just won't go away, like Paul Newman's salad dressing. Kids dream about being major league baseball players, firemen, astronauts, doctors, and then one day twenty years later they turn around and they're sitting behind desks wondering why their lives are so awful. The idea didn't persist; their dreams went away, maybe to be replaced by others, but more likely torpedoed by "common sense" or "being realistic" or other people's opinions. The dreams didn't stand up to all the effort it would require to make them come true. And that raises the deciding factor in my definition of a dream:

A dream is a feeling that sticks.

No matter what. Whenever your mind wanders, it seems to turn up at the same Field of Dreams. It's the vision you wake up with in the morning, and it's the last thing you picture before you fall asleep. Every time you think of it, the idea in your head seems to get more vivid, filled in with more detail: You not only want to win a gold medal at the Olympics, you not only can see yourself standing there on the podium, the medal around your neck, but you also can feel the goose bumps as your national anthem is played; the tears are in your eyes. (That's how real a dream can be and should be.) Dreams make you click, juice you, turn you on, excite the living daylights out of you. You cannot wait to get out of bed to continue pursuing your dream. The kind of dream I'm talking about gives meaning to your life. It is the ultimate motivator.

A dream is a feeling that sticks—and propels.

Big dreams bestow on the dreamer extraordinary resilience and endurance. Consider, for example, what it takes to become an award-winning surgeon:

Of course, you have to get good grades in college, prefer-
ably at a prestigious college or university because good
medical schools are tough to get into, and you will need as

much of an edge as possible. Then there is the MCAT, the college boards of medical school. Even if you have all As or a 4.0, you will have to score equally well on the MCAT, which means that during spring break of your junior (and sometimes senior) year, while your friends are frolicking in some sunny clime, you will be cramming for standardized tests. You pull it off, and come July when your proud parents drop you off on the campus of Harvard (or Johns Hopkins or Stanford), you are coping with pangs of anxiety because the competition here will be much tougher than at that prestigious college you aced. You're now up against the top one percent of all the doctor wannabes out there, and you had better be ready to study your brains out for the next four years. The courses on anatomy alone preclude sleeping. You succeed. You graduate from med school. But before you can do anything with your degree the government requires that you complete a residency of at least three years. Three years will get you the title of "general practitioner," the least prestigious specialty in medicine. Your dream is to be a top surgeon, and that means five years for general surgery, seven years for cardiac surgery, or nine years for pediatric cardiology or neurology. Oh yeah, and one more thing: The education during residency is not really much like education at all. Its more like the military, but with ostentatious senior physicians constantly on you, making life as unpleasant as possible, handing you all the worst duties in the name of "toughening you up."

Let's review the numbers: four years of college, four years of medical school, nine years of residency. Did I mention passing the board certification exams? They cost two thousand dollars a pop, are offered only once a year, and are so tough that typically only about 20 to 30 percent pass. To earn the dough and the experience for the exam, most top residents do a one- to four-year fellowship for peanuts on the dollar. If that isn't enough, and it rarely is, thanks to the quarter of a million dollars in tuition loans, residents are usually forced to moonlight. In total, that's almost twenty years since that day in college when you committed to a career in medicine. You already have gray in your hair, major debts, a completely out-of-shape body functioning primarily on caffeine, and the knowledge that your lazy friends from college are now making seven figures in business or on Wall Street—and you are only on the *brink* of becoming a famous surgeon.

But you had this dream. . . . Clearly, to pull off a dream like that you need more than just a high IQ or "a talent for surgery." You had better have a passion burning inside you, a vivid vision and feeling of the life of the great surgeon you want to be. Becoming highly accomplished in any field requires the same kind of all-out commitment. Great performers have a reverie that helps them wade through all the sludge—the necessary, but often overwhelming and disheartening road to success.

Dreams vs. Goals

Goals are results, outcomes. When you chase a dream, goals are the steps you take to get there, the momentary rewards for your commitment. But the best performers are so caught up in the pursuit of their dreams that they barely notice the stops along the way. The problem with goals is that they divert your focus to the little things; goals trap you in the details, most of which are a chore and meaningless in and of themselves. With a goal dominating your mind, you lock yourself into the strategy to get you there. Success then is at the whim of the strategy, rather than your skills, knowledge, creativity, vision, and problem-solving ability. Discoveries—major scientific ones as well as turns in personal interest—are unlikely to happen when you're busy trying to follow a prescribed route.

One reason why movies pull us into their world so easily—why they're so psychologically captivating—is that they skip the minutiae of daily life, only stopping to feature its dramas. You are not likely to see Julia Roberts getting in the shower three times to tackle a bad hair day or Tom Cruise brushing his teeth before the start of a big action sequence. Goal setting will focus your life more on the details. Dream setting will help you stay focused on the drama.

Typical goals are a promotion, a raise in salary, a new BMW, losing ten pounds, bench pressing three hundred, finishing your MBA, getting home in time to attend your daughter's school play. Goals are steps to get from point A (owning an old Ford) to point B (that shiny Beemer). While goal setting can be a useful short-term tool, it limits you to reaching only point B, with your mind fixed on external results. Such short-term planning gets you thinking too mathematically— setting timetables, measuring your progress, always thinking about the next step. Pure Training Mindset. Dreams, on the other hand, are the way you live your life, the thrill you feel every day as you go about pursuing something; the only limit is your imagination. Chasing dreams is a wide-open process; it's about allowing yourself a broad path to success, finding adventure, opening new doors. Classic Trusting Mindset.

Like you, all my life I have heard teachers, coaches, and parents (not my own, thankfully) say, "You need to have goals." "You need a five-year plan." No you don't. As a college professor, I have talked to many smart and ambitious young people who are letting their goals dictate what they do: I will major in finance, spend three years at a big investment firm in New York City, then quit to start my own consulting company, which I will grow for ten years, sell, and then use the capital to start an even bigger C-corp that I can take public, make a pile of dough, and retire at forty-five. The general reaction to that kind of ambitious itinerary is, "That kid's going to be very successful!" My diagnosis: a future case of burnout, or at least unhappiness or emptiness.

It is a myth that success is about setting the right goals and working hard to achieve them. The path to the top is rarely so direct. And the most inspired stories (coincidently belonging to the happiest people) are about achievements that stemmed from unexpected career twists, events, and discoveries of people open to all the possibilities that life may offer them. Carly Fiorina majored in philosophy and medieval studies at Stanford before she took a job in business. Even when she decided to return to school for her MBA, her plan was not to become the first female CEO of a Fortune 20 company—never mind a computer company.

When Barbara Corcoran quit her job as a waitress in Fort Lee, New Jersey, to become a receptionist in Manhattan, she was hardly planning the creation of The Corcoran Group, one of the nation's most successful independent real estate agencies, with more than five hundred sales associates and a sales volume of $2.2 billion. She sold it in 2001 to NRT, a major U.S. real estate brokerage company, for a reported $65 million.

Princeton University geologist Gerta Keller has stirred up the field of geology by daring to suggest that the demise of the dinosaurs was more complicated than science has allowed. Being an academic maverick was hardly on her mind when, in the late 1950s, as one of a dozen children of a Swiss dairy farmer, she dropped out of school at fourteen, became a seamstress, then a waitress, then traveled to England and then Australia, where she was shot by a bank robber trying to steal her car to make his getaway. Barely surviving, she moved to the United States, passed the high school equivalency test, finished college by taking out loans, and then got her doctorate at Stanford. Not a lot of planning in that amazing career path.

When Jack Kemp was an All-American quarterback at Occidental College and then a star for the Buffalo Bills, it never occurred to him that he would become a congressman with an expertise in taxes, and he surely didn't plan on being Bob Dole's running mate in the 1988 presidential campaign. When Colin Powell decided to make a career of the army, he definitely was not plotting his route to being a four-star general, never mind advising presidents Reagan and George H. W. Bush, or becoming Supreme Commander of NATO and Chairman of the Joint Chiefs; when he retired from the military, he was not mapping out his route to becoming the next secretary of state with the further goal of invading Iraq to topple his former nemesis, Saddam Hussein. If he had set any one of those posts as his goal, he might not have put himself in the way of divergent opportunities—the opportunities at the real heart of his success.

But It Must Be Your Dream

A dream need not excite anyone else on the planet. One person's dream can be another's nightmare. Some dream of being president of the United States; for others, *including* successful politicians, the White House seems like a lose-lose situation—shouldering the problems of the world along with attacks from critics on both the right and left. The thought of being a trader on Wall Street, for example, does nothing for me. I can't imagine that would be any fun. But I have a number of clients whose eyes light up when they talk about risking millions in the purchase and sale of stocks and the lightning pace at which decisions that determine a corporation's fate must be made. I certainly don't discourage them. In fact, I get excited listening to them talk about chasing their dreams.

My job is to help people find a dream that is not their mother's or father's or significant other's but *their* dream, and then to hold on to it, or find a combination of things that juice them. Some people need more than one dream to make life interesting, like Vaughn Walwyn and Paul Newman.

The Best Dreams Are Unrealistic

In buttoned-up societies like our own, people with big dreams can strike the rest of us as irrational or arrogant, if not a little bit strange. How many times do you think Thomas Edison or Walt Disney or Bill Gates heard the words, "Who do you think you are?" The good little American citizen is not supposed to get too big for his britches.

And we Americans are not alone in our pleasure at sticking big pins in big dreams. The English have a phrase, "tall poppies": When anyone grows beyond a "normal" level, his neighbors should cut him down to size, and fast. The Irish call it "begrudgery." Succeed even a little bit, and everyone in town will come up with a way to knock you down. And from what I know about life in France, Germany, and Italy, and most everywhere else, the pressure on someone who decides not to stay in lockstep with the majority is equally intense.

To hell with them. Exceptional thinkers ignore their critics and go about their business making history (or, like Paul Newman, use the scorn of the naysayers to fuel the quest). I earn a living helping people become better performers, and to do that I want to know what their dreams are. I have never wasted a second trying to decide whether a dream was "realistic" or not. It is not my job to evaluate dreams; my job is to try to help people identify the thing in life that gets them so excited they can't sit still. I have learned not to pause on how outrageous or silly someone's dream might seem by reminding myself of the extraordinary things people accomplish every day. No dream is impossible if it really gives meaning to your life. Even the dream with the lowest probability of being achieved can provide you with a lifetime of excitement, helping you step over the trivial disappointments in life, giving you something to work toward, making you feel content that you are living life to the fullest, right to the end of your days. Being "realistic" is too often an excuse for not working hard enough to improve. It also happens to be a significant source of unhappiness.

I often ask my students to come up with an absolutely impossible dream. The usual answers are "flying like a bird" or "playing professional hockey as a woman." I casually remind them of the Wright Brothers or of Manon Rehaum, a goalie who in 1995 was the first woman to play in a National Hockey League game, or of Canadian Olympic hockey all-star Haley Wickenheiser, who was invited to training camp in 1998 by the Philadelphia Flyers. The best answer I ever got was "Czar of Russia." We all agreed that today it would indeed *seem* impossible to become the Russian czar. After all, the Russians replaced Communism not with the old monarchy but with democracy. But then again, not so long ago most people in the world thought that any kind of political change in Russia was "unrealistic." Changing the government of a country may indeed be an incredible long shot, but if you really believe in it, history has proven it can be done. (No doubt critics of Russian President Putin have already pointed out that he thinks he's the new czar.)

The Difficulty of Dreaming Big in the Second Millennium

America has always been a country for dreamers. The men who "invented America" dreamed of a new kind of nation where freedom ruled, rather than a king or a particular religion. We tend to forget that our country was created from scratch by a group of British colonial lawyers and intellectuals. It began with an idea of a new democratic republic, independent of Britain—a notion that was considered foolish if not absolutely mad by two thirds of their fellow colonists, not to mention the British Parliament. But men like Adams, Jefferson, and Franklin turned their dream into the American Dream.

For the impoverished migrants and squatters who helped that dream evolve into a world power within a few generations, and for the millions of immigrants who built the United States into a dominant global force by the mid-twentieth century, to dream of achieving more in life than their parents was not difficult. My friend Bob Rotella loves telling the story of how his own grandfather, at age thirteen and living in a poor village in the south of Italy in the nineteenth century, told his girlfriend that he would create a way for them to live happily ever after. Rotella's grandfather talked his way into a job on a ship, sailed to America, and made his way to rural Rutland, Vermont, where he found a job in a marble quarry. ("Rutland, Vermont," as Rotella likes to joke, "is a tough place to find *today*.") Three years later, the girl made her own way to Vermont, and they married and built a house. But Bob's grandfather fell victim to a tragic accident at the quarry. Bob's grandmother was left with eight kids to raise all by herself through harsh New England winters and the Great Depression. Bob's father had to take a job in a barbershop at age nine to help support the family. All the children grew up happy and healthy. Bob's own father raised five boys, all of whom earned Ph.D.s.

There are literally millions of stories like that in America, all built on the dream of becoming middle class. But today, most people are middle class. Not so long ago people boasted about being "an average American." But what's "average" in the new millennium? These days, "average" in the United States is a middle-class home owner with 2.45 kids and a two-car garage. But average is also being on your third or fourth job; constantly grumbling about your boss; being upside down with credit card debt; divorced or on the verge of a split; having lousy, estranged relationships with your children; being overweight by at least thirty pounds, and on your way to your first heart attack.

If you want more than that in life, you will have to come up with a better dream.

So—What's Your Dream?

When athletes, musicians, surgeons, and business executives come to me for help, they often spend the first hour telling me how much they love what they do. When they finish, I ask them, "Well, what do you want to talk about with me?" Then they spend the next two hours complaining about all the things that are wrong with their careers— how certain people or things are preventing them from achieving what they want to achieve. My response goes something like this: "Well, you certainly don't *sound* like someone who loves what you do." That tends to throw them off balance a bit, and before they can protest, I like to ask, "What do you *really* want to do?" or, "If you could do anything at all, what would it be?"

The answer to that question is your dream. For the physician, it may be that she loves the smiles little kids give her when she takes their minds off being sick. For the musician it may be the energy of a packed concert hall. For the human resources professional, it could be a congratulatory handshake upon signing a hotshot engineer, or for an executive, patting a veteran employee on the back who just hit the million-dollar sales mark. They don't need to change careers. They need to regain sight of their dreams and remember that pursuing them is top priority. The hours spent in my office talking about all the problems in their professions demonstrate that they've lost touch with their dreams.

When you have nothing to do, where does your mind wander? Chances are that's where your dream lies. It is, after all, your life, and you get to write your own autobiography, you get to produce the movie. What gets in, what gets cut out, what you say at your acceptance speech—it's all up to you. Sure, you will need advice along the way; yes, you will need support from friends and family. But as soon as you hear someone trying to warn you off your dream, as soon as anyone starts telling you to be "realistic," cross that person off your invitation list. To help my students get the hang of what a real dream is, I might give them this assignment:

- Compile a list of ten real people you know or have heard about who are pursuing a dream, the one thing that excites them more than anything, that gets them out of bed every morning with a smile on their face, that really turns them on.
- But . . . they have to be doing something that you could not imagine yourself doing, something that you think is boring, pointless, risky, unachievable, unrealistic, or just plain weird.

Make your own list, and once you have finished that lineup and thought about these people and what turns them on, you will have learned a lot about what real dreams are made of. What idea is rattling around in your head that never seems to go away? What do you really want to be when you grow up—or, better, what did you want to be before you grew up and learned how to "know better?"

Remember: The kind of dream I am talking about is a feeling that excites you, that sticks, that propels you and gives meaning to your life. If your dream strikes you as too wild, too improbable, don't worry. If it's possible in your head, it qualifies as a good dream. Now all you have to do is commit yourself to that vision of your future and pursue it full speed ahead.

CHAPTER 5

Hard Work Is Not the Answer

You know the type: The first person at the office, the last to leave, never takes a break, grinds right through lunch, always eager to take on a new project, constantly working on skills and self-improvement, months of unused vacation and personal days piled up. This is the kind of eager beaver who is so "committed" that they sacrifice personal and family time for the organization. They are in it "for the long term." They give it "110 percent!"

Our culture loves these people, considering them the very definition of the word *dedication*. When the company's fortunes are dipping, the boss is bound to call a meeting to fire up the troops: "We're not performing up to shareholder standards," he warns. "We have to step it up." And he is likely to point to an employee: "You all need to be more like Joe. He's always here working, giving his all for the team." Coaches in particular adore their Joes—the player who may not be the most talented but trains harder than anyone else. The coach's favorite, the teacher's pet, the perfect employee, the ideal citizen—such performers have become the embodiment of the cherished American value that sacrifice and hard work open doors.

Not necessarily. The kind of person who's always tending to "just one more thing" before calling it a day—the person that some (including myself) might call a "grunt"—can be a liability. Those who place too much value on the notion of laboring harder than everyone else can be doing themselves—not to mention their real ambitions, their self-confidence, and their families—a disservice. Yes, on paper they get a lot done. But there is a big difference between hard work and *great* work. To sacrifice in the name of commitment is often to put your own potential on hold, as well as your happiness. And while Americans love the person who "gives it his all" and are critical of the naturally gifted performer who "makes it look easy," as a coach, CEO, or head of surgery, I will take the natural performer over the grinder every time.

Don't get me wrong. I am not against honest labor. Perseverance plays a role in making your dreams come true. But over the past ten years of studying elite performers, I've discovered that the greatest define commitment as much more than diligence and conscientiousness. To them, commitment, like confidence, is a special kind of thinking—a single-minded sense of purpose that is fueled by the energy of a personal vision. In this redefinition of the term, the truly committed person has something that wires her. She doesn't think twice about doing whatever it takes—including working *less* and playing *more*—to pursue her vision, no matter how little (or how much) glory or money is involved.

If you are killing yourself just for a salary raise or to impress the boss or to please your parents (or to win a date with that very attractive coworker), you are not genuinely committed—and probably low on self-confidence. (Confident people are very motivated and not, as most assume, the other way around.) Hard work will no more make you an inspired performer than practicing your penmanship will earn you a Pulitzer Prize for poetry. And if you're saying "yes" to every project and sitting on every committee while ignoring your wife and kids or your health in the cause of "getting ahead," why aren't you getting ahead? Why are you skipping your daughter's piano recital? Being exceptional is not about being everything and everywhere.

The Myth of the "110 Percent" Solution

Few things were more useful in turning the dream that was "America" into the richest and most powerful nation in the world than what historians have called "the Protestant work ethic," which taught that financial success was not an obstacle to heavenly reward. The earliest arrivals to the American colonies were thrilled to find themselves in a place where opportunities were as boundless as the fertile land. Europe's poor and striving majority had been stuck in the toiling classes for as far as time could record, no matter how much effort they put in. But over the next two centuries, millions of European immigrants to America proved that if you worked hard, you could boost your family quickly into the middle class. Enterprise and conscientiousness were considered virtues. "The Lord helps those who help themselves," Benjamin Franklin famously wrote in *Poor Richard's Almanac*, the nation's first self-help bestseller. It was evidently a lesson Franklin had learned at the knee of his own father, Josiah, a Puritan immigrant from England who prospered as a Boston candle maker. On Josiah's tombstone, his son inscribed, DILIGENCE IS HIS CALLING.

This notion that arduous labor was next to godliness became part of the national narrative: It was hard work, for example, that opened the frontier; it was hard work that built the railroads (the nation's first Internet); and it was hard work that, allegedly, created the world's richest economy and all those industrious American millionaires. By the 1990s, twentysomething software geeks camping out in their offices were making billions; CEOs were celebrities, and one of them—Hewlett Packard's Carly Fiorina—was the first woman to run a Fortune 20 company. Suddenly, working "24/7" was not only virtuous and the surest route to success, it had become sexy.

Even after the late 1990s dot-com bubble burst, sending the US economy into free fall, employee work ethic vaulted forward into the twenty-first century, still the principle measure of corporate virtue. Easy money was gone; it was time to get back to the basics of what built this country: hour upon hour of plugging away at the office to get ahead. Top managers will still argue that more than two weeks of vacation is for idlers, or sissy Europeans. (The average vacation time in France is at least four weeks; in Norway, it's eight!) Human resource analysts cite the United States' superior GNP to prove their point—and to keep people in the office. So many American strivers have bought into this that they actually boast about the vacation time they *haven't* used. So strong is this cultural idea that hard work really pays off that it is okay in our society to fail—as long as you were giving greater effort than anyone else.

This is not a good thing. As admirable as honest labor can be, it is not the answer to every problem or failure. The Protestant work ethic may have been great at building a nation, but those intent on building an extraordinary life for themselves will have to redefine their sense of commitment to mean something more than putting their nose to the grindstone. A pat on the back can become addictive; everyone wants to be appreciated. But it can also be manipulative, intentionally or not. Becoming a master of your profession is more than the robotlike effort of honing a set of skills; it's craftsmanship, something that doesn't translate from mere effort. I remember taking a sculpture class in college one summer. Every sophomore at Dartmouth is required to be on campus for summer term, but the atmosphere is lax and outdoorsy and focused on creative ways to learn. Students call it "Camp Dartmouth." I was still relying on my workmanlike attitude. I was playing baseball at the time and figured I'd take advantage of my reduced course load to train hard. Since my reading list was light, I poured extra time into my sculpture class and was sure all the hard work would earn me an A. When August rolled around, and I picked up my grades, I was shocked at what I saw next to SART 16: B+. I went to the professor. I informed him that I had been in the studio far more hours than any other student in the class, and surely I deserved an A. Dr. Lee smiled; he knew I played baseball. "If you take more batting practice than your opponents," he asked, "will you be certain to win more games?" It was really the first time I had not been rewarded for my assiduous dedication, but his logic was impeccable.

His words were also a revelation of how less work and more play could create opportunities for genuine creativity and breaking away from the pack. While I was punching the clock for overtime, other students were thinking about ways to make art.

Another way to understand the limits of hard work (and to borrow from a *Far Side* cartoon by Gary Larson, another exceptional thinker) is to imagine yourself in a room with one door that only opens inward. No matter how hard you try to push the door open, it will not budge. You're putting so much effort into pushing, it does not occur to you that there might be another solution. If you just stopped for a moment and thought about the door dilemma, you might realize that all it takes is to *pull* the door open. Sometimes it is difficult to see the easy solution to a problem because we are busy working too hard.

There are already so many obstacles to success—why turn your own sense of "commitment" into another hurdle?

Overmotivated Underachievers

A few years ago, I got a call from a young lawyer who said he needed help to pass the New York State Bar Exam. That goal hardly seemed a major challenge for someone like John Aspland, who recently had graduated first in his class from one of the top law schools in the nation and immediately got a very lucrative offer to join a prestigious New York City firm. John had spent more than eight hours a day over the past half year preparing for the bar. From early morning through the afternoon he reviewed what he had learned in law school and what he had to know for the state exam; he went home for dinner, barely having time to catch a glimpse of his new baby, and then went back to the law library to study into the night. John turned studying for the bar exam into a full-time job. He was determined to outdo everyone. He headed into the grueling two-day, twelve-hour-and-fifteen-minute test as full of New York State law as a budding attorney could be.

And when the list of passing candidates was posted four months later, John's name was not on it; he had failed the exam. John was stunned; he had never failed at anything before. Worse still, the big law firm he was set to join (with an enviably nifty starting salary) withdrew its job offer. John's all-out effort had not paid off. His fast-track career all of a sudden seemed to be going backward. It was October; he had to find a job; he had large sums of school loans to grapple with. If he didn't want to waste a year, he'd have to study and sit for the test the next time it was offered, in February.

John was so desperate to pass he was willing to seek out a stranger whose expertise he'd never contemplated before. "I'm not quite sure what you do," he said to me over the phone, "but someone told me that you could help me." His self-diagnosis was that he had "choked under pressure." I asked him about the test and how he had prepared. From his answers, I quickly realized that dealing with pressure was not his problem. John had cruised through the cutthroat competition frenzy of law school without blinking, undoubtedly due mainly to his intelligence, but also from his experience as a standout college rugby player. And he really did enjoy the law and seemed fully committed to creating a successful legal career.

John Aspland, however, was a classic case of "overcommitment." His problem was not that he didn't study enough; he had studied *too much*. Those long days in the library memorizing New York State law had made the test seem even bigger and harder than it was. After months of studying methodically but not very efficiently, John had not only worn himself out, he had depleted his confidence, too. As traditional commitment rises, self-confidence often heads south. The more time you put in, the more you sacrifice, and the more your brain subconsciously begins to think that there must be a good reason to have given up eating properly, exercising, and enjoying your friends and family. The brain concludes that you must be up against some enormous obstacle. Otherwise, why would you be expending this unusual amount of effort? The body then goes into emergency mode: Nutrients are burned for short bursts instead of for sustained energy, which is best for long-term memory; muscle is catabolized; fat is stored rather than burned, increasing fatigue; dehydration levels rise; and sleep-wake cycles are thrown out of whack, impairing consistent concentration. As our bodies gear up to take on the "enemy," they switch on the wrong kinds of systems for passing an exam. The pancreas, for instance, goes on alert, effectively robbing glucose from the brain to boost the rest of the body into panic mode. Without proper glucose, the brain is hamstrung; we cannot think clearly. Hormone levels are skewed, influencing our emotions, which also make it difficult to recall information and maintain a consistent mindset. At the most basic psychological and physiological levels, it's red-alert time—definitely not the way to take on a two-day, twelve-hour-plus marathon of problem solving, critical analysis, legal writing, and clear judgment.

John had fallen into this vicious cycle of overwork and anxiety, which easily can spin its victims deeper into faulty commitment: "The more the better" attitude toward work causes psychophysiological detriment; productivity and progress also take a hit. Believing the myth of hard work, the sufferer concludes that he must not have been committed enough, so he decides to work even harder. The result is total Training Mindset, or what performance psychologists call an "overmotivated underachiever"—a person who, by every objective measure, is talented and able, yet does not perform anywhere near his potential, despite massive amounts of effort.

In a culture in which diligence is a virtue, overmotivated underachievers have an irresistible appeal. They're "coachable." They'll hammer away at any request or suggestion you give them; and they'll break their backs trying for you. It's no wonder that when I talk to groups of coaches or managers about my take on commitment, I can feel the tension in the room. Most coaches have spent their careers trying to get hormone-stoked adolescents (distracted by sex, drugs, peer approval, and once in a while even schoolwork) to focus on the personal discipline it takes to become a top athlete; most managers fill their days pushing uninspired workers to maximize their effort and minimize their breaks. Most coaches and managers, in fact, were overmotivated underachievers themselves, who succeeded because they worked hard at their modest talents but fell short of greatness. All that work, however, made them great "students of the game," perfect preparation for their career. The downside is that they are likely to see themselves in, and overreward, the diligent hustler. Meanwhile, they berate the supremely talented performer who has never had to train hard to succeed. "If I had just half your talent," coaches say (and have said probably since the first Olympic Games in ancient Greece in 776 B.C.), "I would have been the greatest player of my generation." It is an unlikely boast. Why? Because gifted, intuitive performers think very differently from your typical overmotivated underachiever. Coaches and managers tend to think that the bigger the obstacle, the more you have to bear down, that if you win the wind sprints at practice every day, or crank away more hours on the clock, you're going to succeed. Great performers don't think obstacles are a big deal. They watch the grinders choke at go-time and say, "Thank God I'm not like that."

Do my descriptions of the overmotivated underachiever sound like someone you know? Are *you* an overmotivated underachiever? Let me nudge you toward an honest answer:

You Might Be Overmotivated If...

- You spend so much time at the office or on the road that when you come home your two year old asks your wife, "Who's he?"
- You are delaying your own dreams to achieve your boss's. When questioned about this, you say in all earnestness, "Everyone has to pay their dues."
- You work all the time but never enjoy it or feel fulfilled—and rationalize it by saying, "That's the price of success."

- You cling to the notion that effort will get you past any obstacle.
- You work 24/7 to boost your career, but you can't get past a plateau; all that work has so far only made you a candidate for divorce or a heart attack.
- Your boss or partner asks you to stay late to prepare for a presentation that's coming up next week. When you do it, reluctantly, you think it's proof of how committed you are.
- You constantly complain that it's not fair when someone who's never in the office before 9:00 is given a promotion. Or when you watch sports you dump on athletes for not hustling out every play: "How can they be paying that guy millions of dollars?"
- You always perform better when you are practicing or preparing than when your work really counts; the more important the performance, the worse you do.
- You are good at your job—but never when the boss, recruiters, or anyone else you might want to impress is looking over your shoulder.
- You just "know" you are better than you're showing, but you can't seem to bring out your best.

Taking the Cure

At least John Aspland seemed to realize that he couldn't have worked any harder. But when I asked him how he had prepared his mind for the bar exam, he assured me that he had studied nonstop, memorizing as much material as he could. John misunderstood my question. I wanted to know not what he was filling his mind with, but *how* he was filling it. What was his attitude going into that examination room, and then at his desk before he opened the question book? I wanted to know whether he actually had thought about the test *independently* of the material. "What do you mean?" he protested. "The test *is* the material." I explained that one's attitude toward a test and state of mind

entering the examination room—how refreshed you feel, how ener-
gized you are, how confident you must be—can play as important a
role in such an ordeal as the information you have memorized. He admitted that during the entire year's preparation for the bar exam he
had not given the quality of his thinking toward the test a moment's
thought.

I suspect that most of the readers of this book are beyond their
test-taking days. Yet the examination room remains one of the greatest sources of high anxiety in most people's lives, and bad memories
(not to mention bad grades) have a long-term effect on how many
people prepare for the challenges in the rest of their lives. (How many
people do you know who still have anxiety dreams about being late for
tests, or arriving at the wrong room for a big exam, or showing up
without any clothes on?) Taking a test is no different from preparing
for a presentation to a client or the board. Most people in their work
lives are required to master a certain amount of information related to
their job or product. And when employment is tight and downsizing is
in the air, progress reports, quarterly evaluations by bosses, and peer
reviews can have a lot more riding on them than a passing grade in
Bio 101. A big career is a long line of important tests, and how you
prepare can be the difference between gaining the reputation as a
"clutch performer," a failure, or just one of the masses.

I told John that he had to change his entire thinking about the
exam. My advice for preparing for the next test sitting—six short
months away—was to spend not more time studying, but *less*. To
be sure, he had to review the material. But he also had to practice his
attitude. I suggested he restructure his preparation time into two
phases:

1. He needed to rehearse his perception of taking the exam:
   He had done the work and he was ready to prove it.
2. He needed to develop a study and practice exam schedule that trained his energy, his attitude, and his approach at least as much as it honed his knowledge of
   New York State law.

I got John into a routine of working in small chunks of time. His previous studying style had been to grind all day with a few breaks for food and time with his wife and baby. I suggested he begin by starting his next round of preparation by putting in a couple of hours at the books, taking a break for a workout at the gym, and then returning to his desk to take a practice test. After that, he was free to spend the rest of the day with his family. In the evening I allowed him to return to the law, but only for another practice test, and not to jam extra material into his head.

For someone like John, accustomed to putting in eight- to twelve-hour days studying, this new schedule was going to feel as if he were wasting a lot of time. But if a practice test shows that you've got certain stuff nailed while other topics need some improvement, working on material you already know is wasting time. A few days later, you can review it to assure yourself that the information has stuck, and then move on. Once you change your study habits, you will soon see that by getting in some exercise, decent meals, and more time with your family or friends, you will be able to work with more intensity and efficiency when you return to your books. That efficiency, combined with rest and sitting for practice tests, translates into greater retention.

It took John several weeks to get comfortable with his new schedule, which eventually became two-hour blocks of studying interspersed with four hours off every day. Initially, taking twice as much time off as studying seemed a backward routine for preparing for an exam, but I assured John of several things: He had six more months to prepare for a test that he had already spent over a quarter decade preparing for; after three years of law school, plus almost another year preparing for two attempts at the bar exam, a smart guy like John was bound to know a heck of a lot of law. And what he didn't know would come out in the practice tests, which I encouraged him to take every day. John had to stop questioning his work ethic, and he definitely had to stop beating himself up. His main focus now should be on his attitude toward the exam. With the proper kind of commitment, he was bound to boost his confidence up to the level of his legal knowledge.

Above all, John had to start enjoying the test process as a way of showing how much law he knew. Before he dove into a practice exam, I advised him to leave it closed on his desk for a few minutes and give himself some time to consider how he wanted to think during the test. The attitude he had to practice was one of confidence—total belief in his preparation and knowledge that would translate into a pure Trusting Mindset. John had to remind himself that there were bound to be questions he could not answer. But who cares? There will be plenty more that he will hit out of the park, and he ought to have a great time with that stuff as well as an absolute blast grappling with the bears (just as he did when taking on bigger opponents in rugby). I also asked him to imagine other law students taking the test and then recall how stressed and overcommitted his fellow examinees were the last time. I told him to smile at the thought of how absurd people become under pressure and to remind himself that he would be as ready as he could be, and was about to have some fun proving it. I also wanted John to understand—and *rehearse*—that his attitude alone was bound to give him an edge on most of the other examinees.

During the entire year he had prepared for the first exam, he had taken only *three* practice tests. For the six months running up to the next sitting, John took a practice test every day. By the time the second exam came around, taking exams was as much a part of his daily routine as brushing his teeth. Instead of spending all this time cramming, he actually was performing under pressure—the best way to turn his new mindset into a habit.

He was raring to go. But I had one last tip for him: Don't bring any books to the examination room. Trying to add a few final facts into your head minutes before the exam is not only useless (a year and a half's study is unlikely to be much improved by five minutes more), it is bound to increase anxiety and reduce trust. Instead, I advised him to look around the room at the other people preparing for the test— flipping though their books for last-minute information, pacing around the room, already biting their pencils. I told John to take an inventory of their expressions and nervous tics, and then ask himself, "Do I want to look like that?" Of course not. Those people are not having any fun at all. Most of them would be dwelling on failing the test. I wanted John to be thinking about passing it. I also wanted him to get a good laugh at all the weird behavior that takes place in examination rooms. Legend has it that a candidate once sprinted up and down the aisles, sharing with her fellow test-takers the following essential bit of information: "I am covenant, and I am running with the land!" On more than one occasion, a guy wearing diapers has been spotted. Noticing such wacky things was likely to put John into the confident mindset required to do well on such an important test.

After the test, we talked, and John said he thought it went quite well. "Whatever my score is, it will be a good one because I had a really good time," he told me. "And you were right about the room. Before the test people were so crazed that they were doing all kinds of bizarre things. One guy was in the back of the room doing tai chi." John reported that he actually had laughed out loud as he scanned the room, which unfortunately made his neighbors even more nervous but put him in a playful mood. Were there questions that he didn't know the answers to? "Well, yeah," he said. "But that doesn't matter. I expected that." The stuff he knew, he really knew, and he was confident that he had done well on those sections. I was delighted because from what I was hearing, I could tell that John had done extremely well.

As it turned out, we both fell short in our predictions on how well John did. He did not just pass the New York State Bar—he got the highest score for that sitting. As a result, he got a number of good offers from prestigious New York City law firms. He turned them down. He knew that the big firms require young associates to put in punishing hours at work, which might be okay for single people, but John and his wife intended to have a second child, and he was also committed to spending time with his family. Besides, he'd just learned through the bar exam process that grinding out long hours wouldn't make him a great attorney; he had gotten the feel for the kind of passion, single-minded attitude, and well thought out strategy required for real commitment. John accepted an offer from a good firm in the state capital, and now when he works hard or around the clock, it's based on desire, not self-sacrifice.

Once a classic case of an overmotivated underachiever mired in the Training Mindset, John Aspland learned how to work less and trust the Trusting Mindset—and it changed his life. He now lives and breathes the commitment of an overachiever.

CHAPTER 6

Definitely Put All Your Eggs in One Basket

Back in the early 1970s, sociologist Darrel Siedentop, now the dean of the College of Education at Ohio State University, was conducting research on human development in sport. In his free time, he was a passionate gardener who had landscaped his large backyard beautifully with a well-mowed lawn surrounding his pride and joy, a lovely flower garden. One afternoon, he came home from work, headed for the garden, and was appalled at what he saw. Someone had been tramping through his flower beds. Staking out the scene of the crime the next day, he heard some voices in the yard, and there were his culprits: neighborhood kids who were using his yard as their after-school football field, diving for touchdown catches into his soft flower beds.

Siedentop was furious. But he also was an accomplished scholar who studied social motivation. He had an idea. He emerged from the house and called the kids over. Instead of threatening them, as they expected, or punishing them (or worse, calling their parents), he informed the football players that he was delighted that they loved his flower garden as much as he did. He invited them to keep coming over after school, and to encourage them, he offered to pay them a dollar apiece to play in his backyard. The kids could not believe their good luck.

Not only could they continue their football games in this great field, but they would also get paid for it, just like professional athletes! After school the very next day, they met in the sociologist's yard to play, and, sure enough, he paid them each a dollar. Every day, they showed up and collected their fee. Within a couple of weeks, however, they came less and less, and soon stopped showing up altogether.

Siedentop not only had his garden back, he also had data for the motivation chapter in his landmark 1972 book *Development and Control of Behavior in Sport and Physical Education.* The story of his "accidental" study is a staple today in psychology and sociology classrooms around the globe for explaining the difference between *intrinsic* and *extrinsic* motivation. The neighborhood kids, Professor Siedentop wrote, initially used his flower bed for their end zone because it was fun. They loved playing football, his plush green yard provided the neighborhood's most inviting field, and diving for catches into a soft flower bed had the extra kick of seeming like they were scoring in the colorfully painted end zones of the Rose Bowl. But when he started paying the kids, he began to change their motivation. Soon they were coming to his yard not for the joy of a pickup game of football, but to make a buck. Their motivation had been shifted from internal—"Hey, let's play"—to external—"That weird guy will give us a dollar again." Siedentop's conclusion: Commitment that is personally driven is stronger and more enduring than commitment hinging upon outside rewards. It's comparable to playing the violin because you love the sound and rhythm and feel as opposed to your mother loving the idea that you're playing the violin. "But you are musically gifted!" your mother might protest. And you actually might be extremely talented. But you will never turn into a great musician because, as the old saying goes, "your heart isn't in it."

I see the problem of extrinsic commitment all the time with medical students and young residents. They study and work crushing hours at the hospital, doing everything expected of them—from thirty-six straight hours on their feet staring at radiology films to the never-pleasant task of cleaning out impacted bowels—but not doing it very well. The reason: Their hearts aren't in it. They have chosen medicine because their parents were thrilled by the idea of a doctor in the family, because guidance counselors encouraged them in that direction, or because they were seduced by the prestige and income doctors earn. Inevitably, they burn out. The same holds true for Wall Street traders and analysts attracted to the financial services business for the year-end bonuses and massive fortunes hanging out at the end of the stick. They go nonstop, never straying out of eyeshot of a stock ticker, saying "yes" to every request from the boss, keeping themselves awake with coffee and amphetamines. They think their commitment is impressive, until they find themselves checking into therapy for ulcers and depression. This is not healthy commitment.

Most people can recognize these extreme cases. But it blows me away just how many folks object when I suggest that they, too, may be over- or extrinsically motivated. When I say in one of my lectures that commitment needs to be something more than sacrificing your own dreams and time with family and friends, someone will inevitably jump up in the question period to argue that without that Spartan ideal shaming him into the office every day, he would start dogging it on the job, cutting corners, taking days off. "No," I explain. "Once you lift the guilt, if you end up dogging it, it's because you realize that what you're doing with your life doesn't juice you." Find something that does, and not only will you enjoy yourself on the job, the work will also seem to be taking care of itself.

Dedication is necessary to success, yes. But it must be the *right kind* of dedication. If you've got lofty, creative, vivid dreams that you want to turn into reality, you must also be abnormal in the way that you view commitment. It doesn't mean going top speed in every aspect of your life, day and night. Making great stuff happen is not about multitasking or sheer effort. You must make choices about the areas where you most want to separate yourself from the pack. When people buy into the demonstration of work ethic, throwing themselves into everything, the result is halfhearted commitment in too many areas. To be committed to everything is to be committed to nothing.

The kind of commitment I find among the best performers across virtually every field is a single-minded passion for what they do, an unwavering desire for excellence in the way they think and the way they work. Genuine commitment is what launches you out of bed in the morning, and through your day with a spring in your step.

When I described my version of true commitment to a friend who enjoys the poetry of the great Irish writer William Butler Yeats as much as watching baseball and playing golf, he pointed to a line from a poem Yeats wrote during World War I, "An Irish Airman Foresees His Death":

> *A lonely impulse of delight*
> *Drove to this tumult in the clouds.*

That "lonely impulse of delight" is at the center of genuine commitment.

To help my students see the difference between what traditionally passes for commitment—what I call "unhealthy commitment"—and real, sustainable, performance-enhancing, "healthy commitment," I put the following three lists on the board:

HEALTHY COMMITMENT	UNHEALTHY COMMITMENT	LACK OF COMMITMENT
Being Passionate	Having a Spartan Ideal	Being an Occasional
Striving for Excellence	Striving for Perfection	Player
Earning It	Sacrificing	Being Victim to Obstacle
Finding a Way to Win	Paying the Price	Making Things Easy
Loving the Extra Mile	Forcing an Extra Mile	Giving in to Frustration
Chasing a Dream	Always Focusing on	Lacking Inner Desire
Doing It for Yourself	Mistakes	Going Through the
Focusing on Successes	Delaying Gratification	Motions
Feeling Dedication	Always Working	Doing Just the Big
Being Intense	Neurotic, OCD	Things

HEALTHY COMMITMENT	UNHEALTHY COMMITMENT	LACK OF COMMITMENT
Being Optimistic	Logging in the Hours	Being Lazy
Playing	Being Pessimistic	Not Really Wanting It
Going for It	Covering Your Bases	Not Sustaining It Daily
Expressing Freedom	Preventing Failure	Thinking Negatively
	Taking Responsibility	Making Excuses
The Stuff of Dreams;		Cheating
Doesn't Feel *Like*	*Can Work, But Isn't*	Blaming Others
Work	*Fulfilling*	
		You'll Be at the Whim
		of Circumstance

What I want you to come to grips with is the difference between going all out because you think hard work is one of the Ten Commandments or because you think it is what your boss or shareholders expect and reward, and going all out because it thrills you. Great performers truly cannot get enough of what they do. As Mozart famously said as he was dying at age thirty-five, "I am finished before I have even begun to enjoy my talent."

The Passion of Real Commitment

When people warn, "Don't put all your eggs in one basket," exceptional thinkers laugh them off; putting all their eggs in one basket is a secret to their success. To outsiders, their behavior can seem obsessive, monomaniacal, or downright crazy. So crazy, in fact, that some think they really should be "committed"—to a *mental institution*. That's just how differently great performers think. They decide what they want out of life and work and *commit* to that choice with the single-minded focus we usually identify only with starving artists who endure poverty and/or the scorn of popular taste to pursue their artistic passions. It's a useful model for the kind of commitment I am describing. For while many artists have become rich, I have never heard of a great one who chose to be an artist for the money or the fame. The best in every field do what they do because:

> *They simply cannot imagine themselves doing anything else;*
> *they don't want to imagine doing anything else.*

They love selling porcelain or farm equipment, making deals or music, or repairing watches or automobiles; the thrill of standing before a jury or a classroom, transplanting hearts, playing tennis, or sitting down to write is what gets their system flowing. The genuinely committed person is so into his pursuit that he would do it even if, as the famously "crazy" American poet Delmore Schwartz once said of crafting poetry, "no else seems to read what he writes."

In 2003, Martina Navratilova was back at Wimbledon, twenty-five years after the young Czechoslovakian tennis player electrified center court, clinching the first of her nine Wimbledon singles championships. Martina and her doubles partner were rated number six in the world and had a good chance to win Wimbledon again. But everyone wanted to know why Martina, about to turn forty-seven years old, was still submitting her body to the exhaustive travel and pounding physiological stress of big-time tennis. "I just love playing," said Martina, who proceeded to win the mixed-doubles championship for her twentieth victory at Wimbledon and set a new record.* When critics wondered why Bill Cosby was still acting in TV shows in the 1990s, years after making $250 million off the syndication sale of his breakthrough megahit, *The Cosby Show,* he just shook his head in wonder: "Comedy is what I do." While in the middle of taping a new series in New York, Cosby flew to Las Vegas one Saturday just to test out a stand-up routine he'd been working on for years about his high school algebra teacher, and then flew immediately back to New York to be

---

*Navratilova has won nine singles championships at Wimbledon, seven women's doubles and four mixed doubles. In her thirty-one-year career, she's captured 340 tournament championships: 167 in singles, 173 in doubles.

back on the set early Monday. It wasn't a whim, gag, or bet. Wealthy enough to donate tens of millions of dollars to medical research and universities, Cosby does stand-up these days simply for the love of making people laugh.

Such childish passion for the process rather than for the rewards is hardly limited to playing games or spinning comedic routines; it is at the foundation of all science and art. Between 1661 and 1666, Isaac Newton sat alone in his study at Cambridge University describing the laws of physics and the mathematics to prove them. He then proceeded to show how the phenomena of the real universe, such as the movements of the sun and the moon, the procession of the earth's axis and rotation, and the rise and fall of tides, all danced to Newton's new tune. The results were an extraordinary feat of genius that overturned the Aristotelian cosmology that had dominated human thought for almost two thousand years. Newton was twenty-four years old! More astonishing was that Newton did not publish his findings for another twenty years, only after a friend wore him out begging him to share his knowledge. He had revolutionized physics to satisfy his own intense desire to explain how God's world actually worked. Newton eventually turned his personal notes into his masterpiece, the *Principia Mathematica*, but only during breaks from his new intellectual obsession, alchemy, the spurious science of turning iron into gold.

True commitment can produce *Principia Mathematica*. It also can produce balderdash. The destination is not the point; the journey is what the greatest performers love. And they go after it with an intensity that most view as nuts, or even irresponsible.

The Intensity of Real Commitment

Think about the most accomplished people you know, the people you admire and envy, and I will bet they are so intensely committed and full of energy that their friends and family complain that it would take a bullet to get them to slow down. Take Billy Blanks, for example, the inventor of Tae Bo, a popular exercise program that combines martial arts, kickboxing, and dance moves. Tae Bo offers a unique and heart-pumping workout that, although the physiology is counterproductive for most people interested in weight loss, is terrifically satisfying. But Tae Bo's popularity has as much to do with Blanks's energetic personality and commitment as it does with the product. Anyone who has seen his infomercials and videos will attest to the appeal of Billy Blanks: "If Tae Bo can make me feel like that and look like that, I want a piece of it," is the typical response.

Billy himself has an inspiring personal story. As a kid, his dyslexia and joint problems made him a school yard joke. But Blanks, the fourth child in a family of fifteen kids, clearly had his classmates out-pointed in the determination department. He absorbed himself in Tae Kwon Do, focusing on overcoming his hip anomaly, and found the activity enthralling. At fourteen, he ditched every other pursuit in a quest to master martial arts, and by 1989 he'd won seven World Karate Championships, held black belts in six forms of martial arts, and was the captain of the United States Olympic Karate team, having accumulated thirty-six gold medals in international competition.

Billy definitely has gotten the last laugh on everyone who poked fun at him and assumed he wouldn't amount to anything. In the past twelve years, as Tae Bo became the exercise of choice for such celebrities as Paula Abdul, Magic Johnson, Pamela Anderson, and Oprah Winfrey, Blanks, now a member of the Karate Hall of Fame, has produced sixteen different tapes featuring him leading various martial-arts inspired routines. He's made millions. He's routinely asked to serve as a fitness consultant, and he's appeared in nineteen big-screen movies. Yet he still goes down to the local Tae Bo center to teach classes. Why? Because he loves the workout, and he loves pushing other people to improve their fitness. In his free time, he wouldn't want to do anything else. When asked why hundreds of thousands of people have become Tae Bo fanatics (and Billy Blanks fans), Blanks says, "Everybody wants to be motivated."

To be sure. But most of his customers pick up his videotapes so they can exercise at home while catching up on phone calls, watching

CNN, or simultaneously listening to self-help cassettes. They are ignoring Blanks's most important lesson: To succeed, particularly early in life, you have to grab on to that thing that will separate you from the herd, something that you love intrinsically, and go for it, all out. You really do have to "put all your eggs in one basket."

Isn't Such Commitment Inevitably Selfish?

Some might also call it "putting blinders on." I call it being *single-minded* in purpose—the kind of mindset that typifies exceptional thinkers. Often clients will worry that if they put in the kind of focus required to spark their careers or make their dreams come true, they would have to borrow from other obligations—to their families or their communities or their companies. They're afraid of turning into that burnt-out surgery resident or that hospitalized commodities trader. But remember, those are not examples of real commitment. I've found that people with the healthy kind of commitment have very full lives.

Can one really have it both ways? Can your career and family dreams both come true? You bet. I suspect you've seen someone who you've envied for their dual success in and out of the office; perhaps you've wondered how they juggle it all. I'm hoping you yourself have experienced this kind of combined happiness, even if just for a moment in a single day. (You eat breakfast with your family and each person shares the energy of what they're looking forward to doing during the day; you high-five your kid as you drop her off for school and you tell each other, "Kick ass today"; your first call after losing a big client is to your spouse, who replies, "I'm behind you. We'll get an even bigger one"; you close a deal at the office and get up on your desk to do a mock celebratory dance with the purpose of making your team members laugh.)

It's not about juggling or honing your organizational skills, or reducing your intensity in one area so that you can raise it in another to be "balanced." It's finding ways to tie your various interests together and make them part of the same basket. If great excitement comes from your work, you don't have to leave it at the office. Bring it home and allow it to flow into your family life. It is not a crime to love your work more than mowing the grass or even coaching your kid's Little League team. The common mistake people make is to try to compartmentalize the energy that drives them. I can't stand the phrase, "Hold on, let me put on my marketing hat," (or boss hat, or student hat, or mommy hat). Having multiple personalities is a psychological disorder. The more we try to segregate one part of our personality or life from another, the less effective we will be—and the more we'll need counseling. The most enlightening professionals I've worked with bring their family and personal pursuits to the office—sometimes literally. I've known doctors who enjoy whiffleball games in hospital corridors and executives with basketball hoops in their conference rooms. Shared intensity can integrate the ideas, while perspectives and experiences from home and such after-work activities as competitive sports, sailing, and mountain climbing can enrich your work day.

An old friend of mine who is now a principle design engineer for a medical device company in Silicon Valley is a good example of healthy commitment. Misunderstood, like most exceptional thinkers, Terry Davison is often criticized for his "irresponsibility": He brings his two 100-pound dogs to the lab (and lets them off their leash!), wears tattered athletic shorts around the office because he is scampering to and from the gym, plays softball (well) and surfs (badly) whenever he can get the chance, creates his own vocabulary and wild nicknames for coworkers, and generally keeps people off center. If you didn't know him, you'd think he was nuts. Trying to fit him into a traditional corporate mold would convince you that he'd never be a success. But Terry currently owns more than fifteen patents, and his engineering feats have more than once saved the company. He's not a master of multitasking; he doesn't wear separate hats for each of his hobbies and job functions. Instead, everything he does is focused on being intensively creative. He doesn't partition out his "dog-owner" life and leave his beasts (pudgers, as he calls them) at home or at the kennel. He finds a way to involve them in changing the mindset of his whole office, making it a stimulating, rich environment with a greater purpose, instead of an uptight lab. And in the end, integration of his commitments not only makes him more efficient at what he does, but also improves his and everyone else's performance. Terry would have wholeheartedly agreed with "adventure capitalist" Richard Branson, who said that his balloon flights and business ventures "form a seamless series of challenges."

When I lecture on commitment to my classes at Rice, I often use the example of "Mattress Mac," a legendary figure in Rice's hometown of Houston. Jim MacIngvale (a.k.a. "Mattress Mac") is one of Houston's wealthiest businessmen. Mac made his money not by prospecting for oil, as so many old Houstonians did, but through his single-minded aspiration to help people afford a better life. From his early days of selling mattresses and bed sets to the city's growing middle class, to his innovations in warehousing and same-day shipping of furniture to his customers, Mac was ambitious. But each of his ventures was tied to one overriding idea: "Being relevant for people," as Mac puts it. The company's commercials on local television, featuring "Mattress Mac" with a wad of cash in his hand promoting his wares, are famously amateurish and irritating; but they helped increase the store's visibility without creating costs that would be transferred to customers. Mention "Gallery Furniture" to anyone from the Houston area, and they are likely to launch into an imitation of Mac's boisterous, in-your-face slogan: "Buy it today. Have it today. Gallery Furniture will . . . SAVE YOU MONEY."

Customers often are surprised to find Mac himself greeting them at the door or handing them an autographed football or basketball. He personally oversees his warehouse outlet every single day. Most days, he's there from sunup to sundown. And the man devotes equally as much energy to serving the community. He's a relentless proponent of youth sport programs and the world's single largest benefactor of tennis, a role that includes flying five hundred lucky kids to the French Open in Paris every year. He built a state-of-the-art tennis club that has hosted the U.S. Clay Court Championships and U.S. Open, and he cut a deal to host the Masters Cup in Houston every year. He built and also funds the Houston Rockets' practice facility; he helped steer a bid to bring the 2012 Olympic Games to Houston; and he created a new college football championship now known as "The Houston Bowl." All of these activities and all the energy he puts into them serve the same mission that has fueled MacIngvale since he started selling mattresses under a roadside tent decades ago: improving the quality of life in Houston. That's the basket he puts every single one of his eggs into—and Mac has plenty of eggs!

"What Happens if I Commit Totally— and Then Drop My Egg Basket?"

My clients often wonder whether they should have a backup plan in case they full short of achieving their dreams. "To commit to a career in music I will have to drop out of college," they explain. "But if I don't make it, then I will be stuck without a college degree." Or, "If I start my own business, it will take all my savings; if I fail, how will I pay for my children's education?" Such worries are a rational approach to life, but not the approach exceptional thinkers take to achieve great things.

For starters, thinking about contingency plans even before you've begun to chase your dream shows a certain lack of confidence—and also might be evidence of a lack of real passion. I've discovered that those inclined to initiate backup plans too quickly often are trying to rationalize their way out of taking a risk in life or out of truly committing to an ambition. No, you might not make it as a professional musician. But if you don't, you can always go back to college. It's not as if you will become less intelligent in pursuing your dream as a musician, and the experience you pick up in the process is bound to be useful in whatever career you choose next. If the failure of your new business gobbles up all your savings, that doesn't mean your kids will never go to college. You saved money before, and you can do it again; there are also plenty of loans and grants and scholarships out there, if you're willing to look. Don't let such excuses hold you back.

In fact, I am hard-pressed to come up with a scenario in which the backup plan is not something you can do later. What about leaving a great job to take a flyer with an idea for a new business or to join a start-up company? What if you'd be parting with a job that paid hand-somely and a boss who treats you like a son? "Are you crazy?" your friends, your father, or your spouse will ask. But you are not crazy, just exception-al. If the new job or company doesn't work, for one reason or another, your ability to think exceptionally got you a great job be-fore, and it will again—with a host of added skills and experiences that your previous position couldn't have taught you. If one boss liked you, chances are you're a talented and congenial person who can de-liver, and there is another boss out there who will appreciate your contribution as an exceptional thinker just as much. Or your first em-ployer likely will respect you even more for your initiative and offer you another position.

If you fall flat on your face or go bankrupt, so what? Exceptional thinkers know that they're going to fail, and failure does not change how smart or talented they are, or how much their loved ones love them, or their long-term potential; bankruptcy is not the end of their world, but just one more challenge to show how good they really are. Anyone who has made a costly mistake in business or in the markets will concede how painful it was, but they will also be quick to add how much smarter and tougher failure has made them for meeting the next challenges in their career (in fact, astute executives have been known to go bankrupt in some ventures *intentionally* as an effective long-term business strategy). Before giving in to second thoughts about taking a risk, consider those people who turned down going to work for the infant IBM or Kodak or Xerox or Microsoft—all because they were worried about putting all their eggs in a new basket.

I don't care if you're twenty years into a career and suddenly say, "You know, I always wanted to be a doctor (or lawyer or engineer or minister or chef or orchard owner or teacher or Peace Corps volun-teer)." People shift careers all the time in middle age and, more im-portant, they tend to be a better doctor or minister or whatever as a result of having spent a decade or two doing something else. It's amazing how hard people work to find a reason why they need a backup plan. All that says to me is that they are too entrenched in the old-fashioned notion of commitment. If Plan A is what thrills you, don't waste your time ironing out the details for Plan B.

Let's try one more objection I often get: What if you want two things passionately, but both are extremely difficult and require total commitment? What if, for the sake of argument, you want to play on the PGA Tour or break a world record in your sport and also be a doctor? Easy. Go for both. You might have to select an order of preference, but that is just a decision along the path to making both happen. Success in a sport is generally age-dependent, so maybe that dream comes first. Yes, getting through medical school and the various residency requirements to specialize can take a decade or so. But if the idea fires you up, just keep a picture of Roger Bannister on your desk. He was the first person to break the four-minute mile—and he did it while he was in medical school. Or pattern yourself after Yogi Berra's Spring Training roommate, Bobby Brown, who attended medical school in the off season. Although it took him longer than other students to graduate, Brown became a cardiologist and decades later was named president of the American League. Or better yet, put up a picture of Tenley Albright, who won a gold medal in figure skating at the 1956 Winter Olympics, and then went on to graduate from Harvard Medical School at a time when very few women—never mind women Olympic Gold Medalists—became physicians.

Many great athletes have gone on to equally impressive careers in business and the law: Superstar quarterbacks Roger Staubach and Fran Tarkenton became wealthy entrepreneurs; San Francisco quarterback Steve Young earned his law degree while winning Super Bowls, as did his center, Bart Oates. (Teammates joked that they called the snap count in Latin!) Byron "Whizzer" White, the most famous football player of his generation, was appointed to the U.S. Supreme Court by President Kennedy. The Minnesota Vikings' Hall of Famer Alan Page sits on the Minnesota Supreme Court. I doubt whether Justices White or Page told their teammates, "It's okay if football doesn't work out for me, I have a backup plan. I'm going to be a supreme court justice." They played football with the kind of resolve that earned them Hall of Fame honors, and when it was time to engage in a new calling, they decided to go to law school—with the same put-all-your-eggs-in-one-basket-commitment to becoming good attorneys that they used in athletics.

My friend Oliver Luck, a former quarterback for the Houston Oilers and NCAA academic All-American Hall of Famer, went to law school at the University of Texas after retiring from football in 1986. Looking around for an idea to get him as excited as playing football once did, he signed on as an executive for the NFL and created NFL Europe, which he single-handedly ran as president and CEO. In December of 2001, Luck returned to Houston as CEO of the new Houston Sports Authority, a government agency initiated to finance and construct new sporting venues in the city. By the close of 2003, Houston had three brand-new professional sports arenas, all state of the art: Minute Maid Park (home of the Astros), Reliant Stadium (home of the Texans and the Houston Rodeo), and the Toyota Center (home of the Rockets, Aeros, and Comets). Oliver never had any contingency plans. He simply committed himself to one thing after another, proving that not only can there be a second act in American life, there can be three, four, or more. I recently asked Oliver for his impression of his latest string of accomplishments. He shrugged it off. His mind was already on his next exciting commitment: Figuring out innovative ways to maximize the potential of the city's new structures for concerts, cultural events, international summits, and much crazier ideas—crazy, that is, to nonexceptional thinkers who just don't comprehend people with the kind of commitment or self-confidence of Oliver Luck.

CHAPTER 7

We All Should Wear Ray-Bans to the Office

There is no such thing as too much confidence.

Dr. Bob Rotella

I agree. In fact, as a very confident protégé of Rotella, I would go even further and say that great performers require a measure of confidence that would strike many as absurd, unfounded, and downright irrational. They believe in themselves utterly, without question, even when everyone else is questioning how good (or sane) they are.

How confident is *that?* This confident: Rolling into Tallahassee, Florida, for preseason football camp as an undersized, unproven freshman entering Florida State University's national powerhouse program—with PRIME TIME emblazoned on your license plate. That's what Deion Sanders did in 1985. He had been a left-handed option quarterback in high school but switched to defense in his first year in college because, as he announced to teammates, "I want to be special. Anyone can play quarterback!" Deion insisted that the team create a special poster featuring Deion to be sold at games. Before the opposing team punted, he'd walk over to their bench to warn them that he was going to return the punt for a touchdown—and he'd dare to do that in the opposition's home stadium!

In 1989, the Atlanta Falcons selected Sanders high in the first round of the NFL draft, offering him four hundred thousand dollars. "That's nice," responded Deion, "but I'm worth way more than that. You're going to have to pay me $11 million." By the way, he was already playing *baseball* for the New York Yankees. Drafted by the Yankees in 1988, Deion held out of the NFL draft so he could give college baseball a try. His "hobby" generated a record number of stolen bases, a trip to the College World Series for Florida State, and a pro contract. Did I mention that in college Deion also ran track when he had the time? He won an NCAA four-hundred-meter relay event—wearing a pair of baseball pants—because he had a spare fifteen minutes between games of a doubleheader. Deion hustled back for the start of the second game and proceeded to knock in the winning run.

The Falcons were dumbfounded by Deion's ridiculous salary demand. In the history of the NFL, no defensive back had ever signed for a million dollars, and here was this kid, barely twenty-one years old, who had never played a second in the National Football League, demanding eleven—"to make it fair." The Falcons refused. But Deion knew he was better than the average wage. He also was busy thinking about making the jump to Yankee Stadium, which he pulled off after fewer than one hundred games in the minor leagues—while winning no fans in the New York media by announcing, "Football is what I love; baseball is my girlfriend." By the end of baseball season, the Falcons finally gave Deion a $4.4 million deal, short of the eleven million he had asked for but still the highest salary ever paid to a defensive player.

Pretty outrageous, no? Surely, the definition of "sheer arrogance." The press certainly thought so. They ripped him for not being well conditioned, insisting that no athlete could be in both football and baseball shape at the same time; and they accused him of dogging it in both of his occupations, deriding Deion relentlessly for avoiding tackles *and* striking out against good pitching. They all laughed at the self-annointed "Neon" Deion—who proceeded to run back a punt for a sixty-eight-yard touchdown just five minutes into his first professional game, win Super Bowls with the San Francisco 49ers and Dallas Cowboys, start in the Pro Bowl every year, lead the major league in stolen bases, and hit over .500 in the World Series. Deion Sanders is the only player to hit a home run and score a touchdown in the same week. He's the only person to have suited up for a professional baseball and a professional football game on the same day. He holds the NFL record of running back fourteen interceptions for touchdowns, and he averaged 16.9 yards *every time he handled the ball*. For twelve years, Deion's high-wattage personality, and daily confidence level that seemed to be stuck at "irrational," nettled management—especially his insistence that he should be playing every second of every game, offense and defense—and drove headline writers into overdrive. Deion—well, Deion remained Deion, and he certainly didn't give a damn about what a bunch of overweight sports columnists thought of his mental health. He knew what he was going to accomplish. "When I get the ball, I'm taking it to the house, thinking about scoring every time I touch the ball."

Deion retired in 2001 and soon made a deal with CBS Sports to do commentary as part of their football broadcasting team. Even his biggest critics saw the wisdom in CBS's choice: Deion, who still carried his teenage nickname "Primetime," had the perfect mindset to be in front of a camera. But when Deion announced in late 2003 that his latest dream was to be the coach of his old team, the Atlanta Falcons, the guns were turned back in his direction. "He can't do it," said the critics, pointing out that he had never coached before; "lobbying" for the job was unseemly; it was an insult to the veteran Atlanta coach Dan Reeves, and so on. "I think it would be fun to coach," replied Deion, and then as if to prove himself an exceptional thinker, he added, "I get disturbed when someone in his right mind tells me I can't do it."

Indeed. I'm advising you to aspire to Deion-like levels of confidence. I know, most people are very uncomfortable tooting their own horns. In our culture, it is not considered good manners to talk about yourself or brag about your exploits. What about "modesty" or that bogeyman "overconfidence"? What about the age-old principle of "Don't bite off more than you can chew?" Ignore such warnings; forget being modest. If you're going to become good at what you do, you have to be confident that you're going to succeed; you cannot be afraid to "flaunt it."

"But Deion's a jerk!" People always say that when I raise his example. He may be a jerk. I don't know Deion Sanders personally, though I have known a couple of his former teammates, who talk about him like he is a saint—"the best teammate a guy could ever have." Regardless, whether their public air is interpreted positively or negatively, accurately or not, truly exceptional (and thus confident) thinkers in every field do not worry about such things. Donald Trump surely does not care that many think he's a bit over the top. Do you think Rupert Murdoch cares what you or anyone else thinks about him—or Ted Turner, George Steinbrenner, Oracle's Larry Ellison, Miramax's Harvey Weinstein, or Mark Cuban, the outspoken zillionaire dot-commer who owns the Dallas Mavericks basketball team and has picked up more than a million dollars in fines from the NBA for the brash things he's said? These guys have been hammered in the press for decades for their "arrogance," "overconfidence," and "overreaching"; most of them have been attacked as "crazy" if not downright "evil."

I'm sure you know some extraordinarily successful characters in your own field whose names may not be household words but who could compete with all of the above for the title of "Supreme Jerk." I also will concede that it is harder to find successful women in this category; talented women seem to have a lot harder time getting away with a Trump-like or Steinbrennerian high-handedness in public. But when they charge ahead after their dream, committed and confident, female overachievers also get denounced for being too aggressive, and that other word that begins with a *b* is used a lot, too. (Cf. Madonna, Barbra Streisand, Barbara Walters, Hillary Clinton, and Martha Stewart.)

Genuine confidence is a way of thinking about yourself and your abilities. Confidence is your perception of your own potential; it's a kind of long-term thinking that powers you through the obstacles and tough times, helping you to solve problems and putting you in the way of success. Your confidence is quite a separate matter from your social skills. I could give you a list of real estate tycoons, for example, known for their low profile or dignified charm in public who think Donald Trump is a jerk. But they also know that Trump's (or any other mogul's) social skills are irrelevant when a deal is on the table. As much as you may like to be liked, I would advise you to get rid of that concern when you are performing, and work instead on your confidence and exceptional thinking. You might also consider that no matter how nice a person you are, if you are extraordinarily committed, confident, and successful, there will *always* be someone who will point to you and say, "What a jerk!" The best performers in every field always have a lot of Deion in them, even if the only showing off they do is in their own heads.*

I am not advising you to take a "positive thinking" seminar. When you are up against a tough competitor, a grueling day, a difficult assignment, you cannot create confidence with some kind of on-the-spot routine such as visualizing a happy ending or telling yourself to "be good" or "be strong" or "stay calm." Exceptional performers bring confidence with them. They know what they know and go for it. Confidence is a resolute state of mind by which you believe nothing is impossible. "I am the greatest," proclaimed Muhammad Ali, one of my favorite examples of a supremely confident thinker. Ali used to recite poetry about his prowess in the ring ("float like a butterfly, sting like a bee . . ."); he used his rhymes to call the round in which he would knock out his opponent. Ali boasted, "I'm young, I'm pretty, and I can't possibly be beat." America's tastemakers were appalled by the brash young fighter they called "the Louisville Lip." But Ali's image was snatched up by marketers, his poems were extremely clever, and he did become, indisputably, one of the greatest boxers in history.

---

*But if your spouse, child, or best friend warns you that you've become a blowhard away from your performance arena, you might consider getting some help to improve your social skills.

What bothered people was exactly what made him great: He believed in his success and predicted it, long before he had results to show for it, and against all the oddsmakers.

Overconfidence?—No Such Thing

As Deion once said, "Nobody gets paid to be humble." Elevated levels of confidence are omnipresent among history's greatest overachievers. Benjamin Franklin, one of the most famous men in the world even before he signed the Declaration of Independence, once lamented about humility, "I cannot boast of much success in acquiring the reality of this virtue." The young naval officer Horatio Nelson knew that as the son of a country parson, his prospects for promotion would be slim in class-conscious Great Britain. So he decided to bypass the usual route up the chain of command by becoming a national hero. The crowds that turned out to cheer him after he annihilated Napoleon's fleet at the Battle of Trafalgar were surprised to see a not-so-heroic looking five foot six inch house of bones with one arm and one blind eye. Historians have noted that no admiral had ever been as decisive and as strategically bold at sea as Nelson.

Artists and writers, too, have been known for the same kind of superstar mentality. Neither Picasso nor James Joyce was celebrated for modesty. The American poet Robert Lowell raised many literary eyebrows when he compared himself to Milton, and the novelist Norman Mailer, his contemporary, was declared an "egomaniac" for suggesting that he was as good as Hemingway. When actress Katharine Hepburn once ignored a swarm of autograph hunters, an angry fan yelled at her, "We were the ones who made you!" Hepburn turned around and with fire in her eyes replied, "Like hell you did!" And then hopped into her limo and was driven away. As a young actress starting out, she was cut from several plays. When asked later in her life how she kept going in the face of such public humiliations, Hepburn laughed and said, "I am terribly afraid I just assumed I'd be famous."

If there were a Nobel Prize for confidence, there would not be a shortage of business leaders in the running. In his recent book, *The Mind of the CEO*, Jeffrey Garten, Dean of the Yale School of Management, recalls the first time he met C. Michael Armstrong, the Chairman and CEO of AT&T. Garten was Undersecretary of Commerce and Armstrong, then the CEO of Hughes Electronics, had just been appointed chairman of President Clinton's National Export Strategy. Garten and his colleagues at Commerce had spent weeks preparing for this first meeting with Armstrong to help him get started in his new job of gathering information from US business leaders on how to improve US export policy. Garten and his colleagues were surprised to see Armstrong walk into the conference room without the usual battery of assistants. He shook hands and sat down. Recalls Garten, "I was about to give an overview of the administration's policies and objectives, but I never had a chance . . . 'Here's what we're going to do,' he said, in a tone that indicated he was already running and we had better catch up . . . from the first minute it was his show." And then there's Lee Iacocca, who, despite being terminated for public failures at Ford Motor Company, was so certain he could turn Chrysler around that he agreed to an annual base salary of one dollar! "Right up front, tell people what you're going to accomplish and what you're willing to sacrifice to accomplish it," he said. When Sanford Weil stepped down in 2003 from his position as CEO of Citigroup, *The New York Times* described him as "a brash, voluble man with a robust ego."

Surely the sort of people chosen to run AT&T or GE or Chrysler or Citigroup are likely to have had so much success in their careers that it's little wonder they are loaded with confidence. It's an objection I hear often when I lecture about confidence—and it's wrong. It's not a chicken versus the egg debate. Confidence precedes success. Sit in preseason team meetings all around the country and you will hear coaches warn about overconfidence: "Confidence is the result of years of hard work and focused performance," they preach. But seriously, folks, who would put in all that effort unless they believed they'd come out on top?

One of the drawbacks or our media-saturated world is that we're always looking at people (and companies) in the glow of their most recent impressive victories. We tend to view confidence as a product of accomplishment rather than part of the process that leads there. But supremely confident people were confident long before they achieved anything. Confidence is not the child of their success, but a major factor in it. Deion Sanders was "Primetime" years before he starred on *Monday Night Football* or in the World Series. The young Cassius Clay announced he would "whup" anyone (including the kid who stole his bike) even before he started to study boxing in Louisville with policeman Joe Martin, before his gold medal sweep in the 1960 Rome Olympics, and years before he converted to Islam and renamed himself Muhammad Ali and refused to be drafted during the Vietnam war. ("I've got nothing against those Viet Congs," Ali explained, logically, annoying millions more American sports fans.) Richard Branson, Michael Dell, and Apple cofounder Steve Jobs were confident enough about their abilities to start their businesses as kids, without college degrees. In 1998, after his first appearance on the stand defending Microsoft against widespread charges of monopolistic practices and illegally undercutting the competition, Bill Gates seemed so "arrogant," according to press reports, that he had to be coached on how to appear more personally appealing in public. Sanford Weil grew a small brokerage firm he helped found in 1960 into the major Wall Street player Shearson Loeb Rhoades, which was acquired by American Express in 1981; he created a second financial empire, again starting with a small Baltimore-based financial company, Commercial Credit, and swallowing bigger fish (Primerica, Travelers Insurance, Shearson, Salomon Brothers), he merged with Citicorp in 1998, creating the new company Citigroup.

We rarely see such successful people early in their careers, moving up, falling down, making mistakes and poor decisions, getting their lunch handed to them. Few people know that starting out at GE as a young man, Jack Welch accidentally blew up a warehouse and was sure he would be fired. Luckily, Welch has reported, his boss also was an exceptional thinker who backed self-confident employees. By the time Sandy Weil stepped down at Citicorp, most people had forgotten that he had been squeezed out as the number two at American Express. Few remember that Steve Jobs was booted out of Apple in 1985, only to return twelve years later to save the company. Donny Deutsch, the Chairman and CEO of a hugely successful New York advertising agency with his name on the door, has conceded, "I've always been a guy pegged as having a great ego. But I've never met a guy who has built a business who has not had a great ego. If you can't build your own brand, how do you build brands for people who pay you for it?" Deutsch has boosted such brands as Bank of America, IKEA, Pfizer, Mitsubishi, Coors, and Revlon. But few of his critics or even his fans remember that at the beginning of his advertising career, all the evidence suggested that he was in the wrong line of work.

After college Deutsch worked at Oglivy & Mather for six months, where, by his own account, "I was a terrible account executive. I didn't like it. I was bored." He left ("They would've fired me"), did some traveling, needed some money, went on television's *Match Game* and won five thousand dollars. He then went to work at his father's ad agency. His father fired him. "I wasn't any good," concedes Deutsch. But when his father later announced he was going to sell the agency, Deutsch jumped back in because he knew his father didn't really want to sell. In 1984, he landed his first account for his father's agency, the Tri-State Pontiac Dealers. To get his foot in the door, Deutsch sent a fender to the Pontiac rep's house with a note that read, "We'll cover your rear end." That deal doubled the agency's size, and from there on it was, according to Deutsch, who took over the company from his father in 1992, "a fun ride."

A major part of the fun came in 2000 when he sold his 87 percent share of the company—Deutsch, New York—to Interpublic for $200 million. Deutsch, whose swagger and black-T-shirt-cool-guy style one might easily mistake for belonging to a professional jock, now has his own show on CNBC. Why the new career? "It's easy to play the game and say, 'I'm good at this, and I'm going to keep playing it,'" he says. "The fun is, the juice is, playing other games, facing other challenges, while recognizing who you are and what your competency is." After failing twice in advertising jobs, a person might conclude that he was not any good at advertising. Such early stumbles might cause many to lose their confidence. Not Deutsch, who has proved to be one of the most talented pitchmen of his generation (and not shy about agreeing to that label). He just needed to discover—on his own—that what really got him out of bed in the morning, what blew his hair back, was having some fun in the advertising business. The trade press calls him a "wild man," competitors prefer "yahoo," but no one disputes his talent for advertising. Deutsch says what sets him apart is "the fairy dust" of confidence, and as if to prove it, with a big laugh he announced to one publication, "I can kick the ass of any CEO in advertising."

Superstars think like superstars long before the fans or the press anoint them. What comes first is the confidence. Deion had it to spare long before he had anything to show for it, and, according to Deutsch's father, Donny always had confidence, even when he didn't have a clue how he was going to use it.

Understanding the Science of the Confidence Habit

Confidence is consistency of thinking about what is possible and how to make it possible. How can you believe in something that has not yet happened? We do it all the time, though usually negatively. Most people tend to let negative thoughts and beliefs control them: "I might fail, I might lose. What if I screw up? Yes, I've poured myself into this project, done everything in my power to get it right, but what if the boss doesn't like it?"

To be sure, the future is not knowable, at least in any complete way. Yet the human mind seems wired to demand a complete picture. Gestalt psychology teaches us that a structured whole does not depend on its specific constituents; a drawn figure, for example, will appear complete in our mind and still will have meaning even if the actual representation is lacking or replete with holes. Our mind fills in the blanks based on experience. If you take any sentence in this paragraph and cover up the bottom half of the line of print, you still will be able to read and understand it. Even though your eyes cannot see the entirety of each letter, your brain fills in the gaps. If that sentence were in French and you had never studied the language, your brain would still be able to help you sound out words based on your experience with seeing letters of the alphabet. If it were in Greek, however, with entirely different characters (assuming you didn't know how to read Greek), you wouldn't even be able to sound out the words. Your brain would have no relative information to substitute for the missing data. But when there's familiarity, the Gestalt phenomenon kicks into gear, matching whatever we see to our experience. Try this experiment: Draw the letter C on a piece of paper, then put another piece of paper on top, covering the open half of the letter. Ask people what they see. If you've set it up correctly (so they can't see through the cover sheet, and so forth) most everyone will say they see the letter O, or a zero, or a circle. Their mind is making up information that is not there!

The brain can be even more creative. If you make up a story with a few major facts, tell it to someone, and then go about your business, when you come back later and ask the person to repeat the whole story, they are likely to add more "facts" than you gave them. It's a favorite experiment among cognitive psychologists, particularly those who study eyewitness testimony, that reveals what we call "false memory." If you ask subjects how they know so many details, they are likely to explain that they must have read it in the newspaper or heard it from another friend. To justify the added information, they manufacture an explanation. When confronted with the verity that the story was fiction from the beginning, part of a psychological experiment, they insist that they must have heard about the experiment somewhere!

Then there's the "waterfall effect": When watching a pattern of motion or color for a while, the brain will stick with that pattern even after it has stopped or been changed. The repetitive triggering of perceptual neurons causes activation in the memory areas of the brain that continue to fire after the environmental stimulus ends. By way of our hardwiring, neural signals coming from our memory center override those in the visual or sensory cortex, thus allowing our "habits" of thinking to alter or filter what we actually see, hear, or feel. If, for example, you stare at a grid of red and white checkered squares for a while, and then look at a grid with black and white checkered squares, you will still see red and white, until the brain adjusts with enough neural firing to form a new "memory." Anyone who has been to the movies probably has experienced the waterfall effect when watching the credits roll. We get so used to the rolling letters that even when the credits end and the final, stationary visual pops up (usually the studio trademark) we still have the sensation that the image is moving. The brain is wired for interpretation based on our most common experiences and thoughts. Regardless of the accuracy of the sensory data coming in, because of this filter of experience, we interpret what we're seeing based on our own set of information and are tenacious in defending our decision.

We can look at our future and potential in a similar way, using confidence as the cognitive filter of choice. Though you cannot predict the result of tomorrow's big sales meeting with absolute certainty—the client is notoriously difficult and tightfisted—you have been working hard in preparation for several days and do have a certain amount of reliable information on which to base your expectations. You might know, for example, that the company lacks a resource that your product provides; you know that your product has tested better than anything else on the market. As you play the scene in your mind, the details you've been most attentive to are the ones your brain will use to fill in the gaps in the picture of what will happen. It's up to you what those details are. When you sit in front of a group of potential investors, you cannot know for certain what their ultimate decision will be. Your idea is great, but the history of business is filled with examples of missed opportunities. You can go into that meeting with confidence or not. If you have an appointment with your boss to defend your strategy on a particular deal, you know what you know. How do you feel when you walk into the boss's office?

It's up to you. Confidence is about looking at an incomplete circle and filling in the remaining 60 degrees in a way that will give you a better chance to be successful. It's also about spending enough time looking at circles that when your eyes view an arc, your mind sees a circle. Confidence is not a guarantee of success, but a pattern of thinking that will improve your *likelihood* of success, a tenacious search for ways to make things work. Most people tend to be specialists in projecting "realism," disappointment, or total disaster. They log in an extraordinary amount of thinking about the things that might go wrong. Most people are not great performers as a *result* of their intelligence. Great performers don't get smart; they develop and then rely on their Gestalt-style confidence. But I repeat: It is not something they do on the spot. They don't suddenly stare at black and white checks and see red. They have been staring at red and white so long, either through training or experience, that they're geared for red and white even when presented with the darkest of pictures.

Confidence Is About Possibilities, Not Probabilities

When I ask my clients to tell me about their dreams, they often reply by compiling an odds sheet on their careers as if they were betting on a horse. They've clearly put a lot of thought into the chances of a promotion in the near term, landing a big client, becoming a department head in a few years or a senior VP, getting recruited by a better company, maybe eventually becoming a CEO, or starting their own multimillion dollar company. Many people come to me with the goal of improving their odds. "Who cares about the odds?" I say. "What does that have to do with performance?" The more they stumble trying to explain it to me, the more I see someone who's either not confident or not excited about the prospect of making his dreams come true.

Most people are not inclined to bet on long shots. If someone thinks the odds are 20 to 1 that they'll land a certain account, they are unlikely to bother trying; they certainly won't pour in every ounce of effort and tie up all their free time. I find that when people translate their goals into probabilities, they tend to look for even money or a 50–50 chance. They're into safety over happiness. I advise them to stop thinking about the probabilities and start focusing on the possibilities. Exceptional thinkers are turned on by the concepts in their minds and the feelings in their guts, not by ideas based on some external, mathematical prediction. If what juices them might come true—somehow, someway, someday—they know they'll have a blast trying to figure out how to make that possibility happen. Whether it does or not is immaterial.

Computing the odds against you is one way to make a rational decision. It's also a good way to lower your confidence. If there's something in life you really want, you won't get it or experience it by sitting around doing calculations. By basing your efforts on better criteria than statistical probability, you can save yourself a lot of misery and depression and can then put that energy into finding ways to make the things you believe in come to fruition. "Why risk your reputation?" is a question exceptional thinkers do not understand. What they hate risking is being complacent, bored, or unfulfilled. The best in every business are always looking for the next big challenge.

In 1992, when an IBM board member asked Louis V. Gerstner, Jr., if he was interested in running the company, the former CEO of RJR Nabisco and ex-president of American Express passed. IBM's sales were plummeting, its stock had decreased by 50 percent over the past five years. Gerstner was aware that both *The Wall Street Journal* and the London *Economist* had predicted that IBM was on the verge of becoming another late, great American company. After he got his first look at IBM's current financials and budgets, he saw that the company's sales and profits were declining too fast for comfort, and that its cash position was scary. "On the basis of those documents," he later recalled, "the odds were no better than one in five that IBM could be saved and [they indicated] that I should never take the position." But the board was persistent, Gerstner grew intrigued, and the advice of an old friend also caught his attention: "IBM is the job you've been training for since you left Harvard Business School. Go for it!" Gerstner agreed, thinking that his track record as "a change agent" might be just what the company needed. These were the variables that played into what Gerstner later called "my gluttony for world-class challenges."

To my ears, that's a superstar talking. Gerstner signed on as CEO of IBM, watched profits decline $800 million over four months, and then refocused the company's mission. Ignoring critics who warned that IBM would have to be broken up to survive, Gerstner proceeded to buck the conventional wisdom even further by slashing prices on the company's core (and most profitable) product, mainframe computers. Gerstner even had the self-confidence to say in public, "Computers are magnificent tools, but no machine can replace the human spark." Ten years later, he had pulled off one of the greatest turnarounds in American business history.

Embrace the Unknown

I know it's hard to put yourself in the shoes of superstar athletes and celebrity CEOs who get stoked by hanging it on the line. But I find it a worthwhile imaginative exercise that helps you get inside the heads of exceptional thinkers. They never measure themselves by outcomes; they do not care about how much money they've made, or even their win-loss record. For athletes, enjoyment happens in the moments of greatest tension: the bottom of the ninth, down by a run with two outs, a runner in scoring position, and the bat in your hand, or the final two minutes of the fourth quarter of the Super Bowl ticking away as you step up to center, looking at the NFL's number-one-ranked defense standing between you and a championship. Pure success tends to be about creating opportunity and seeing what you can do with it. For great and supernaturally confident business leaders like Lou Gerstner and Bill Gates and Donny Deutsch, a new challenge is what keeps their work interesting and, as Deutsch would be quick to add, "fun." If the outcome were certain, where would the satisfaction, the excitement, or the fun be?

Confidence is about ignoring external or other people's realities in order to believe in yourself and your ability to make great stuff happen. What "great stuff"? Someone has to make it to the major league, so for thousands of dedicated ball players, the big leagues are a possibility. There are also thousands of CEO positions out there in the marketplace, so any ambitious executive has the option to imagine him- or herself sitting in the corner office. (Also keep in mind that many of the most successful CEOs in American business never had the top job before. GE's Jack Welch and HP's Carly Fiorina are two who immediately immediately come to mind.)

In the 1950s, when Robert Johnson was in elementary school in Freeport, Illinois, what were the odds that he would become a billionaire? What were the odds that he would become the first African American billionaire? What was the probability that he would create Black Entertainment Television (BET), the largest black-owned and -operated company in the country? Zero probability. In Mississippi, where Johnson was born, black kids still could not go to the same schools as white kids, or even drink at the same water fountain. As the son of a factory worker and one of ten kids whose only entrepreneurial experience was a local paper route, Johnson thought such goals were inconceivable. But he did dream of going to college and was the only one of his ten siblings to do so. While at the University of Illinois, he dreamed about joining the foreign service and becoming an ambassador. He took the first step by going to Princeton for a masters degree in international affairs and then accepted a job as an aide to Washington, D.C.'s congressional delegate. One night at a neighbor's party, someone told him that he would make "a good lobbyist for the cable industry." Johnson admitted to knowing nothing about cable TV, but he took the meeting and got the job as vice president of government relations for the National Cable & Telecommunications Association. He quickly learned the business, including how programming could be segmented to a specific audience, which sparked his idea for creating a network aimed at African Americans. With a fifteen thousand dollar bank loan and one major investor who loved the idea, Johnson started BET in

1980. Five years later, BET was profitable and growing. In 2001, Viacom bought the network for $3 billion. Johnson, who remained in charge of BET, made $1.5 billion off the deal.

The history of business is full of such unlikely stories. Do not think of yourself as the puppet master of your life, trying to pull the right strings to make all the steps required to get to one particular destination. Confident people are explorers, navigating their potential, always testing their abilities and talent. Trying to control your life or steer it in one direction or the other is a recipe for frustration; too many things can happen that are unpredictable. The people who say, "I'm going to work here for five years, then get married, then get promoted . . ." will not be prepared for accepting a great but risky job offer, not to mention walking around the corner tomorrow and bumping into the man or woman of their dreams. That is *goal setting,* and as you now know from Chapter 4, the most tenacious goal setters get tied up in the their goal achievement strategies. Steps toward the dream, rather than the dream itself, become the main focus. Yes, you always have the right to choose a new opportunity, but will you recognize it when you are wrapped up in details or minutiae?

Clients faced with an unexpected opportunity often will express to me their concerns about resigning in the middle of a big project or leaving colleagues in the lurch. "Their livelihoods depend on me," they'll say. "I have a responsibility to the company and my fellow employees." Sure, but the company and your colleagues will survive without you. And if your departure causes someone to lose a job, you'll help them find another, write recommendations, hook them into your network. Do not downplay your responsibilities to your own career and family. Robert Johnson, for example, did not tell that person who envisioned him in the cable business that he preferred to stay in his current job—"Thanks for the compliment, but I already have a road map for my life." He was curious about an unforeseen opportunity; he wasn't trying to control his destiny, but to explore it.

And what if that new opportunity doesn't work out? Confident people are not hung up on how things work out because the challenge is what excites them, they're into the process, and they know that whatever happens, they will be able to take advantage of the situation. Too many people let setbacks demolish their confidence. The best performers take it on the chin—in fact, welcome it—and still believe that success is just around the corner. Most often, they use obstacles as the drive behind maintaining high confidence and excitement. Setbacks can be a reason to believe in yourself even more, holding all kinds of experience, knowledge, and data to show you how you will be able to move forward and succeed. Not succeeding can be a window of opportunity, not to mention thrilling. For great thinkers, life would be very boring if it were filled only with easy wins.

The very place where most people lose their confidence—after a failure—is where exceptional thinkers build theirs.

Building Confidence: A Case in Point

Not long ago, I got a call from an old college friend of mine, John Katen, who is one of those naturally confident thinkers. After Dartmouth, John went to work for Andersen Consulting (now Accenture), where he decided, after a few short years, to step off the fast track to start his own IT consulting company. He quickly made it a success and then, in the midst of a downturn in the economy, took a whole year off—without any income—to travel around the world. He had no assurance that when he returned he'd be able to pick up any new clients. And as it turned out, when he got back to the United States, he found the economy even worse. So what did he do? He turned down a series of offers from companies eager to hire him as a consultant! He confidently knew how to position himself for the long term, and these companies were unwilling to pay him his assessed value. He held firm in the market. The world's largest and most prestigious lodging company came knocking, understanding the worth of his skill sets, and thereby giving him the kind of contract that brought the kind of authority he needed to accomplish great things. Two years later, what was initially a short project has turned into an ongoing, highly productive relationship.

Now married, John thought his wife Lynn's employers were ignoring how good she was. He advised Lynn to ask for a promotion and more money. "I can't do that," she said. He had another suggestion: "So work for yourself." He called me for some additional ammunition to persuade his wife to quit her very good job in order to go into business for herself. Lynn was handling federal and state licensing problems for a large American bank. Now that banks are allowed to expand their business around the country, they are required to keep track of all the laws and regulations relating to insurance and financial transactions, which often differ from state to state. Lynn's bank had fallen behind in researching the relevant out-of-state laws, and by her calculations was losing millions of dollars in uncollected revenue. John advised her to research these different norms, and then go to her bosses with a business proposition: For providing, updating, and maintaining a database of regulations specific to each client that would allow the company lawyers to keep up with and qualify the bank for the licensing requirements in every state in the union in which they were doing business, she would charge one hundred dollars an hour.

John spent the weekend designing a database that would accommodate all the licensing information his wife would need and stayed up all night writing the computer program to execute it. He walked her through the entire process of persuading the bank to sign her on as a consultant. The freedom of working on her own (and actually making more money than she was as a full-time bank executive) was her dream. But she continued to resist his advice on very rational grounds: Why would the bank hire a new company run by someone who had never done this before (a one-person company at that), offering a service for out-of-state business that they did not seem to care about? And if they did realize they needed that information, why wouldn't they just use their in-house attorneys? By her measures, the probability that a big bank would give her such a cushy consulting deal struck her as, well . . . she figured that the odds were more favorable for picking the winner of the Kentucky Derby by throwing a dart at a list of the horses running in the race. If she didn't take the bet, at least she still had her secure and well-paying job. A lot was at stake.

I agreed that Lynn was not thinking confidently enough; she was too hung up on the probabilities and the costs of this career change. As competitive as business might be, it is not a horse race. Executives, middle managers, salespeople, engineers, and laborers on the plant floor or assembly line beat the odds all the time simply by trying to accomplish what is possible. I advised John to get her to focus on the *way* she wanted to live her life, and then start focusing on the things she knew she could do to make her ideal life a reality. With her experience in licensing deals, which she was already executing for the bank, she could easily research and collect the licensing laws and regulations for any state in the nation as effectively as any lawyer—and her hourly rate of one hundred dollars was likely to be considerably cheaper. With her national licensing database in hand, she would have information the bank did not possess, and a proprietary system for using it. She would be solving the bank's problems in advance. In response to objection, Lynn could point out the high internal cost: If the bank decided to develop a similar database on its own, it would be outside the scope of their current attorneys' contracts and a highly inefficient use of their time. They'd likely have to involve a staff of systems management people that would be wasting more of the bank's resources doing the legwork that she had already done. She also could point to the millions of dollars that the bank already had failed to collect. Surely, saving anyone that kind of money, never mind a major American bank, was worth one hundred dollars an hour.

Might the bank pass? Absolutely. Might she be jeopardizing her present position? Of course. Were the odds against her? Probably. But she had no control of the bank's decision-making process. And focusing on the likelihood of any venture is just plain depressing and distracting. Instead, she should focus on what she was confident she could do easily: compile her database, make her pitch, and wait for the bank's decision. Most important of all, she should remind herself that she was already frustrated and constantly complaining about her current job. She should begin thinking instead about the feelings and day-to-day experiences of setting up her own consulting firm, tackling tough problems, being her own boss, and having a schedule flexible enough that she could pack a bag whenever her crazy husband decided to take some time off and travel around the world. I advised John to remind Lynn that clinging to the probabilities that the bank would reject her business proposal would adversely effect her delivery, only making it less possible and less likely that she ever would get to live her dream of working for herself.

A few weeks later, John called to inform me that Lynn was on her way into the consulting business—and in heaven over her new situation. "I had all these great ideas, and without the confidence to act on them I wouldn't be able to help people who had real needs," Lynn recently told me.

The Confidence Checklist

Clients come to me with all sorts of problems: They're in a "slump," they're choking under pressure, they're not performing as well as they ought to or want to. Often, their real problem is low confidence. Long before they make an important sales call or meet with their boss or the board, they begin thinking about what might go astray, and end up doubting their ability. Like Lynn, they actually are rehearsing potential disasters rather than programming their heads for success and developing confident solutions to roadblocks.

I'm often amazed at how quickly people forget what got them where they are in the first place. The person who is frozen with anxiety over a meeting with the board to discuss the financial condition of the company has managed to ignore the simplest fact of the situation: He's being called in to solve a problem, to help move the company forward, to give knowledge or defend viable strategic moves. Instead of thinking about how he might screw up, he ought to be focusing on the steps he's going to take and why they're good ones. Lynn Katen already

knew more about banking regulations around the country than anyone else at her bank. Once she started acting on that fact, her confidence grew, and so did the bank's confidence in her.

This underscores what I think is a fundamental aspect of confidence:

Action

And the action you take has absolutely nothing to do with a personal in-service in "self-talk." If the road ahead does not excite you,
it's unlikely that you'll be able to persuade yourself to enjoy it. Even if
you could, the result would not be confidence. Confidence is a vision
coupled with the *execution* of that vision—knowing and going. As one
of my other favorite "overconfident" athletes, Joe Namath (whose autobiography is titled *I Can't Wait 'Til Tomorrow Because I Get Better
Looking Every Day*), used to say, "To be a leader, you have to make
people follow you, and nobody wants to follow someone who does not
know where he is going."

Confidence is one of the most misunderstood aspects of high performance, and I find it useful to remind my students and clients what
confidence is *not*:

Confidence is not your track record.

You make a big sale, close a deal, or hit one out of the park, and you feel
great. But that delight is not to be confused with a real and durable
confidence. First comes confidence, then success. Otherwise, there
would be no billionaires or candidates for the White House. In fact,
people who base their confidence on past or even current successes
often lose their sense of dedication and commitment. It all seems so
easy, so why keep working hard? Worse still, by basing confidence on
your track record, you open yourself up to a nasty fall. When you run
into a series of setbacks or outright failures, you are less likely to be
able to pick yourself up and fight back. Bouncing back is even harder
if your confidence comes from outside factors: depending on the approval of your spouse or college classmates, on the bottom line of

your business, on your coach or the critics, on the opinions of analysts reviewing your stock at Merrill Lynch or in *The Wall Street Journal*. This is what psychologists call "dependent confidence." We see this a lot among athletes who are extremely confident under a coach who thinks they're a real "go-to" player. But when they graduate from high school or college or move to the next level and run into a coach who may not be as impressed, their confidence—and their ability to perform at high levels—evaporates.

Soon after Arnold Schwarzenegger arrived in the United States in 1968, he made a prediction: He would become a movie star, make millions, marry a glamorous woman, and wield political power. The young Schwarzenegger's past stacked up quite heavily against such dreams: He was an Austrian bodybuilder short on money . . . and on English. But he didn't rely on feedback from others to decide how he would approach his future. Whatever you think of Arnold's acting or his politics, it is hard to deny his brilliance as a confident thinker.

Confidence is not a button to be pushed.

After I lecture to students or a group of businesspeople about confidence, I will inevitably get a call or e-mail from someone that says, "I tried that confidence thing yesterday, and it didn't work." Typically, they had an exam, showed up twenty minutes early, and sat in the room "thinking confidently." And they failed the exam. They were on the basketball court, tried to think confidently as they made a shot, but the ball didn't go in. Or they had an important meeting or a sale to make, thought confidently, and got no results. Evidently, they had not been listening very carefully to my lecture. There is no guaranteed one-to-one relationship between confidence and success. If every time you thought confidently, you scored, then everyone would be supremely confident (and I wouldn't have a job). You do not push the confidence button and watch success slide out of the slot, like a can of Coke. You've got to rehearse it—a lot! Sticking with confident thinking in the face of adversity and for a long enough haul is the purity of confidence itself—and the definition of an exceptional thinker.

Confidence does not change your physical skills.
If you do not have the right skills or proper training, you are not likely to set your field on fire, no matter how confidently you try to think. Confidence will not suddenly make up for five years of not going to the gym, or for your lack of business experience. Wise entrepreneurs and businessmen know the difference between a good business plan and a bad one. The reason the board sought out Lou Gerstner and kept pressing him to consider running IBM was that he had seasoning as a "change agent." And Gerstner eventually took the job because he was confident that he could bust his ass to pull it off. Confidence doesn't replace preparation. Quite the opposite; confidence is about having the belief and impetus to improve your knowledge base and expand your skill sets, and the gumption to put in years of hard work behind the scenes while it isn't yet paying off.

Confidence is not about "building self-esteem."
Believing in yourself is important. But it had better be based on something specific, now or in the future. There has been a movement in elementary education to "build children's esteem" by telling the kids that they're all wonderful. The trouble is, the kids don't buy it. If they can't read or are failing math, no matter how much a teacher tells them they are brilliant, they know they're screwing up. If they know their teachers are handing them B.S. in one area, they assume they're getting B.S. in all areas; the teachers have lost credibility, and the kids stop listening to them altogether. Worse, they may think their teachers are lying to hide the truth. And the supposed upside is bad, too. If any pupil actually buys the "self-esteem" message, the result will not be real confidence but "dependent confidence."

Confidence is different from "false confidence."
False confidence is the intrapersonal version of the self-esteem movement: We tell ourselves we're great when we know full well that it's not true. With a little swagger and some expensive tailoring, you may be able to persuade the head of Human Resources that you are the

best person for the job. But if the skill or the experience is not there, you will not be the best person, and deep down you will know it, which is a major ingredient for *low* confidence. You can give yourself positive affirmations all day that you're rich, but if your bank account is in the red, your mind will respond, "Yeah, pal, whatever." The brain reacts the same way that kids do when teachers try to con them into feeling good about themselves; you will end up disbelieving the cheer-leader in your head and set your mind up for shutting down on you. Confidence needs to be based on tangible facts and solutions, inner talent, things you can build upon, potential, actions you can take, di-rections in which you are determined to head.

Confidence should not be confused with strategy.

You hear it in sports all the time, particularly when a good team loses to a so-so squad: "You were overconfident!" coaches scream. They are mistaking confidence for strategy. The confident team generally loses to the poorer team not because of the way they thought, but because of ineffective plans or poor preparation. Since you had a better record and more individual skill, you didn't watch the game films, you didn't do the drills or the extra conditioning that you ordinarily do before a game. Overconfidence didn't beat you; your preparation did.

Scaling *down* your confidence level is hardly the answer; then you'd go into the game without preparation *and* without confidence. When a great-thinking salesman with a great product hits it off badly with a customer or blows a deal, his confidence was not at fault; his pitch was. When a talented young attorney hangs out her shingle and confidently goes after high profile clients, charging top dollar, and proceeds to lose the cases, the word is bound to get around: "Her overconfidence ruined a potentially brilliant legal career," people will say. No, her business strategy is what sucked; she needed to build her practice via word-of-mouth referrals—the strongest kind—and go for the slow growth that is the most sustainable. Her confidence level was just right, and if she combined it with the right strategy, she'd be a superstar. If, on the other hand, she kept the same strategy but scrapped her confidence, she'd be even *worse* off.

Confidence is not arrogance.

To be sure, there are people out there who want to believe that too much passion or big dreams or even success are marks of arrogance. Success just annoys the hell out of some people, and they are eager to cut you down. Today, to become president of the United States requires being a specialist in self-deprecation. No one likes an "arrogant" politician. But imagine the kind of drive and self-confidence it takes to think that you can handle the biggest job in the world? I've found that the way confidence is *displayed* is a matter of perception and taste. When Joe Namath was asked a year later about his brash prediction of winning Super Bowl III, he pointed out that a reporter had asked him who was going to win. "What was I supposed to say— that the other team was going to win?" Namath was not arrogant; the press simply chose to perceive him that way.

You can decide if you want to keep your confidence in your head, share it with those around you or with your competitors, or announce it to the mass public. Tom Hanks selects the first option; Deion Sanders chooses the latter. Madonna goes public; Oprah plays the mother of us all. They all have the same level of internal confidence.

Of course, you might be misunderstood. *Real* arrogance, however, called "social arrogance," is thinking that you are better than other people in general. Confidence has nothing to do with your worth as a human being, or with a comparison of yourself to others.

*   *   *

That is everything that I know about how the minds of the best performers work. In my own research and consulting, all big careers tap into the same mindset: Deion-like confidence, all-your-eggs-in-one-basket commitment, "unrealistic" dreams to go with your own Yogiesque view of reality, and the more pressure the better for putting your skills and talent on display. And when the going gets toughest, the best performers work less; their minds are full of "nothing," totally trusting. That's my model for joining the ranks of all of those overachievers you admire or envy.

With this knowledge in hand, some of my students and clients are ready to enjoy the fruits of overachievement. They make the decision to start thinking exception-ally. If they need more practice, they at least know what they need to work on. Some have plenty of confidence, but were stymied by their "overwork ethic." Others might have been too into goal setting while ignoring their real dreams. Some need work on commitment or believing in themselves in the face of adversity. Still others haven't been able to separate anxiety from their body's natural response to pressure. Some just may need to stop looking through other people's microscopes. Typically, the biggest challenge is to be able to access the Trusting Mindset regularly, and at will.

Many clients, however, look at me and say, "Okay, I've got the model, now give me the steps that it will take for me to learn how to become more confident, committed, unrealistic, and trusting." My answer is short and simple: "No can do." Remember what I said in the very first pages of this book: I do not have the secret formula or 12-step program that will make you a success. *You* have to do that. And now you can. I've taken you inside the minds of overachievers; if you want to join their number, reshape your own mind to follow the same patterns. If you really understand exceptional thinking, you won't be waiting for me to hand over the secrets to the brotherhood. The only real secret is:

It's not what you do; it's how *you do it.*

That I can help you with. Start modeling your thinking after Klammer and Russell, Dell and Branson, Gerstner and Deutsch. And to tee that thinking up, jump into Part II. Through working with hundreds of talented performers in all different kinds of fields, I've discovered some guiding approaches that make exceptional thinking far more efficient, effective, and fun—the real juice for working in the first place. You are in the midst of breaking old habits and creating new ones. Overachievement is right around the corner. . . .

PART II

Becoming
an Overachiever

CHAPTER 8

Closing Billion-Dollar Deals—
"One Pitch at a Time"

On July 6, 2003, with five hundred meters left to go in the first stage of the three-week, 2,130-mile bicycle race known as the Tour de France, the most grueling endurance event in all of sport, Spanish rider José Enrique Gutierrez slipped in a turn. His bike spun through the peloton, clipping pedals and spokes, causing a massive crash that sent thirty-five riders to the ground. Tyler Hamilton, a thirty-two-year-old American cyclist and captain of the CSC Tiscali, the team sponsored by a Danish computer-software company, went flying over his handlebars at thirty miles per hour, hitting the pavement squarely with his right shoulder and fracturing his collarbone in two places.

A single collarbone injury is enough to keep even the toughest extreme sport athlete in bed for six weeks. A part of the body impossible to put a cast on, a broken collarbone will hurt with every footstep and turn of the head; a simple cough can knock you out. But there was Hamilton the next day, walking gingerly up to the starting line, his shoulder heavily bandaged, his bike adjusted with three layers of foam padding to spare him some pain from the two-thousand-plus miles of bumpy roads of rural France that lay ahead. Did falling again worry him? Hamilton didn't understand the question. Falling wasn't in his mental frame of reference. Only the next mile of road was. The CSC Tiscali team was facing Stage Two, and they needed their captain.

Cycling analysts were blown away by his courage, and wagered that he could suck up enough pain to get to the mountain stages before he'd have to quit. At l'Alpe d'Huez, when the vertical climb set in, twenty-two healthy riders dropped out. Hamilton kept going. As more competitors fell behind, Hamilton, a perennial second fiddle to his fellow American Lance Armstrong, gained on Armstrong, who was favored to win his fifth Tour de France. Just two weeks later, Hamilton found himself grinding solo out ahead of the pack on a knee-liquefying 122.45-mile, 3000-plus-foot ascent through the Pyrenees Mountains. Astonishingly, Hamilton captured his first-ever Tour stage victory and moved into sixth place overall.

Critics charged that Hamilton must have been faking the injury in order to psych out the competition, just as Lance had feigned exhaustion in 2002 to gain advantage in the mountains. His CSC team physicians had to appear on French television—the Tour de France is taken very seriously in that country—with X rays of Hamilton's collarbone that showed clearly the two fractures, forming a *V*. Hamilton pressed on to finish the 2003 Tour de France in fourth place, a mere six minutes and seventeen seconds behind the winner, Armstrong. Prior Tour winners called it the gutsiest performance in sports history. Hamilton hadn't lent a moment's thought during the race to impressing anyone. In fact, he was grinding his teeth so hard to endure the pain that he later had to have eleven teeth replaced. "I just took it day to day," Hamilton explained.

That, I think, is the most valuable lesson to take from Hamilton's ride. His courage was certainly awe-inspiring, but anyone intent on becoming an overachiever should heed his concentration. For twenty-four straight days, Tyler Hamilton thought only of what he had to do, right then and there, to keep his bike moving. He was, as psychologists say, "totally in the present." As a result, a man who couldn't even use his right arm to shake hands without excruciating pain rode the race of his life and almost dethroned the Tour's most successful cyclist. It was Hamilton's extraordinary level of concentration that made that achievement possible.

Many people are unable to come even close to such intense focus because they find it extremely difficult to ignore their surroundings. Their tendency to be self-conscious overwhelms their desire to be in the present; their cerebral cortex never gives them a moment's rest. Many others are so overwhelmed by the chaos of everyday life that they think the only route to true concentration is to have only one thing to do. They end up spending too much time trying to clear away the brush of each workday, removing presumed obstacles to concentration, trying to make their workloads lighter, their schedules less hectic. But they might be ridding themselves of the very stuff that can help them focus exceptionally.

The fascinating and extremely instructive thing about performing in adverse conditions is how it actually can narrow your concentration for you. We see it often in sports: Tiger Woods has a sleepless night due to food poisoning, is dehydrated and weak at tee time the next morning, but somehow soldiers through the eighteen holes and shoots sixty-five for the best round of the day! Another golfer, K. J. Choi, copes with a terrible pain in his gut through the final round of the 2002 Tampa Bay Classic. Grimacing and clutching his abdomen between swings of the club, he wins by seven strokes, to capture his second ever PGA Tour victory. The next day he is in the hospital for an appendectomy. "When I first started out the day I did feel some pain and uneasiness, to be honest," Choi said through an interpreter. "I just said to myself, 'I'll just take it hole by hole.'"

Sickness has also been known to focus the minds of the best performers in the world of business: They wake up the morning of the biggest negotiation of the year with a stomach bug; rescheduling might blow the deal, and they cannot afford to cancel. So they trudge off to the meeting, woozy and nauseated. Too sick to want to do anything but finish the meeting and get home to the security of their own private bathroom, they skip the usual gamesmanship and the back-and-forth one-upmanship over the details, focusing instead on the most significant pieces of the negotiation, one at a time, and make the deal. It is a strategy that would never make it into a Harvard Business School case study, but a deal gets signed with record-breaking efficiency, all because illness increased their concentration.

Perhaps you have experienced this yourself. When conditions are that bad, the only way to make it through is to focus intently on what you have to do in the immediacy of this very second. Your total attention and energy are poured into executing a task despite all the pain and misery, leaving no room in your brain to think about anything else, no room for distractions, no room for mistakes.

Fortunately, concentration is a voluntary act; you don't have to get sick or hurt to attain intense focus. What you need is to find a centerpiece to your performance—one that is as simple and as absorbing as feeling awful. And one that is immediate, specific to this very moment. When athletes say, "I was in the present," that's what they mean; they were wholly focused on what they were doing right then, moment to moment; they cared about nothing else except executing the current action. When they say, "It was as if time stood still," or "The audience disappeared," they are describing a mental condition free of all perceptual distractions. It's what the great Harvard philosopher William James, who was also one of the pioneers of psychology at the turn of the twentieth century, once described as "public solitude"—the ability to be among other people, sometimes hundreds or thousands of them, and still be in your own little world of focused performance.

So alien is this state of public solitude to how we humans are designed to operate—as dominated by our cerebral cortex as we are—that most people describe the experience as "mystical" or "spiritual." But it is really quite an ordinary biological phenomenon. The trouble is, we tend to think of getting there as requiring a *lack* of distractions. I hear it from executives all the time: "I've got deadlines out the wazoo; everybody wants something from me; how can I concentrate?" Performing in the present is not about making all these things go away. Rather, it's hooking on to one thing—often the most sensory-absorbing thing—and committing all your energy to it. Hamilton's pain and the deal-makers' discomfort are extreme examples. But no matter what your field, you can take any job and find the simplest, most specific, most immediate task and use it to narrow your focus, thus enhancing your performance. You can approach your work sales pitch by sales pitch, negotiation by negotiation, case by case, meeting by meeting, interview by interview, phone call by phone call, e-mail by e-mail, paragraph by paragraph.

In the rest of this chapter, I will show you how athletes, business executives, and diplomats do this. Narrowing the focus of your concentration is so easy that even little kids can learn how to do it. But first you must:

Forget "Cause and Effect"

Learning to be in the present will be impossible without understanding a principle that I have already discussed:

Performance is distinct from outcome.

Few things have been more ingrained in our minds than the notion that everything we do has consequences. For every performance there is a result that will either be success or failure, a win or a loss. Thinking otherwise goes against all logic (and a common understanding of physics). But exceptional thinkers aren't interested in being logical; and while the principle that every cause has an effect may rule in the physical world, making it in the world of high-level performance means *not* paying attention to the results of every move you make. Keeping each stage of a performance independent of the next is another definition of "being in the present."

This counterintuitive separation of the many discrete moments of a given performance is most easily understood, once again, by looking at sports, particularly those games in which there are distinct action moments over a time span, such as in golf or baseball. Coaches and sport psychologists tell pitchers to throw "one pitch at a time"; we instruct golfers to play "one shot at a time." But doesn't one pitch or golf shot influence the next one? Surely, for example, if you hit the ball in the woods instead of the middle of the fairway, that result will affect not only your next shot but also your score on that hole and thus your total for the round. Well, yes and no. It is true that for most players, hitting one bad shot will affect the next one, physically. A player may have trouble hitting from the rough, or be forced to use a larger club. A bad shot is likely to have psychological effects, too, lowering a player's confidence or undermining the pleasure of the game. Such errant shots can affect the overall score.

But they don't have to. Anyone who has played or watched golf knows that it is possible to hook one from a perfect fairway lie into a pond or the sand traps garnishing the green—and it's possible to knock it stiff from the deep rough. A bad shot can just as easily lead to a great shot—if you are thinking in the present—as it can a second miscue. If you're not in the present, you may recall previous failures to get the ball in the hole, or fast forward in your mind to the low probability of getting up and down from a tough position, or the increased likelihood of flying it over the green. As your cerebral cortex fires up, you'll cling to notions such as "shots from the fairway have greater *odds* of hitting the green, the ball's spin is more easily controllable, there is a wider margin for error." And all the while, you'll be reducing your performance level.

It's worth reemphasizing: Great players don't think in terms of probability; they think in terms of *possibility*. They know they have a chance to put a good swing on the ball at their feet. They don't concern themselves with any other shot, past or future. They know it's possible to make a birdie from the rough so they don't spend time contemplating what devastating things might happen if they miss their target. They just focus on the shot in front of them and play it with abandon. And they typically recover from a bad shot with a brilliant one. When legendary golfer Ben Hogan began a round poorly, he used to say, "Well, that's why they have eighteen holes." Top performers manage to separate each stage of their game from the overall score. A player who thinks exceptionally can hit, as golfers say, "one shot at a time"—as if that one shot were the only shot he would hit all week, as if there were no fairway, no green, no cup. Another way to look at it: If a golfer scores seventy, he will have hit seventy separate shots or played seventy different games.

That's the second key to performing in the present: separating the results from the execution—the effect from the cause—and doing so independently with each element of your work.

"Never Give a Pitch Away"

No one was better at separating execution from results than Pete Rose. During Pete's long, productive, and controversial baseball career (1963–1986), he racked up a series of Hall of Fame statistics: three National League batting titles, regular season and World Series MVPs, the modern National League record of hitting safely in forty-four straight games, ten seasons with more than two hundred hits, the most five-hit games, and a career total of 4,256 hits, the most ever in the history of baseball—a record which he broke at age forty-four. Baseball fans know that Rose has not been elected to the Hall of Fame because in 1989 he accepted a lifetime suspension from baseball for gambling on the game. Rose has confessed to being an inveterate gambler, and, as I write, in his new book he has finally come clean to betting on the Cincinnati Reds. Speculation about whether Pete Rose actually has told the whole story about his gambling on baseball is bound to continue, and you probably have your own opinion about whether he should be allowed into baseball's shrine. I would never offer Pete Rose as an exemplar for how to live your life, but you can certainly learn a lot from his thinking on the field.

In the course of researching my doctoral dissertation on mental control in elite performers, I spent two days talking to Rose about the psychology of hitting. No one I have interviewed has been as aware of or as articulate about the importance of mental conditioning as Pete Rose. "Most sports are mind games because most everybody in the big leagues—whatever sport you talk about—has the ability to be there or he wouldn't have made it," Rose told me. "It boils down to the guy that is mentally strong." Then he added, "I wouldn't have been such a successful player if I wasn't mentally strong." Not blessed with tremendous physical gifts—not base-stealing fast, not home-run-launching powerful—Pete made up for his shortcomings with his intensity on the field. He ran to first base even when he was walked. He was *the* inventor of the headfirst slide. His rare style of play prompted Hall of Fame Yankee pitcher Whitey Ford to dub him "Charlie Hustle."

I routinely give a copy of the sixty-page abridged transcript of my Rose interview to clients, athletes and nonathletes alike. I wish they could have been there. Even sitting on a leather sofa in his PJs, he was as focused on my questions as he was on a World Series pitch, and he responded with the in-the-moment intensity for which he is famous. "In all my career," Rose told me, and with extraordinary self-confidence, I might add, "I was the only player who never gave a pitch away." Of all the records he holds in baseball, that's the one Pete cherishes the most. Of course, no one else even keeps that statistic, which is only more evidence that Rose was an exceptional thinker living in his own world.

What does that mean—"Never give a pitch away"? No matter what else was going on in the game or in his personal life, Pete Rose, the batter, focused on every pitch that was thrown to him as if it were the only pitch he would see in his life. For Pete, time stood still; nothing mattered more than the ball coming his way. Rose locked his eyes on the pitcher and so filled his head with images of rawhide and stitches that there was no room left over for other thoughts—no thoughts about the previous pitch or how successful the pitcher was, no thoughts about his desire to get a hit, to win the game, or the status of his batting average or his future in baseball. It was just him and the pitcher "going to war," as he put it, over this one pitch.

At the plate, Pete was the maestro of focus. Nothing got in the way of his concentration. Nothing. In 1979, just after being traded to the Philadelphia Phillies, while Rose was in the locker room before a game, a stranger walked up to him. Sitting in his sliding shorts, he couldn't even say, "How'd you get in here?" before the guy served him a set of divorce papers. Pete stuck the legal documents in his locker, went out on the field, and proceeded to get four hits in four times at bat. He followed the performance by racking up hits in 22 of his next 29 at-bats. That first year with the Phillies was full of personal problems for Rose; in addition to the divorce, he also faced paternity suits. On the field, however, Rose was his same old spectacular self, batting .331 with 208 hits, 40 doubles, only 32 strikeouts, and an unstoppable on-base percentage of .418. His new teammates were amazed, knowing full well that in a similar situation they would have been mightily distracted. How did the Hit King do it? "Well," Rose explained to me, "I figured that I could get sued for divorce and go 0 for 4 or get sued and go 4 for 4. I'd rather go 4 for 4."

That was the way Pete Rose approached his job of hitting baseballs, for his entire career. Actually, it was more than a job; for Rose, hitting was "war" and his attitude was, "You are not going to beat me." He studied the motions of pitchers before the game and during the season, noticing how their arms looked when they threw a fastball, a curve, or a slider. He broke down each game to every single pitch during his at-bats. If he fouled one off, he would step out of the batter's box and check his strategy and focus for the next one. And to increase his odds of winning the daily war between batter and pitcher, he ingrained the approach of thinking and preparing for a particular pitcher in the on-deck circle. Once he was at the plate, though, he was in the middle of a battle armed solely with intense concentration.

The same kind of self-imposed, narrow concentration translates to any job, big or small. In recent years, I have worked quite a bit with physicians at the University of Virginia, Baylor, and the University of Texas medical schools. When I discuss how Pete Rose thinks in the batter's box, they understand immediately the connection and application to their own mindset.

How Distracted Are You Prepared for Your Heart Surgeon to Be?

As impressive as it might be to show your stuff when it's go-time in a big game, imagine what it's like when a patient's life is in the balance.

My favorite story about how doctors handle that kind of pressure came from Dr. Curt Tribble, a renowned heart surgeon at the University of Virginia Medical School. Luckily, Curt learned about moment-to-moment concentration early in his career.

Curt was a highly motivated student. In medical school and residency, he flourished under the direction of experienced attending physicians. His intelligence and drive garnered invitations to operate on the best surgical teams. He received supervision from nationally acclaimed surgeons. At the conclusion of his training, all of his ambition earned him a position on the faculty at the University of Virginia. As a faculty member, however, Curt could no longer depend on senior physicians to guide him through residency. *He* was now the attending physician. But he was also a junior staff member, and that meant being assigned all the junior help—the least experienced students, the lowest-ranked nurses. His procedures were scheduled in the old hospital building, not the newly built, high-tech facility that people associate with the University of Virginia today.

Needless to say, Curt was antsy about the first heart procedure he would conduct on his own with no senior surgeon looking over his shoulder to ensure a successful result. The pressure went up a notch when the patient wheeled over from the cardiac catheterization lab was a man already in extremely critical condition, his blood pressure way down with a blocked artery. "Basically," Curt explained, "the guy was having a heart attack in the hall and dying right there."

With time running out, the surgical team moved him into the operating room and scrubbed up as quickly as possible. Curt was rattled, thinking to himself: "I want to do right by the patient." But he recalls being "uneasy about the outcome"—so much so that his state of mind that day was still clear to him years later when he told me the story. "I'm thinking in a general sense that this is likely not to go well," he recalled. And then, as they headed into the OR, the cardiologist caught Curt by the arm: "By the way, you'd probably like to know that this guy was our most recent mayor and there are a lot people from the newspapers and TV stations who will want to talk to you about this when you're done."

It was hardly what a young surgeon wanted to hear: The Mayor was cooling right there on the table, and the world was waiting outside to find out the result! According to Curt, the cardiac team had no chance to contemplate the best way to pull this off; they had a heart to work on, and they had to fly. Curt quickly realized that he couldn't do the operation by trying to control the outcome. His top priorities were the incisions and stitches. Curt was smart enough not to try to force a particular outcome, nor did he risk stopping to weigh the consequences of what he was doing. He made the crucial decision to let the instincts he'd built up through years of training take over, let his hands go to work, and deal with everything else another time.

Happily, the mayor came through beautifully, with a full recovery.

"I kind of had several epiphanies during that morning that have served me well ever since," Curt recalled. No matter what your field, it would be useful to keep what that young doctor learned in mind. Epiphany Number One: Curt learned not to get ahead of himself. An exceptional performer is absorbed in the actions of the moment, no matter what's at stake. Epiphany Number Two: Curt realized that it's important to let results be just that—by-products of what you are doing. You can't try to control wins and losses, no matter how important those wins and losses might be. Heart surgeons like to say that every time you actually think about getting a stitch right, you are likely to get a stitch wrong. During that operation on the mayor, Curt discovered that for a surgeon who is *really* good mentally, heart surgery should be no different than tossing a set of keys across the room—a free act, closed loop, but also intent and engaged.

Dr. Tribble also gained insight into one of the most important lessons of thinking in the present, Epiphany Number Three: No matter how much or how little prior experience or practice you have, no matter what your skill level at the time you are about to perform, you must, for the moment, let go of any inclination to judge yourself.

Even in Business? What About the "Bottom Line"?

To be sure, few activities in life are more result oriented than business transactions. Most businesspeople would insist that their measure of success is the profit and loss statement; everything in corporate America is done with an eye on "the bottom line." Yet managers and their staff still have to execute the tasks of the day; they are constantly on call to pull off a series of very different roles with different goals in mind, often under tight time constraints. Successful businesses require people who can get the job done with skill and precision, effectiveness, and efficiency. And as we have seen, nothing discourages the concentration necessary to perform well at go-time more than worrying about the outcome, letting tasks pile together or influence one another, focusing on the past or the future. Mastering the art of being in the present can be an extraordinary tool for business success.

My friend Bob McNair is a billionaire businessman who spent $750 million for the rights to bring the NFL Texans to Houston, built cutting-edge Reliant Stadium for $325 million, and then to help pay the bills persuaded the NFL to stage the Super Bowl there in only its second year in the league. How did he pull it off? McNair is often lauded for his interpersonal skills. A common marvel from people who meet him is, "He has more projects on his desk than anyone in the city, more people clamoring to get his attention, and yet he carefully listened to every word I said." Bob's secret, however, isn't executive training in communication at Harvard Business School. When McNair sits down to do business, he merely concentrates on one project at a time, focusing his attention solely on the person sitting in front of him. He confesses that he's not any good at juggling several things at once, but when he speaks with someone, personally or on the phone, he wants to know everything about them. He treats everyone like an old friend that he's eager to catch up with. That single-minded focus gets him into the present, and because of it no one is a better deal closer with literally billions on the line than Bob McNair.

Segmenting your work is an effective way to narrow your concentration no matter what business you may be in. You don't have to condition yourself like a Tour de France rider or professional ballplayer, or own a near-billion-dollar NFL franchise. You just have to *think* like those people do. If you are a business executive, you must think about what you have to do right now, immediately, to take the next step (like Tyler Hamilton). If you are in sales, you must key on the most appealing aspect of your product and pour all of your senses into it, focusing on the task at hand regardless of whatever else is happening in your life (like Pete Rose), keeping each sales pitch distinct, like it's the only thing you'll do today (like Pete Rose at the plate). If you are a business executive, turn off your cell phone and Blackberry, put your checklist and corporate calendar away, and let the person on the other side of your desk consume your attention completely (like Bob McNair). And whatever your job is, don't bother to think about the consequences, positive or negative, of your efforts. Just lose yourself in the execution of your strategy for execution's sake alone (like Dr. Tribble). Treat every task you do as a separate performance.

At certain times, salespeople, for example, are performing (i.e., selling), and during others, they are either preparing to sell or evaluating a sales call. The superior salesperson will be free and loose during the sale, attending to the client's responses. Her focus always will be on the interaction, the relationship, and never on the result of the sale. Like performers in other arenas, salespeople can get frustrated with a poor performance or lose confidence as a result of a rejection. Those feelings can get carried into the next meeting. The result: the wrong kind of concentration and thus subpar execution. Similarly, an executive in any kind of business might blow up in front of his own staff, then start processing the reasons and consequences as he enters an important meeting with the company's CEO or board. His performance will be further compromised as he tries to "make up" for the past or "get a leg up" for the future. In her best-selling memoir, *Madame Secretary*, Madeleine Albright, the first female secretary of state in U.S. history, offers one of her daily "to do" lists: "1) Call

Senator Helms; 2) Call King Hussein; 3) Call Foreign Minister Moussa; 4) Make other Congressional calls; 5) Prepare for China meeting; 6) Buy nonfat yogurt." You can bet that Secretary Albright did not bring her state of mind from Senator Helms to King Hussein—and after the meeting about China, she certainly wasn't in the same mindset in the store where she bought her nonfat yogurt. In another part of the book, she describes having a "screaming match" with the National Security Adviser in the first Clinton administration and then going home to knit two caps for her grandchildren. Though Albright doesn't explain how she became so skilled at compartmentalizing her concentration to the different stages of her performance day, I would suspect that she had to work very hard over the years as a wife, mother, university professor, and diplomat to define each task specifically, take the time to reset her mindset in between, and train herself to "be in the present."

I suspect that you have experienced this kind of total absorption often in your own busy life. The key to high performance is being able to switch it on at will. No problem. Narrowing your focus by segmenting specific tasks to get yourself thinking "in the present" is so easy that even little kids with severe attention deficit disorders can learn how to do it.

Focusing the Unfocused

When Mary Kirk Cunningham, a member of the U.S. Track and Field team with a top-ten time in the United States in the 10K racewalk, wasn't preparing for the 1996 Olympics in Atlanta, she was teaching third grade in the Arlington public school system. One of her biggest challenges was getting a classroom of twenty-five rambunctious eight- and nine-year-olds to focus on the various tasks of their school day— from learning multiplication tables and dealing with the added stress of taking standardized tests to the daily chaos of getting dressed at the end of school and finding their way to the right bus. Any parent (or former third-grader) can be sympathetic to what teachers like Mary Kirk, as she prefers to be called, are up against, but her job was further complicated by the presence in the class of several kids who had been diagnosed with severe attention-deficit/hyperactivity disorder (ADHD). In my terms, the school day was filled with distractions to thinking in the present; for children with ADHD, a typically activity-packed school day can be a nightmare.

I got to know Mary Kirk in 1995 when she enrolled in a one-credit continuing and executive education course that I offered over a couple of Saturdays at the Northern Virginia satellite of the University of Virginia. On a break one evening during the course, she asked me if I would help her racewalking team prepare for the Olympic trials. I agreed, and began working regularly with the team and with Mary Kirk individually. It was fun, and we made great strides in improving their race times.

Even more gratifying was when Mary Kirk later told me how the kind of mental conditioning we worked on to keep her focused in a race could help her students increase their powers of concentration and improve their performances on standardized tests. A lot of my clients actually relate stories about passing overachievement principles to their children: "As I was working on my mindset, my daughter really picked up on it; we ought to teach the stuff in every school," I hear. Mary Kirk is a great case in point. She worked especially hard with her ADHD kids to come up with strategies to help them focus on the various activities of their day, from learning an academic skill to what she referred to as "the biggest waste of time" for a teacher— getting the kids packed up at the end of the day and ready for the buses that will take them home. "They've been in school all day," she explained, "they're ready to go home, it's loud, and about ten things are going on in their heads at once." To achieve focus, Mary Kirk asked the kids to think about something in their school day that was challenging, like an upcoming test, or a conflict they were having with one of their classmates and picture themselves working through it. That not only streamlined their thinking; it gave the kids additional time to practice problem solving with "one-pitch" attention. "They had an opportunity every single day to do that," notes Kirk.

When the buses were about to be called, Mary Kirk would ask her students to switch to thinking about something exciting that happened during the day that they could tell their parents. "It worked great!" she recalls. "There was no rushing out, no chaos. They had something very specific that they had concentrated on that they were ready to discuss with their families." Parents noticed the change immediately. When they asked their kids what they did in school that day, instead of getting the age-old reply, "Nothing," the kids had something that they had thought distinctly about and were eager to share at home. Along the way, Mary Kirk's third-graders had put themselves so "in the moment" that it didn't even occur to them to push and shove and yell and run out the door.

For most of us, our days are not a whole lot different from being in kindergarten: You're moving from meeting to meeting. An engineer goes from the computer to the lab then back to the computer. A manager meets with his staff and then has lunch with his own boss. A public relations or marketing executive must spend hours with clients, more hours designing the right kind of campaigns, and then even more stressful time presenting results to superiors and to the clients for approval. A lawyer researches cases, depositions, rehearses arguments for court, all the while fielding phone calls concerning any number of new cases. These days, doctors must devote their days to trying to keep their businesses as well as their patients alive.

Overwhelmed by the details and distractions of their busy lives, most people try to eliminate as many as possible "to give myself time to focus on what's important." The typical result is that they waste too much time trying to sweep away the small stuff and still don't manage to focus, or they get caught up in writing and rewriting "to-do" lists, further frustrating themselves with the volume. My recommendation is simple:

Don't rearrange your work; rearrange your focus.

Instead of looking forward to the end of a hectic project one month from now (or the end of a day, just like kindergarteners do), embrace the chaos and let it help you narrow your focus.

I actually have recommended to some clients to create even *more* chaos at work so that getting any work done at all will force them to be in the present. It's a variation of the newspaper reporter on deadline: If your job depends on getting things done in a busy, noisy area, your brain will find a way to concentrate. The human brain is designed that way. When you set up the environment to require extraordinary concentration, it's more likely you'll get into the present. I have been known to make this recommendation to clients particularly flummoxed by distractions: The next time you consider taking a sick day because you feel awful, go to work instead and discover how easy it can be to find a remedy for your illness in your brain's ability to lose itself in concentration. By focusing on one task in one moment (the more specific the better) and free of results, time will disappear—and so will your misery or whatever else has been distracting you. More important, you will find that your performance goes up a notch—just like Tyler Hamilton.

Explaining "in the present," time-oriented concentration is one way I guide my clients toward overachievement. But spatial concentration is just as valuable. In the next chapter I will explain some of the science behind maximum focus and prove to you why, when people ask you after one triumph or another what you were thinking, you only can come up with worn clichés, making you sound the same as a celebrity performer—because you are thinking exactly like them (or perhaps better put, "not thinking," exactly like them).

CHAPTER 9

Target Shooting

For the past four years, I have been advising members of the rising national powerhouse Rice tennis team on how to improve their mental games. We work a lot on building concentration so they can stay in the present. To help players learn to achieve this kind of focus, I tell them that before they hit every shot, they should pick a target. For the rookies on the team, their response is typically one of confusion. They've always thought "targets" belonged to sports such as riflery and archery in which the point is to hit a bull's-eye, or to shooting-oriented games such as golf, lacrosse, soccer, and basketball. Tennis, however, is a game of lobs and drop shots, baseline volleying and coming to the net. The idea is not to hit a target; it's to get to forehands and backhands and rocket them over the net, to move your opponent and set up shots that cannot be returned. In its simplest form, all you have to do is keep the ball over the net and in the court, and therein lies the problem for too many tennis players: They just hit the ball. Though they might hit it with power consistently, they do so without aiming at a particular spot. At the most, they will target regions of the court: right, left, down the middle, deep on the baseline, or short over the net. But the mind works much more efficiently when it has something particular to key in on. The right side of the tennis court is a large area; that's a vague instruction for your brain. Tennis players can aim much more specifically, and when they do, their games improve.

I even advise distance runners to become target shooters. They look at me as if I've suddenly lost my mind: "You know I'm a runner, right?" In the mid-nineties I worked with a marathon runner who began focusing on each stride. He thought about the pavement, picking out the patch of asphalt in front of him where his foot would land next and feeling the pavement glide underneath him. He would think about one step at a time, shifting his eyes from the left foot to the right foot and back, watching one spot, and then the next, and the next. The repetitive nature of this running style left no room for other possible perceptions or "targets" that might have invaded his mind during a run. He didn't think about the gut-wrenching hills coming up in the course, he didn't see his fellow runners, and he never gave a thought to his position in the race. He simply kept putting one foot down after another.

After we'd worked on target shooting for a few months, he started reporting to me that he'd finish marathons with a lot more energy left in the tank. His thinking was becoming so efficient that his body was free to turn it up a notch. Scientifically, his brain was using less energy mentally processing the race, leaving more glucose and oxygen for his muscles. Similarly, tennis players can exhaust themselves analyzing each shift in momentum, processing every bit of strategy and counter-strategy. By the final set, the mind has turned to Jell-O; players complain that in long matches it's hard to keep their concentration going. The remedy is to simplify and narrow what you think about: Just go out target shooting. The tennis player can try to hit every shot to a spot as specific and small as possible—about the size of a tennis ball usually works for most people. Your brain will stop hogging nutrients and stop robbing the rest of your system of fuel.

Have you ever left the office after sitting at your desk all day, and your legs felt as tired as if you'd just completed a triathlon? How did your body get so fatigued without any physical exertion? Mentally, you were processing so much information that your brain could only get the job done by sequestering glycogen, amino acids, enzymes, and oxygen from your muscles. It is no different from running marathons, physiologically. If you approach your work with increased focus, you'll prevent muscle catabolism. You'll be a better performer during the day *and* be able to work out at the gym, play with your kids, or just plain enjoy the evening. One of the best ways to narrow your focus is to become a target shooter.

Of course, the point isn't actually to hit a spot; you get no points for accuracy in business (or tennis). It's about having something to fill your mind with, vividly and completely. Target shooting isn't counting the number of times you nail your objective, or measuring the distance you miss by . . . which brings us to a core fundamental of spatial concentration:

Target shooting is all about what happens before *you pull the trigger.*

It's not about staring really hard at something, trying to force yourself from being distracted by other sights. And it's not about spending time assessing whether it's the "correct" target or if your opponent is expecting you to go for that target. Worrying too much about the spot itself is likely to distract you from the task at hand. So what do I mean when I say "pick a target"? Just that, pick one—get your eyes to select the finest, most detailed, most immediate element of your performance, and then simply react to what your eyes see. In fast-paced careers, like trading, emergency medicine, news broadcasting, and most military duties, there will be a lot of target selection going on in short periods of time, making it even more crucial to just look and shoot—which, as we have seen, is another definition of the Trusting Mindset and just how we want to think under pressure.

Where you find your target is limited only by your imagination. Even in business, plenty of targets are available—if you are trying to think exceptionally, that is.

Targeting Business

The metaphor of a target has been a business cliché forever, as in "the company made its targeted earnings last quarter." For most business-people, "target" means an outcome, something to shoot for in sales, earnings, or profits. But—a point always worth repeating—focusing on outcomes is a detour from total concentration. In a business-related performance:

Your target should be a key in the process of what you are doing.

In sales, for example, the target is not making the sale but doing what is most likely to lead to the sale. In most cases, you will be able to pick out your target beforehand. Often, it will be the sales strategy for a particular client. What do you know before going into the sale? The product you will know cold—why it is good in a specific way and why it is good for a specific client. No good salesperson will meet with a prospective client without doing as much research as possible about the person or the company. The target, therefore, will be based on the most effective strategy to sell this particular client your partic-ular product, not on a vague notion of being a good salesperson, not a general approach to selling, not just a good handshake or a confident bounce in your step.

Once you've selected a focused, research-backed target, execute it single-mindedly and without reservation. If you start second-guessing your strategy and switch to another in the middle of the sale, you will have taken your mind's eye off the target. Such doubt (and the subse-quent loss of concentration) is more likely to cost you the sale than a bad strategy is. Nor can you think about the results of this sale or a previous one. To cut your brain's natural tendency to evaluate your strategy or to conjure up a memory of prior sales calls, you must have a target that's positive in nature, in the present, and vivid. And you must be decisive about your target.

Sales is a lot like putting in golf: You examine the line of the putt between the ball and the hole. What is the condition of the green's surface or slope—flat, downhill, uphill? That will determine the speed of the ball and how hard you must hit it. Will the ball break left or right? Once the golfer has factored in those variables, he can pick a spot on the green and putt the ball toward that target. Notice that the target is not the bottom of the cup; that's the desired result. See the target, internalize it, let it dominate your mind with no other thoughts about score, sinking the putt, past or future putts. Then hit it straight. When expert putters miss, they don't say, "I am a terrible putter." They say, "I picked the wrong target." Similarly, in sales, once you've figured out your target—a sales strategy, in this case—you take aim by pursuing that strategy to the hilt and get totally absorbed in it so that every one of your senses is geared toward it. It's just another straight putt. Locking into a highly specific target, you will sell at your best, and if you do your best and still fail, it was not because you were a bad salesman. You were doing what you thought it would take and loving the process. You just had the wrong target.

Let's say you're a sales rep for a small poultry farm. You're selling organic, free-range chicken, for instance, and your customer is a deli. If the deli has always gone with the usual fare, do you detect a curiosity about the organic product? That could be the target: to work that curiosity, to increase it, to get the customer so intrigued by the prospect of marketing a new product that he might buy your stuff, even though it might be a little more expensive. Every aspect of your skill as a salesman should zero in on finding that spark of interest and working it. Perhaps in the course of conversation, he notes that his business is down among a certain kind of upscale, more educated consumer. If you're target shooting, you'll be able to turn your attention to it, like a laser beam. It will require some improvisation, but good salespeople are skilled at responding to the situation. You might turn your sales pitch to the data highlighting the appeal of organic chicken to the very customers he's missing, who believe that organically raised chicken might be better for their health than birds filled with growth hormones. "Let me tell you why those people will come into your deli (or restaurant or supermarket) to buy organic, free-range chicken . . ." Working that line of sales is what will be engaging and fun. You'll enjoy the conversation for the sake of the conversation, for the interesting information exchanged. You won't be watching the clock or hypersensitive to negative signals; you won't be pushing the sale too hard, trying to force it; you won't be overloading the customer with irrelevant or counterproductive information; you won't be second guessing your approach or thinking about your appearance. Why? Because those things are not there, or you're blocking them out? No, they're still there, and a salesperson's performance easily could be affected by them. But not yours; you're too locked into a specific target.

The target can be an attitude, body language, a twinkle of interest in the eyes. It could even be a book or a magazine on the desk or a picture on the wall. "Hey, you're a fisherman (have gone on safari to Tanzania, have two daughters), too?" There is nothing like shared interests to grab a reluctant client's attention. Reading the client may be part of your strategy, looking for a lure to one of your products. See it and work it, concentrating on that and nothing else.

If you're in human resources, your target could be employee morale; if you're an ad writer it's likely the brand image you're trying to project. If you're in surgery, the target is usually an incision or stitch site. For a musician, the target rarely is the notes on the page, at least for the best performers; instead it's an internal emotion or a person in the audience who is clearly being moved by your playing. In architecture, the visual arts, and most fields of engineering, the most effective target is often a design in your head, or a particular brush or pencil stroke, or a soldering point. Whatever your line of work, there's a key element of what you're doing that can soak up all your attention.

The Target Is in Your Mind: The Science of Maximum Focus

The runner or tennis player or business executive or surgeon who has picked a target has found something to help focus their attention on what they themselves are doing, not on any number of things that are outside their control or tangential to their performance. The spot they pick keeps them focused on each movement, much the same way that injured Tour de France cyclist Tyler Hamilton poured attention into pedaling and thus seemed to forget that he had a broken collarbone. To be sure, all of the above examples begin by looking at something. The real common thread, though, is that the target is in the mind, taking it over, occupying it, like an invading army. The sneaker mark in the deuce court, the shadow on the road, the emotional response of the client across the desk—all are in their minds and no longer in their eyes when performers actually pull the trigger. When a golfer takes his backswing, he actually is no longer looking at his target; it's in his mind. When a runner is locked into footprints on the pavement, it's an image in her head; she actually may be gazing toward the horizon. And when a tennis player is gunning for the line, his physical vision is fully buried in the ball.

The fact that one's eyes are actively doing one thing while one's head is absorbed in the target leaves no room to do or think anything else. That is precisely why the body works so efficiently in such moments: You can't process strategy or mechanics, and you definitely cannot assess long-term consequences. In short, picking a target and filling your mind with it streamlines what you are doing, makes it simple, clear, uncomplicated. A target connects your actions with the vision in your head.

In the 1999 movie *For the Love of the Game,* Kevin Costner plays Billy Chapel, an aging Hall-of-Fame-bound baseball pitcher in the final appearance of his career. In the action sequences, he is on the mound in a dogfight in his rival's home stadium: The fans are going crazy, the pressure is intense, and Billy Chapel is trying to gather himself. "Clear the mechanism," he says to himself, and suddenly the roar of the crowd is muffled. Everything around him gets blurred except his point of view of the catcher's mitt. He's in the Zone—or at least, the Hollywood version of the Zone.

In real life it doesn't work that way. No matter how much we might want to block out all distractions during an important situation, so long as we are awake or not in a coma, the sensory system is in full gear, receiving stimuli and sending signals to the brain. Each of our senses is actually a chemical/mechanical device. The ear picks up sound waves through the vibration of small bones called "ossicles"; contact from objects alters the structure of skin cell membranes; light waves are absorbed by the cornea and reflected onto the retina; food particles cause a chemical reaction in the papillae on the tongue. While each sensation stimulates an electrical signal to the brain, the cause is purely mechanical or chemical. And, therefore, no matter how hard the Hollywood pitcher tries to "clear the mechanism," the mechanism is going to continue being physically manipulated by incoming information. Like a ball bearing dropped down a track in a physics lab, sensory perceptions keep rolling. If you blow on a moving ball bearing or try to nudge it from the track, it keeps going because, as Newton's Third Law of Motion long ago explained, things in motion tend to stay in motion, unless something extremely significant interferes. Similarly, as much as a pitcher might want to make the distracting sights and sounds go away—not to mention all those memories of games past, when batters raked the next pitch out of the park—he will not be able to make that happen, *unless something extremely significant gets in the way.*

That "significant something" can be the right target.

I suspect that you have experienced the benefit of a target already during those occasional times when you have become so engrossed in one activity or another that the rest of your sensations seem to have stepped out for a coffee break. Such a target is, to give an extreme example, why armed-robbery victims make such poor eyewitnesses. When the police ask them to describe the thieves and exactly what happened, victims often draw a blank or give a very superficial account of the events. Why? "All I could see was the gun aimed at me," a typical explanation goes. No matter how many other people were in the room and no matter what they were doing, the victim literally only had eyes for the weapon. Like Tyler Hamilton being forced into intense concentration in order to get through the Tour de France in spite of his pain, the robbery victim experiences an unusual mental compression by the presence of a gun—an item that dominates attention entirely. Does that mean your other senses have been shut down? No, your cortex is still receiving the same information, but when neurons are firing, they cannot stop and refire; they have a refractory period before they can fire again. So, despite the flood of incoming data, your mind is already too busy to process other information consciously. When you are buried in a gripping novel, you don't hear the train passing by, or smell the dog slobbering on his old bone, or see the kids running through the living room, tracking mud everywhere.

The gun in a stickup is the kind of target that I have in mind—not something to aim at, but something that occupies the mind, takes it over entirely, like, well, a ski-masked man with a gun. There are certain activities whose very nature demand such intense all-sense concentration that they take up all the processing of the cortex—or else. The mountain climber moves up the face of the cliff locking her eyes on each handhold, grabbing it, making sure her grip is firm, listening for any loose rock; she steps onto a jutting stone, one foot, then another, testing its solidity, all the while sensing the tension on her safety wire. Skilled climbers work their way cautiously up a steep face, seemingly part of the mountain; they get absorbed in their work because in their line of work a distraction can be fatal. There is no room in their minds for anything but what it takes to make this particular climb, one hold and one step at a time.

Similarly, race car drivers will put every sense into a turn. They see it, hear it, feel it, smell it. When I was at the University of Virginia, Bob Rotella invited the legendary race car driver Richard Petty, "The King," to speak to a class. Petty, who was one of Bob's clients, talked about the experience and the psychological thrill of racing cars at nearly 200 m.p.h. for a living, and in the question period a student wondered, "Is it hard to stay focused with all the steel flying around you?" Petty, with a record two hundred NASCAR victories, more than double his next closest competitor, was amused by the question, but his answer remains extremely revealing about the kind of mindset a top performer requires: "I have never once in my career had to practice being focused," I recall him saying. "I do it automatically," he explained. "If I am not focused on a point in the track right ahead of me, I'll crash." Petty also confessed amazement that golfers and baseball players could find the same kind of target intensity without having death staring them in the face during every performance. Petty's answer was a variation of Samuel Johnson's famous line that "when a man knows he's going to be hanged in a fortnight, it concentrates his mind wonderfully."

At a less death-defying level, the threat of a deadline can keep a newspaper reporter in the middle of a busy newsroom oblivious to the cacophony of colleagues working the phones all around him. The reporter is not trying to block out things to write the story; on the contrary, banging out his story, turning notes into sentences and paragraphs, trying to beat the clock but writing quality prose is what makes him unaware of the noise around him.

Anyone can do the same at will. In fact, psychologists can replicate the reporter's or race car driver's narrow focus in the laboratory by tricking people's perceptions. All it takes is a sensory deprivation chamber—a silent, soundproof, colorless, odorless room, designed as a light vacuum from which no light waves can enter or leave, leaving you literally "in the dark." Subjects are fed "fake" sensory stimuli, such as the walls rotating. Even though the brain is being fed kinesthetic signals that prove they are not moving, subjects will try to grab something to keep themselves from falling. The experience has manipulated their concentration, narrowing their focus to the image they're receiving rather than the reality. The result shows us that you can use the power of concentration to alter any reality. In one experiment, scientists built a special chamber that lacked reference points to distance and depth. At one end the ceiling was just a few feet from the floor. In that corner, they propped up a child's teddy bear. Subjects were asked to look inside the room and estimate the height of the bear they saw. Most reported that the bear was between eight and ten feet high! The explanation for this mistake is easy enough: Most rooms are eight to ten feet high, and the subjects assumed that since the bear filled their sight, from floor to ceiling, it must be equivalent to the size of the room. Lacking a complete set of data, subjects could only key in on the relationship between the bear and the ceiling; i.e., concentration tailors performance output.

Notice also that this wasn't simply a physical sensory experience—the eyes seeing a big bear. The actual height of the teddy bear was about a foot, and subjects in the experiment would have had plenty of memory data on how tall stuffed animals usually are. But in the experiment, information was processed and framed according to each person's immediate *experience*. Participants were not encouraged or given the time to "think it over." The open feedback system of our brains, with all sorts of neurons stimulating each other, is constantly shifting sensory information between the cortex's short-term and long-term memory centers. The more sensory data that's processed, the more memories and analysis enter the mix, slowing the system down and increasing the chances for distraction. Not only are we bombarded by the data from our five senses, but information is also being processed from our "sixth sense," the cognitive function of the brain that assesses the input of the five senses and makes judgments, associations, and decisions. Getting a desired performance result will be difficult if you add memory and calculation to the concentration equation.

If you attend to all the information around and inside you, though, won't you have a more complete and accurate picture of the world? Absolutely. But if you remember Yogi Berra's take on the world, the "correct" reality isn't one that will help you perform to your utmost. Whatever the desired performance—be it connecting with a client, moving an audience, or bringing a giant bear to life—an exhaustive scan for as much "relevant" information as possible will only get in your way. Exceptional thinkers only want to attend to the perceptual cues (visual, tactile, auditory, etc.) that work in their favor and process those one or two simple, narrow targets so intently that their brain is busy with only a small piece of information—creating, in effect, their own sensory deprivation chamber. Exceptional thinkers allow their concentration to affect reality, not the other way around.

Don't "Clear the Mechanism," Fill It Up—with a Target!

There is a difference between putting your effort into thinking about everything *affecting* your performance—all the distractions, evaluations, and consequences—and putting the same effort into thinking about the performance itself. When I'm explaining this to clients, I often use the metaphor of a dead elephant. Suppose a four-ton elephant dropped dead in the middle of your living room one day (a ridiculous image, to be sure, but that's why the metaphor works so well). No matter how hard you tried to sneak past that elephant, to step around it, or to ignore it altogether, you wouldn't be able to. Filling up your entire living room, crushing your sofa and coffee table and pressing up against the windows, this monumental and very dead animal would undoubtedly enter your field of vision. Even if you put on a blindfold or stayed away from the living room, the smell alone would bowl you over.

The same thing happens when you try *not* to think about something. It will still get into your head. And the harder you try to ignore it, the starker the image will be when it pops back into your mind. Try this classic experiment: Close your eyes and don't think of a tall giraffe. What occupied your mind's eye? Yup, a tall giraffe! The solution is not to *remove* a thought, image, or feeling from your brain, but to summon up a new one to replace it. The more you absorb your thinking in an alternative target, the more the unpleasant or performance-hampering information gets pushed out, without your having to think about it. If you now want to get rid of that image of the giraffe, instruct yourself to close your eyes and picture a fuzzy tarantula, or a spectacular waterfall, or anything else equally dramatic.

Billy Chapel in *For Love of the Game* was very lucky that Pete Rose was not at the plate. While Costner's character was trying to "clear the mechanism" of distractions, Rose would have been filling his mechanism up with a tight, specific, vivid target. Senses are mechanical;

the only way to control them is to manipulate them mechanically. To avoid distraction by the usual sights, sounds, and other sensations of the baseball stadium, the player will have to make sure his vision, hearing, and the other divisions of his sensory system are too occupied to process potential distractions. Pete would have been studying Chapel's move to the plate all season as well as during the game. In the on-deck circle, he would have settled on his hitting strategy for this particular battle in the "war" between himself and the pitcher. When his turn at the plate came, all Rose would be thinking about would be, "see the ball, hit the ball."

Of course, most players do not get into such an intense state of concentration as easily as Pete Rose did. In that ability to "see the ball" rests a lot of neuroscience. To get a clearer sense of the mechanics required for such targeted focus, I offer another analogy: Imagine six buckets (representing the five senses plus the sixth sense of cognition and memory) all attached to each other. If each bucket were filled to the brim with a different liquid (water in one, oil in another, beer in a third, etc.), and the contraption were moved, there is a good chance that the contents of the buckets would spill over, polluting each other. If, however, you fill each bucket with the same liquid, the danger of messing up the other buckets vanishes.

Take the example of an advertising copywriter. Embarking on an assignment, a copywriter might think about her company's track record or the importance of the result, or weigh the dollars on the line compared to other projects waiting on her desk; she might call the client six or seven times to see how they feel about various slogans; she might read copy for competitors' products; she might flip through past successful and unsuccessful ad campaigns; she might attend to the hubbub of colleagues working on other ventures around the office; she might look at the clock. All of these actions would impair concentration. Instead of trying to block out these potential distractions, though, an ad writer should try to get one thing to stimulate her sensory systems, and stimulate them garishly. The best candidate is of course the product's brand image. Say it's a sports car. The ad writer should feel the tight cornering, hear the purr of the engine, smell the new leather, see the shine of the red paint and the blur of the trees passing by. The goal is to fill up the entire sensory system with aspects of "sportscarness" that are particular to effective performance in the current moment—generating visceral emotion about the product, in an ad writer's case—and in the course of that kind of total absorption with that target, the rest of the sights, sounds, thoughts, and other ordinary demands of a busy office will fade into the background.

Extraneous or performance-impeding details will become inconsequential, not because you somehow blocked them out of your mind, but because your brain is already too full to process any more sensations. Once a copywriter's vision is locked on the red paint of that sports car, her visual cortex is not likely to receive other images; the hair cells in her ears are already vibrating with the sound of the car engine so that they are not likely to pick up the noise of neighboring desks, nor stir up memories of past shouting matches with disagreeable clients; the smell of the leather will even prevent odors from hindering her. Of course, something unexpected could interfere; a colleague charging into the room or a truck backfiring out on the street would "break her concentration." But if the writer's sensory system is filled with appropriate aspects of performance as vividly and as detailed as possible, the break will be transitory and a quick refocus will already be teed up.

Isn't that the experience that Richard Petty was describing? The race car driver is entirely engaged in controlling that speeding car around the dangerous curves of the speedway. The mountain climber grabs a piece of the mountain, holds the rock and feels it to make sure it won't break away. Those handholds begin to look big and sturdy; they start feeling easier to grasp. In such situations of concentrated focus, the target will not only seem bigger, but time will also become distorted.

And *actively* so. While Richard Petty, the mountain climber, the salesman, and the ad writer are "lost" in their work, they are not missing a moment of what is going on. In the Zone, they definitely are not "zoned out."

Super Pilot, Not Autopilot

Absorption is a prime quality of the Trusting Mindset. Your mind is so fully occupied that it loses all sense of time and space. Universal to the reports from the Zone are the experience of being one with what you're doing, a lack of self-consciousness, and such simple control of the performance that there is a sense of effortlessness. What could be more pleasant than such a feeling of transcendence? That is why athletes and actors have described it as "mystical" or "religious"; it is also why psychologists have dubbed it "peak performance," "optimal experience," and "flow."

But consciousness can be distorted in different ways, and in analyzing optimal experience, researchers often make the mistake of assuming that the same symptoms are always caused by the same mental state. When we realize that we have driven for miles down the highway without noticing any turns or signs, particularly the one for the exit we were planning to take miles back, we have experienced one kind of loss of self-consciousness. But it has happened because our mind has been wandering—to the song on the radio, the countryside, our cell phone conversation, or picking out constellations on a brilliantly starry night through the open top of the convertible. We have been unconscious of the fact that we have been driving a large and dangerous missile at 65 m.p.h. That is an example of autopilot, and it is hardly what the auto insurance industry has in mind when they describe an "attentive" driver.

The truly focused driver is absorbed in all the things required to keep his car under control and to navigate the roads safely. When Richard Petty careens around the Daytona International Speedway at 200 m.p.h., his consciousness, too, is in an altered state. The condition of Petty's brain on the racetrack, though, is quite different from his brain on the drive from the hotel to the "office." During the race, he definitely is not missing any turns. A great race car driver is not just aware of his car and the track; he becomes the car.

As I was writing this section, I was riveted with concentration. If a friend or colleague had walked into my office, I would not have realized it. If they'd said something or touched me on the shoulder I would have jumped. I was truly focused on my writing, but at no time was I spaced out or in a state of dissociation. Writing a chapter of a book requires a clear plan for what you want to include and the order in which that information is to be delivered. But the fun and the challenge of writing comes when you get absorbed in the outline, moving from a list of ideas to filling them out with vivid arguments, research, and illustrations. I knew exactly the point I was trying to make, the information that I had to convey, but some of my best stuff came only when I was fully occupied imagining the points in action. And when my editor attacks all this with her red pencil, I don't expect it to be a passive autopilot experience. She will be wondering why I wrote one thing and not another, scratching out a paragraph, jotting a question in the margin, her mind actively engaged by the editing process. Like Richard Petty, she will not be thinking about anything else other than what she is editing—not the way she wants market my book, not the sale of foreign rights, not the other book she must also begin editing. I would like to think that she will be so caught up in making the ideas clear and powerful that she will lose track of time and might even forget her lunch date at one of those elegant and expensive restaurants that New York editors frequent.

The true exceptional performer is on *super* pilot. Every single sense, every fiber of his body is brought together in what he is doing. True, he is "lost" in his work, but he is not missing a thing. So while the experiences of autopilot and super pilot have the same markings—a loss of self-consciousness, immersion in the present—they are on different ends of the concentration continuum. Or, put more specifically: A performer on super pilot is buried in the right target, while a performer on autopilot is buried in the wrong target!

The standard descriptions of peak performance found in Mihaly Csikszentmihalyi's accounts of "flow" and in Jim Loehr's descriptions of "full engagement" seem to miss this distinction. Both try to get inside the heads of the best performers to explain, in Csikszentmihalyi's words, "the state in which people are so involved nothing seems to matter," in which they lose track of space and time and feel that extreme sense of exhilaration that athletes have for decades called "the Zone." They both recognize that concentration is a key tool to get into the top performer's mindset. Csikszentmihalyi notes that the kind of concentration experienced in flow requires "a complete focusing of attention on the task at hand—thus leaving no room in the mind for irrelevant information."* I agree. "In flow," he writes, "there is no room for self-scrutiny." I agree. He also uses the example of the mountain climber making a difficult ascent: "He is totally taken up in the mountaineering role. He is 100 percent climber, or he would not survive." Csikszentmihalyi points to a clear connection between intense concentration and flow states. I agree. The significant characteristic of this mental state, according to Csikszentmihalyi, is "loss of self-consciousness." Some people, he says, are naturally better at this than others; they are able easily "to screen out stimulation and to focus only on what they decide is relevant for the moment." I agree. These people tend to be so "intrinsically motivated" that they are not bothered by distractions. I agree. But Csikszentmihalyi concludes that the neurological evidence is insufficient to prove whether flow causes the concentration, or concentration causes the flow.

I disagree. My own research over the past decade indicates that learning how to concentrate intensely opens the door to the experience of ultimate performance available to every performer. Csikszentmihalyi seems to identify the exhilaration and intense focus of the top performer with the mental state of autopilot. My own research puts high performance at the other end of the awareness scale, on super pilot, where the performer's mind is actively engaged. And while Csikszentmihalyi believes that we can learn how to increase the flow in our lives, the sketchiest section of his book comprises his in-

---

Flow: The Psychology of Optimal Experience, by Mihaly Csikszentmihalyi, a well-respected University of Illinois research psychologist, is a summary of two decades of skilled academic research on the sense of "exhilaration" everyone feels when they are performing effortlessly. See pages 58 ff.

structions for how this might actually happen. Like most of the current self-improvement gurus, he places too much importance on the perfection of *skills,* not to mention the role of "steps" and "goals" and "evaluation"—the very things that, in my opinion, become obstacles to a high performer's mindset. "The essential steps," according to Csikszentmihalyi, for transforming even the most ordinary physical acts, such as walking down a city street or hiking through the woods, into experiences of flow are:

> (a) to set an overall goal, and as many sub-goals as are realistically feasible; (b) to find ways of measuring progress in terms of goals chosen; (c) to keep evaluating what one is doing, and to keep making finer and finer distinctions in the challenges involved in the activity; (d) to develop the skills necessary to interact with the opportunities available; and (e) to keep raising the stakes if the activity becomes boring.

I cannot imagine how anyone can think so much about "goals" and "progress" (another term, after all, for "outcome") and simultaneously have the brain efficiently narrow to a clear, simple, in-the-present target. To me, that is a classic example of trying to be in the Trusting Mindset by using the Training Mindset, like a golfer working on the mechanics of his swing on the eighteenth hole of a major tournament or a businessman trying to close a deal by trying to remember a checklist his business-school professor put on the board in a class on how to negotiate your way to "yes." When the Training Mindset is turned on, performance suffers. The cerebral cortex is a stern taskmaster, and the last thing you need when you're under the gun is someone telling you what to do.

Jim Loehr, who has cowritten two books on how to improve performance, has thought long and hard about success and almost gets it. He understands that stress is a *sine qua non* of high performance and sings its praises. He also recognizes the importance of commitment in top performers.* But when it comes to the psychology of performance and the mindset of top performers, he seems mired in standard methods of "stress management" and "time management"; worse still, he advises an exhausting number of pencil-and-paper "exercises" that propagate the myths of "self-control" and "self-talk." His latest book, *The Power of Full Engagement*, written with Tony Schwartz, takes into account all the variables for improving performance that most of us performance psychologists would recommend: finding something that excites you every day, confidence, commitment, intrinsic motivation, focus, and the "power of full engagement." But anyone eager to become the kind of "corporate athlete" Loehr and Schwartz are promoting must also "commit to their *training* system," which requires wannabes to fill out "personal development" logs and worksheets tracking their "vision," "ritual building strategy," and "accountability."

Such a systematic approach, I would argue, is likely to encourage a Training Mindset rather than the Trusting one found among the best performers. Nothing derails efforts to find the Zone more than the natural tendency to be too programmatic or evaluative when trying to improve performance. To know you will be assessing your performance daily is to introduce second-guessing during performance; to have too many steps is to risk thinking more about the steps than actually performing and staying in the present.

Many have sworn by the Loehr-Schwartz "development plans," but when you look closely at the individual cases they cite, you will discover people who went from being poor performers to being average performers. They improved, to be sure, but now they're stuck at mediocrity. (I'm assuming you want to be better than that.) Such a programmatic approach to top performance ignores the neurological fact that the minds of the best players are in a special state. To develop those kinds of exceptional habits of thinking actually requires thinking that way rather than thinking in the opposite mode, which is what

---

Stress for Success, by Jim Loehr and Mark McCormack (Time Books, 1998), and *The Power of Full Engagement*, by Jim Loehr and Tony Schwartz (Free Press, 2003).

happens when you spend so much time during the day writing in a diary about how successfully you are following someone else's steps toward fulfillment. By definition, focus is where your eyes and senses are, not your mind—thinking less, not thinking more.

Loehr also remains too enamored with "self-talk" and "visualization" techniques, which, as I have discovered in my own research and consulting work pan out, only for a minority of clients. For the rest, trying to visualize or talk themselves into high performance is a detour away from it.

Of course, trying to achieve intense, target-specific concentration may not be easy initially. Do not expect to be an exceptional thinker the first time you try to get there. If getting into the Trusting Mindset were so easy, we'd all be Tiger Woods or Dr. Curt Tribble. Frankly, super pilot eludes most professional athletes and top executives; the rest of us can't expect to stroll right in. Like most worthwhile things in life, achieving the focus required for enhancing performance will take some hard work and some repetitions. But, oh, how rewarding it is when you log in the practice and start experiencing the benefits of exceptional thinking.

Yes, some people, like Yogi Berra, Tiger Woods, Bob McNair, and Madeleine Albright, can achieve high levels of concentration naturally. They were born with a more ingrained instinct to focus. They are not, however, genetically different from the rest of us; their brain physiology works the same way as ours. We who are naturally distracted by life have to learn how to become more target specific, and being intentional about focus is likely to be a strange experience.

In fact, the kind of programming most people do mentally before they enter any task tends to be quite accidental. When they step into the limelight, they take with them whatever was bombarding them the moment before. Whether it's a boss criticizing their work, a V.P. dropping by the office to hand over a stack of documents he needs reviewed, or ten thousand screaming fans, it enters people's thoughts. That's what they're teed up to think when they perform, as opposed to being intentional, decisive about what they pay attention to. The vast majority of performers will let their cortex assimilate data from any sense, and then deal with those sensations in the middle of performance. It's like kids during Halloween who are told that when they enter the haunted house, they will be confronted with all sorts of scary and gross things. And then they are blindfolded and told to stick their hands into a bowl of eyeballs, which is really a bowl of grapes. They have keyed themselves up to be scared. It works.

You can also key yourself up to be focused. It takes practice, to be sure. But you can master it quite readily when you think of it as a choice you can actually make: Decide what your target is *before* you perform; make it singular, specific, process-oriented, vivid. And get into that kind of intentional concentration routinely.

CHAPTER 10

Making It Routine

"Houston, we've had a problem here."

There aren't very many people who don't get chills when they hear Jim Lovell's famous understatement from outer space to NASA's Mission Control Center at the Johnson Space Center in Houston. On April 13, 1970, command module pilot Jack Swigert was radioed a directive to stir the cryo tanks aboard Apollo 13. When he flipped the switch, Apollo 13's destination immediately changed. The spacecraft was no longer headed for the Fra Mauro highlands on the surface of the Moon but back to Earth—if it could get there.

"The problem" turned out to be an explosion in space that nearly killed the three astronauts manning Apollo 13, and it held the entire nation in suspense for four long days, ending in a triumph of split-second engineering, human courage, and heroism. Turning that disaster into a success took an incredible amount of exceptional thinking from all members of the flight team. Lovell, Swigert, and fellow astronaut Fred Haise get most of the credit in that department, but I think one of the greatest lessons in high performance comes from Gene Kranz, the flight director. Long before there was a problem, before the mission even was launched, Kranz made sure everyone on the Apollo 13 team was prepared for success, teed up to think exceptionally.

Astronauts spend an exorbitant amount of time training, both physically and mentally; they're keenly interested in the role of the mind in high-stakes situations. Because of my work, I've had the pleasure of being invited to NASA's Johnson Space Center on a number of occasions. On one trip, I was asked to speak to the NASA "Founders Group" that represents the original team of pilots, engineers, and scientists—including Jim Lovell and Gene Kranz—who moved to Houston at President Johnson's request to start the space program. My lecture on longevity and "psychological hardiness" soon got sidetracked to a discussion of Gene Kranz's famous collection of vests.

After graduating from college in 1954 with a degree in Aeronautical Engineering, Gene was commissioned in the U.S. Air Force, where he flew high performance jet fighter aircraft. In 1960, he joined NASA "without any real idea of what I would be doing" and worked his way up to the top of Mission Control, serving as flight director for both Apollo 13 and Apollo 11, the historic mission in which Neil Armstrong would become the first man to walk on the Moon. Before nearly sixty NASA missions over thirty-seven years, the first order of business for Gene Kranz on the floor of the MCC was always the same: He donned a new vest that his wife stitched for him. "It became almost as important as anything else that needed to take place before a launch," he told the audience that day.

Gene Kranz's vest routine took on the air of a sacred ritual. He would arrive at the control center and organize all the necessary pre-flight activities. Before countdown, he'd pause to unwrap the box that contained the vest and slip it on, tugging it snuggly into place to the applause of all the controllers. Occasionally, he'd take some ribbing: "Looks like you bought that one off a Gypsy, Gene." His response was always matter-of-fact, something to the effect of, "Save it for splashdown," confirming to everyone that this was not fun and games, but a significant part of the launch procedure. As Gene described it, he'd then turn on the MCC microphone and run down the "go/no-go" checklist for each control station, succinctly, one at a time. For decades, this had been Gene Kranz's systematic way of getting himself focused and locked in—and, at the same time, getting his team in a similar mental position.

Performance psychologists call this a "preperformance routine," and anyone intent on becoming a top performer will need one. As performers, we have to divide our lives in half between preparing and performing—between facing pressure and not facing pressure. A routine helps you make the transition. In every career, we have to shift from ordinary workaday activities to moments when we are required to execute to the best of our ability. The doctor moves from pre-op to surgery. The manager moves from preparing a presentation to delivering it. A salesman moves from planning his strategy for a particular pitch, or compiling promotional materials, to delivering them, to making the call. Or the salesman, manager, and doctor are on the golf course in the morning and get paged to the office—a patient needs immediate care or a cornerstone client is threatening to cancel an account. They have to rush back to their jobs ready to perform.

We also experience occasions when something breaks our concentration, for one reason or another, and we have to find a way back into the performance mode. The executive steps before the board for a scheduled presentation, does a brilliant job, and goes back to the office, and while she relishes the day's triumph. Her boss calls to say that the board loved the presentation, but they have some questions. How does she match her previous performance? And before you think that sounds straightforward enough, consider that the surgeon might have had an argument with his spouse minutes before a scheduled operation, or maybe a nurse just quit. How does he alter those intense feelings in order to deal with the patient on the operating table? Analogously, your sales client does not want to hear about how many putts you missed during the morning's round. You need something that can help you reset your thinking for the next task at hand. Engineers must transition from the design board or cad program to the lab, to the boss's office, to meetings with sales reps. College professors, too, need to think differently as they approach the lecture podium than they did in their office preparing the lecture. The executive making a presentation to the board or conferring with a major client is surely in a different mode than when he's going over departmental strategy with his staff. Prosecutors and defense attorneys have to go to a different place mentally when they're standing before a judge and jury.

It happens all the time, in *and* out of the office. Bad day at work, but it's your child's birthday. Snap out of it, man! Or good day at work, but you come home to learn that your son got turned down by the college of his choice or that your husband just totaled the car. Even more frustrating: You've had an amazing day, the best ever, and you come home and everything is just absolutely normal! Sometimes we are able to switch our attitude on the fly, but without a systematic, practiced method for shifting gears, you'll be left at the whim of circumstance—your thinking will be brought down by obstacles, setbacks, and unexpected turns during the day.

Even positive things will disrupt the performer's mindset. At that extraordinary moment when Apollo 11 touched down on the Moon, "The people in the viewing room," Gene Kranz reported, "started applauding and stomping their feet on the floor. And it came through into the control room. The chill that I felt at that instant literally made me speechless, and I had a hard time getting going with the Stay/No Stay decisions we had to make. We were dangerously close to running out of fuel, so we had to figure out, in about seventeen seconds, if we could shut down and walk on the Moon, or if we had to lift off. I usually hit my fist whenever I really needed to focus. That time I pounded my arm so hard on the console that I broke my pencil and had a bruise that stayed with me for days afterward."

Most people do not realize that they already possess some elements of a preperformance routine, like Kranz's vest or hitting his fist. Most people don't realize that they purposefully can change their mood or how they think. They leave it to chance. You don't need to do that. You now know what makes an exceptional thinker, and I hope you already are in the process of testing your levels of confidence and commitment, putting yourself in the way of pressure in an effort to practice your new approach. When you backslide a bit, though, or when it's time to step up your new skill in order to perform at the next level, having a routine makes all the difference.

The Preperformance Routine

A preperformance routine can help make transitions to the performance mindset easier, as well as keeping you thinking exceptionally amid distractions, obstacles, and interruptions. But while such routines often involve physical movement, they have nothing to do with physical preparation.

A preperformance routine is about getting your mind *ready to perform.*

The elements in your routine basically are unimportant. What you physically do may not necessarily be related to the physical requirements of your performance. I know at first this seems counterintuitive. Frankly, golf pros and golf announcers are largely to blame for this. "You must have a pre-shot routine," they advise, correctly. "You must do the same thing before every shot." Not precisely. Tiger Woods tends to do a series of physical things, moving between discussing yardage and a target with his caddy to hitting the ball. Typically, he stands behind the ball, staring at his target; he takes one or two relatively slow practice swings, then, staring at the target, he tugs at his shirt to loosen up his shoulders, addresses the ball, gets comfortable in his stance, and makes his swing. On the face of it, it looks like he's got a kind of "12-step program." Any avid Tiger fan could write out every single step (including some subtle motions I've neglected to mention). Golf announcers love to point out the various quirks unique to certain players. (I mean, they have to say something to fill that airtime, right?) And viewers are listening. Amateur golfers all around the world are staring at their targets and loosening their shoulders à la Tiger Woods, or looking once at the hole and then putting, like Davis Love, figuring that if they imitate their favorite pro's routine, they might be able to improve their games.

It does not work that way. What you actually do as your routine does not matter, as long as it helps you focus and trust your skills. You will not get very far by watching the nearest overachiever in your office go through her preperformance routine. In fact, anyone who's trying to re-create someone else's physical routine is going to be thinking far too much about what he's doing. He's going to be working too hard on what he does *before* his performance. And while he may get very good at it, and be able to repeat the routine without a flaw, it's time wasted that should be spent setting up his mind for the actual performance. Preperformance routines should be designed to get you to *think* clearly and simply during an upcoming event—to be confident, to focus, to take advantage of the physical response a pressure situation sparks. When that star in your firm or field paces around the room before a big meeting (or goes to the gym for a workout or simply closes the door of his office) he is not rehearsing his spiel any more than Tiger Woods, standing behind the ball taking a few warm-up strokes, is practicing his swing. Tiger's swing does not really need much more practice; that top performer you admire has taken thousands of meetings and come out a winner in most of them. He and Tiger are using their preperformance routines to get their minds into the right condition to allow all their talent and years of practice to do their thing.

Put another way, that little routine is a tool for making the transition between training and trusting—two opposing mindsets. To move from being calculating and deliberate to being loose and locked on, you can't be asking yourself whether you've executed your routine correctly; you can't be examining its physical components. That's the Training Mindset, which is not where you want to be as you enter into a performance. A routine is nothing more than a symbolic gesture, a mental exercise in thinking in the present, free of evaluation, having fun. How those thoughts are manifested physically represents the routine that other people see. To try to come up with the routine first, and then assume it will prepare your mind, is backward. I repeat:

An effective routine is not *specific things that you do every time.*

The worst thing you can do is let your routine dominate your performance; if you tell yourself that you have to walk into the room confidently, shake hands all around, unbutton your jacket, sit down, and take a swig of water, you will be practicing the routine itself, not how you're thinking. You'll make your mind much too active. As you move and count, you will be filling your mind with your routine, rather than with confidence that it will all play itself out, or with a target—your strategy for the presentation, for example.

New clients sometimes get excited about showing me the routine they've worked out. "Doctor J, check this out . . ." I already know their routine is not serving the right purpose; it's rote and controlled. It's funny how many times a client has run through their routine for me and then asked, "Okay, now what do I do?" That's the same question your mind asks if you're dead set on an exact number of practice trials. Once you've finished them you still have to execute the performance. You still need a transition! The purpose of a routine is to move smoothly into the performance, not to check one thing off and then check the next.

An effective routine is about feeling and rhythm.

Think of it as a lot less like a countdown and a lot more like a warm-up dance. To get the right feeling going you might need to change your routine occasionally, or extend it or shorten it. Watch Tiger Woods more closely. He does not always go through the exact same motions. He doesn't complete a routine for the sake of completing a routine; he uses his pre-shot time to get to the point where he feels loose and confident; he has a target in mind and trusts his swing. Most amateurs are thinking, "Do your routine." Tiger is thinking, "The ball is going there, and I can feel it," or "I'll use this stroke," or "This is going to be fun." And then he takes aim and hits the shot— one that he probably has hit a million times before—and nails it. How many practice swings does it take? Usually one or two, but sometimes he takes three or more, as many as he needs for confidence to take over, as many as he needs for his eyes to get locked in.

Sometimes he tugs at his shirt harder than others, sometimes he won't touch his shirt at all. Sometimes he rocks back and forth a dozen times, setting his feet comfortably; other times his feet just hit a comfortable spot right way. And he rarely spends much time standing over the ball looking at it; by the time he gets there, his routine has blended into the shot itself. He just reacts to his target and feel, letting them flow into his club. The next time you are watching one of the major golf tournaments, make a note: Tiger also will back off the ball and go through his routine again. This is crucial to understanding preperformance routines: If the routine does not become part of the execution—in other words, if you flow through your routine and your mind is still not ready—don't proceed. Stop and do it again, or alter the routine.

When I'm giving a lecture, my own routine generally goes like this: I take my coat off and/or roll up my sleeves. I click through my Power-Point slides or write topic headers on the board, flashing an illustration in my mind (momentarily, rapidly) that goes with each concept (and in time to whatever music I was listening to on the way to the lecture). I put my notes down, stroll across the front of the room (sometimes with a subtle dance step), tug at my belt or adjust my shirt, pick out someone in the audience to smile or wink at, and then say something like, "Let's rock and roll." Notice: There is a lot of room in here for variation. My routine is about thinking creatively, pictorially, rather than rote regurgitation; it's about getting a feel for the tempo of my delivery, and getting into a playful, fun mood. It's *not* a deliberate series of actions, a to-do list, or cramming specific phrases into my mind. And if my routine doesn't get me visual and loose? I do it again; it doesn't take but a minute or two, and I know the audience would rather start a little late than sit through a stodgy, uninspired lecture.

Warning!

The two most overused (and overrated) routines in psychology are visualization and relaxation. I made my case against relaxation in

Chapter 2; fight-or-flight physical symptoms are something to take advantage of, not stifle. Visualizing your performance ahead of time (the perfect shot, the perfect presentation, the Platonic ideal of the sales call or negotiation) is likely to disappoint performers who, being human, are far from perfect. When the performance that comes out does not match the performance in your mind, you're thrown right back into the Training Mindset, comparing, overevaluating, analyzing where you went wrong. The task of every preperformance routine is to help you use your physical response to pressure as an edge, to help you make that transition into a state of intense, in-the-moment concentration, and to help you eliminate assessment, judgment, and critique.

Where Will I Find the Time?

Often clients will insist that they are too pressed for time. How can they fit preperformance routines into their busy agendas? It's a strange question, a bit like asking how can you possibly make time to fall in love or be a good parent or even do your job. The right routine, properly ingrained, not only will help you concentrate more consistently, it will also increase your efficiency in every aspect of your life.

I recall one occasion when a student of mine at the University of Virginia, who dreamed of becoming a great musician, complained that she never seemed to find enough time to practice. Classes, exams, the theoretical study of sound—everything seemed to be getting in the way of making music. She wanted to devote large blocks of time to playing but could only find an hour here and an hour there. I told her she needed a "a pre-shot routine." She was incredulous. "Isn't that for golfers?" she queried. I asked her how she thought the players on UVA's golf team handled all their course work, papers, and exams, while still managing to log in rounds of golf every day—productive, focused rounds. She'd never thought about it before. I told her that if the golf team approached their game the way she approached music, they'd finish last in the conference for sure.

"When you're doing homework," I explained, "you're thinking about how much it's getting in the way of your music. You're not studying very effectively. You choke on your exams. Then you think you have to put more time studying because of your poor scores, or when you do go to the practice studio, you're thinking about how little time you have, or how soon you have to get back to your books. Your music doesn't get any better. You carry that with you into class and don't pay attention. It's a vicious cycle. Meanwhile, the golf team is practicing a routine to help them prepare to play well on the course, and then another routine to prepare to perform well in their studying. You need to start thinking like they do."

We came up with a routine for her: closing her books, stacking them in a sorted order so when she returned she could pick up right where she left off, then heading to the practice studio, where she'd go through some stretching, loosen up her arms, her hands, her fingers, and play her favorite piece once, without thought, just to enjoy it, before getting into the material she needed to work on. When she returned to the library, she'd sit down, line up three or four highlighters, set the alarm on her watch for two hours, and then say to herself, "GO!" She was becoming systematic about how she approached each of her performances, and it translated into efficiency. She set herself up to be fully committed to each endeavor, with reinforcing methods to mark starts and stops. Her grades rose and all of a sudden she found her music was flowing more freely.

Musicians, like golfers, have to put their minds in the right place—trusting, confident, enjoying the pressure, being in the present, and so forth. Otherwise, no amount of practice or "time management" will make them better. The same is true in all professions: If you are stuck in the Training Mindset, evaluating yourself, or thinking in the past or future, you will not perform up to your potential. You will waste a lot of time, be an inefficient performer, and likely assume you need to manage your time better. In reality, you need to manage your *thinking* better. I see physicians and attorneys chewing up hours during the day programming their palm pilots or entering their schedules into expensive day organization software on their laptops. They could be using that time to perform—or in the case of residents and law clerks, to sleep! But they feel they are disorganized or inefficient, all because they haven't learned how to make transitions between points in their day, or they are not living up to their potential because they can't get from the Training Mindset to the Trusting Mindset. They need to work on getting into a performance mindset rather than logging extra practice time to prepare.

I advised the young musician to pay a visit to Trax, a tiny little hole-in-the-wall bar in Charlottesville tucked between the University of Virginia campus and the medical school. I told her to try to be the first one there on a night when The Dave Matthews Band was playing. Back then, Dave had just moved to Charlottesville. He was bartending and playing local gigs while also assembling his now famous band, trying to create his own recording label, Bama Rags, and lining up an aggressive college tour. I advised the UVA student to watch what Dave did before playing and in between sets. For a musician with a hundred other things on his plate and still not having made it big yet, he was the epitome of performing in the present. And the rest of the guys in the band truly loved what they were doing; you could see it in the way they played and hear it in their sound.

The music student came to class a couple of weeks later and in discussion group told everyone, "That guy Dave Matthews is going to be rich." She'd had a chance to talk with the members of the band before they started playing and asked Dave if he had a preperformance routine. "Of course!" he replied without hesitation. "You can't be successful without one." He went on to explain to her that in each facet of his career, from writing to jamming, from working on his voice to recording and performing, even when he was downtown, away from music, he'd stop and intentionally commit himself to only what he was doing at present. It wasn't so much of a warm-up or stretching routine, but a mental check to get himself away from the multitasker's mindset. In those days, the Dave Matthews Band was going all out for stardom, which meant a lot of work in a lot of areas, and a lot of travel. It would have been easy for them to get caught up in scheduling and time management. But for someone who thought as exceptionally as Dave, that would have been *wasting* time, not managing it. Sure, sometimes he'd get so absorbed in one performance that it would hurt another. But if he'd tried to avoid that, nobody outside of Charlottesville and South Africa would probably know of him today.

The UVA student, of course, had seen the future: Less than a year after she went to Trax, the Dave Matthews Band had sold 150,000 albums on their own label, had jumped onto the HORDE Tour, and were getting ready to sign a deal with RCA. The rest is, as they say, music history.

Designing a Routine

It doesn't matter what is in a routine, as long as it gets your head where it needs to be. Nor does it matter what other people think of your routine.

When major league shortstop Nomar Garciaparra stands at the plate and seems to fiddle with his batting gloves a hundred times and replace his feet, kicking his toes into the dirt with equal obsessiveness, he's not counting, he's not tightening the Velcro; what he's really doing is focusing his mind on hitting a baseball. Garciaparra's batter's glove and foot action drives some fans to distraction. Other players, however, know he's just doing what it takes to get comfortable and ready at the plate—to feel loose and rhythmic, to narrow his thinking, and to have his timing set. The great athletes don't give a damn whether other people think their routines look stupid or are a waste of time. It's their routine, and it is they who ultimately will be responsible for their performance. And they don't waste any time measuring their routines against what others are doing to get mentally ready, either. What works best to get them to think exceptionally is what counts; whether someone else is doing more or less in preparation is irrelevant, and attending to that is a potential ticket *out* of a great mindset.

For players with the quirkiest routines, mocked by opponents, fans and the press, performing well is the best revenge. Al ("the Mad Hungarian") Hrabosky used to talk to the ball between pitches. A hard-throwing reliever for the St. Louis Cardinals, Hrabosky understood two things about his pitching: (1) focusing on the ball helped him move past evaluation and get excited for the upcoming pitch (and thus stay "in the present"); and (2) his antics would disrupt opposing hitters' routines and thus give him a psychological advantage. Hrabosky would demonstratively curse the baseball in his hand, fire it into his glove, and then throw it past the hitter. Except, that is, the hitters who themselves had great routines. On those occasions, the result was a matchup that opened the door for truly remarkable performances, the best against the best, the kind of exciting moments in a game that usually make the highlight reel for SportsCenter. Hrabosky once cursed at the ball and then tried to throw it by Henry Aaron, one of baseball's all-time great hitters: The Hammer hit it out of the park on a line so hard and low that it made the shortstop's knees bend, and if the bleachers hadn't been there, it probably would still be rolling. When he got back to the dugout, Aaron deadpanned to his teammates, "Let him go find that one and talk to it."

So how do you come up with a routine that works? I often advise clients to start *backward*. Where do they want their routines to get them? Where do they want their minds to be? Most clients simply want to return to the feeling they've had in the past of total control of their skills, being absorbed in the moment, for the sheer pleasure of it. Others are looking for specific aspects of top performance—confidence, perhaps, or a loose and rhythmic feeling, or feeding off pressure. Identifying the psychological product of a solid routine is a critical assignment. Once my clients accept that, the rest usually falls right into place. As they experiment with a number of stretches, movements, and symbolic cues, the ones that foster great thinking almost identify themselves. How? Because these are the moves that work—that help change their thinking under pressure.

I advise clients to turn their memories back to experiences of being on top of their game and identify the things they may have done

before their performances that made them so psychologically exceptional. Imagine you're a marketing manager for a major pharmaceutical company who came up with an extremely successful campaign for
getting a new product to the market. It all took place a few months
ago, and here's how it happened: You had been brainstorming all
morning, all your best people sitting in the conference room for hours
racking their brains but getting nowhere. You broke for lunch. Ex-
hausted and starving but with all your notes in your hand, afraid to
misplace them, you pinned them up on the bulletin board in your office and headed out to get a sandwich, which you brought back to the
office. You turned on the radio, sat down, and enjoyed that sandwich.
Listening to some tunes, you stared at the bulletin board on which
the notes from the morning's meeting were hanging. As you chewed
rhythmically you noticed something—and then it hit you. The new
campaign fell into place.

Here's how you might design a routine from that experience that
would help bring out the clever marketer in you the next time around:
The key to your creativity would be finding a way to get loose after a
brainstorming session—pinning up your notes and leaving the office
(signaling your brain to stop training), listening to music (putting you
in an artistic mindset), and directing a Zen-like gaze at the wall (letting your brain get absorbed in your target and just trusting it). You
certainly would avoid sitting in all-day meetings, one after another,
racking your brain for a week or more. So do you also avoid researching the market segment or fiddling with graphics on your computer?
No, you need to do that. But your most creative moments seem to
come when you get away from the details for a while. You therefore
have to design a routine that builds in breaks from the grind of brainstorming, that allows you distractions so your creativity can go to work
on what it's learned in those meetings and be sparked again when you
just trust your notes.

You need the brainstorming meeting, but not for the entire morning. Set it for an hour or so and tell your staff that when that time is
up, you'll all be breaking for lunch, no matter what. From the meeting
to securing a sandwich, call home to talk to your spouse or arrange a

weekend trip with the kids—anything that will keep you from brooding on the pharmaceutical campaign. Then head back to the office with your lunch, flip on the radio, relax in your chair, eat your sandwich, and let the notes on the wall fill your brain. What happens if nothing comes to mind? Try the same routine later in the afternoon. Make it a break for coffee or a quick trip to the gym. If that doesn't work, so what? Definitely do not spend the rest of the day chewing up time in a conference; don't wreck your evening with family or friends fretting over your missing ad layout. Great ad campaigns are hardly ever born in one day, and they are least likely to come to you when your brain is fried.

Many of my clients who are businesspeople are amazed by how much they get done by having a routine that simply gives them a way of transiting into performance mode. They used to start one project and stick with it until they got results, ignoring their other projects. Work has a way of filling the available hours. Give yourself a weekend to finish that report (or clean out the garage), and it will take the *entire* weekend. But if your routine sets the rhythm for your work day, you will finish things within that preordained time. If a needed solution doesn't come to you, put it aside for a while. But when you return to that project, go through your routine again.

To maximize your potential in whatever you might do for a living, you need to get into that mental state in which your focus is most intense, in which you trust your abilities, experience, and the work you've already done. The purpose of any routine is to help you make that all-important transition between preparing to perform and actually performing. Also, your routine should never be a chore. The best performers enjoy everything about what they are doing, including their routines.

No matter your profession, you can look back to those moments when everything seemed to be coming together at once. If you're a surgeon, what did you do between pre-op and surgery before your best cases that got you so immediately into the groove? When you're scrubbing up, putting on surgical gloves, checking the arrangement of the scalpels, or setting your eyes on the marks the nurse has made for the incision, where does your mind go? Equally important, what events or actions prior to an operation tend to break your concentration?

For a salesman who prides himself on being "good with people," meeting a new client and winning him over may be what gets him into focus. Confident about his ability to charm a block of ice, the salesman mentally puts away the product stat sheet and closes his notes on the key talking points. He then reminds himself what he loves about the preliminary banter, the setup, and as he greets the new client, he looks him straight in the eye. That could be a good routine. Or maybe you know that the client is a stickler for facts and figures, an engineer who is likely to needle you about the product's specs and performance. To get yourself ready for him, you sit down with your company's engineers and have them grill you. "Come on, be tough on me," you say before each question, and when your engineers ask it, you nod your head, smile, and answer, articulately and persuasively. Just that one nod of the head could be enough to get your mind confident and in the present, locked on the product as your target, rather than stuck on the client's resistance to your product or the odds against the sale.

What helps you get into the groove with one client or with one performance might not necessarily work with another. But analyzing what worked for you in the past is a good place to start. Once you get in the habit of using a routine that seems to work for most situations, you can adapt it for special cases.

Notice that these routines do not necessarily involve a series of physical actions. If before each big meeting or negotiation, you go to the bathroom, then make two copies of the price spreadsheet, crack your knuckles, and then pick up the phone to call your client—just for the sake of having a routine—that series of actions is not likely to be adequate preparation for performing. In fact, it might even increase your sense of anxiety: "It worked for the last client, but this one is notoriously difficult to deal with, especially in an economic downturn."

A preperformance routine is "routine" only in the sense that it creates consistent, dependable thinking. When your product is strong and your client is needy, all it might take is sitting down and dialing the number. The following day it might take you thirty minutes before you're ready to make that call. Whatever gets you mentally ready for performing, no matter how dumb it might sound or look, can constitute a routine.

Remember John Aspland and the New York bar exam? Before the test he shut his books and put them away in his knapsack, scanned the room to observe other students freaking out, chuckled, thanked himself for not being that uptight, and looked forward to having some fun problem solving. His routine was to laugh at other people's bizarre routines. When my sister took the test for her license as a clinical psychologist, someone actually pulled out a pet iguana and kissed it before beginning the exam!

Keep in mind: A routine is not a superstition. Confusing the two is a common mistake—the salesman who has a pair of lucky boxer shorts or the executive who always eats two eggs sunny-side up before a big presentation. The critical difference is that superstitions are about superstitions; routines are about exceptional thinking. Yes, superstitions can affect your mindset. When you go into the bathroom before a board meeting, take out your lucky "power" tie and put it on, you'll probably feel pretty good walking out the door. Your confidence might click into place. Fantastic! That's what you want from your routine (although your confidence ideally should be about performing well and not how sharp you look). But if it's a superstition, that day when you forget your lucky tie at the gym or the dog chews it up, you'll fall apart: You'll stop thinking about your presentation and start thinking about how disheveled you look; you'll become filled with doubt and worry.

I've actually received phone calls from clients on the brink of an important performance who've lost their talisman: "Doc, I'm at the cleaners. I've got to be at the office in twenty minutes and my lucky white shirt is now bright pink! What do I do?" I usually try to help them see how foolishly they're thinking: "I guess you'll have to go in naked," I say. "You can't possibly wear a *different* shirt; none of your other shirts have as much experience, they don't know the market like this shirt did."

Ask yourself: "Do I have a routine or a superstition?" If the answer is "superstition," get yourself to think about the elements of your great performances that had nothing to do with your lucky shirt or tie or the inside-out gym socks, the lapel pin, talking to your eight ball, or rubbing the nose of the bust in the hallway as you enter corporate headquarters. Gene Kranz's vest? A routine. The box with his vest almost didn't arrive in time for the Apollo 13 launch. Was he biting his nails, worried that it wouldn't arrive, thinking he might not perform well or be able to get his team focused? No, he said he would have used a NASA cap, or simply told the controllers that this mission was about the panels in front of them and not his vest. That's the mark of an effective routine—the actual elements always can be modified, swapped out when necessary, knowing that the end result is what counts.

Gene was not occupied with whether his routine would be the same as for previous missions or whether it was "working" or not. He understood that a good routine *reduces* evaluation; a good routine will lead you into taking action, immediately. It is a fluid transition—routine into performance—rather then one stage, pause, next stage. You cannot think, "I've done my routine, now I'm ready to perform." Or worse, "I've done my routine, am I ready to go?" That's simply more evaluation, rather than something that takes you seamlessy from the Training to the Trusting Mindset.

Think of the act of tossing a piece of paper into a wastebasket. You mash up the paper as you're checking out exactly where the basket is and then you toss the paper into it, without another moment's thought. The routine is crushing the paper while simultaneously putting your eyes into the trash bucket; that's what helps you focus on what you are about to do. Sighting your target becomes the final cue to react to, the point at which the preperformance routine flows into the performance, where you are so locked on your target that it has filled up your mind, allowing your skills to kick in. No one ever looks at the ball of paper and wonders, "Have I wadded it up enough? Am I really ready to throw it?" When I toss a set of keys to someone, I often jiggle them in my hand to get a feel for what I'm throwing, sense the weight of the keys, and then fling them to the other person. That's what a routine should be: You are neither thinking about the routine nor evaluating it, you're just using it as a cue to make the transition between preparing to make a toss and making the toss, between preparing to pitch a product and selling it, between designing a scientific protocol and conducting an experiment.

Keeping your mind out of the way is the purpose of the preperformance routine; it is the stage for dispensing with evaluation, for benching the cerebral cortex. It is the routine that should help you begin the process of intensely focusing all your sensations on the task at hand, getting in the present, picking out a target—and just doing it.

Making It Routine

Once you have devised a possible routine to help you think like an exceptional performer, you must condition it. Devising a routine is not enough; you will have to practice that routine. One of the persistent frustrations of my work as a performance psychologist is how often I hear coaches give lip service to the mental game, and then I have to beg them to allow their players to spend some time practicing the way they think. To be sure, it's a lot more difficult to gauge the psychological work players are doing compared to watching them hit line drives in batting practice or run plays on the football field or basketball court. Coaches are right that at the highest levels, the difference between winning and losing is often mental, but they need to honor that by setting aside time for their players to rehearse their routines consistently amids the constant distraction, chaos, and competition.

I also have begged business executives to allow their employees to turn their days upside down and spend less time on workaday matters and more time getting mentally prepared to go to battle. Do you want your staff to be grinders or do you want them to meet challenges with their talent blazing? No one has to teach an MBA how to read a spreadsheet, but most managers have a thing or two to learn about performing their best on a regular basis. They know they have the potential to get into the Trusting Mindset—they've experienced the feeling—but they don't have a clue how to make sure that when the spotlight goes on they'll be ready to put on the kind of show they know is in them. Business schools and in-service training programs are all about how to think critically. As a result, people learn how to prepare exceptionally well, but they're stuck in a practice mindset. It's no wonder they don't perform up to their potential. They need to spend a lot more time learning how to think differently under pressure. They need a well-practiced preperformance routine to make the transition from preparation to performance.

In fact, every degree program in management should have a short course on routines, and every company should do an in-service on identifying the psychological purpose of a routine, crafting steps to simulate those desired "thinking" results, strategizing how to integrate and practice new routines. Schools and organizations also should devote time to developing effective philosophies of performance.

CHAPTER 11

Socrates Never Had a Slump

Having gotten this far into the book, you probably now have a very good idea of how you stack up against exceptional thinkers and what your strengths and weaknesses are as a performer. Do you think like Yogi or Michael Dell or Richard Branson? Billy Blanks, Tyler Hamilton, Deion Sanders, or John Aspland? Paul Newman? Or Bill Russell, Robert Johnson, Gene Kranz, or Jamie Kent? How about Franz Klammer or Donny Deutsch or Bill Cosby . . . or a squirrel? I hope you've already started working on new methods of thinking. But you may be having some trouble, running into obstacles, or backsliding with one mode of thinking or another. Don't worry. It's perfectly normal and an expected part of the process of pursuing greatness. You may be having difficulty with confidence or concentration or commitment. You may be an over-motivated underachiever. The physical symptoms you experience under pressure may have metastasized into high anxiety that keeps you away from the kind of challenging situations that might give your career a boost. You may not have the right routine. You may have been pursuing someone else's dream rather than your own. Or you still may not even know what your real dream is.

If you're like many of my clients, you'd probably like some immediate results. But if you truly want sustainable, lasting success, if you are looking to join the ranks of overachievers, you have to remember that there are no quick fixes. Nor is exceptional thinking, as we have seen, a button to be pushed or a switch to be flipped. And it doesn't have anything to do with the outcome of a given performance. It is a state of mind that you consistently get into, allowing it to be your driving force. It is—I repeat—a habit. And as such, something as monumental as reshaping your own mind will take a lot of practice—many repetitions. Even if we think we're confident or focused or committed when we are preparing for a high-stakes situation, we revert, psychologically and physiologically, to our strongest habits, usually bad ones shaped by the myths of high performance. You need a guide—a beacon—to help you refocus when you veer from your new commitment to exceptional thinking.

You need what I call a "philosophy of performance."

Don't worry. I am not asking you to read Plato or Kant. Being an exceptional thinker does not require being a deep thinker. It has nothing to do with how much knowledge you have or where you are in the search for "the meaning of life." (Although if you develop the kind of philosophy I have in mind, your life will take on a lot more meaning.) I want to get you to think like Yogi Berra, who never made it past the eighth grade. When the game is on, great performers like Yogi, no matter what their field, know how they want to think, and keep thinking that way. Whether in the midst of setbacks, obstacles, or successes, they maintain that consistency by sticking with a well-defined philosophy of performance.

What's the difference between a philosophy of performance and a preperformance routine?

- A philosophy is a consistent, overall approach to what you do and why you do it; it's the framework for handling all the ups and downs that come with being passionate and trying to be great at something.
- A routine is what helps you execute exceptional thinking at the actual moment of performance; it helps you honor your philosophy, one performance at a time.

Defining Your Philosophy of Performance

Legendary UCLA basketball coach John Wooden devised philosophies that served as cornerstones for his team's approach, to keep his players in a mindset that made being successful easier. A favorite was: *We'll always win—if we are given enough time.* If UCLA lost, which it did rarely under Wooden, his players did not accept the result as a loss; they were on their way to winning, but the clock ran out before the team was able to dominate its opponent. It was a great strategy for getting a team to think confidently, to stay free of evaluation and in the present. The same philosophy proves useful in all sorts of areas:

I will end up on top, eventually.

You will beat your competitor in earnings and profits. Maybe not today or tomorrow, but given enough time, it will happen. If your dream is going into business for yourself, it may take years; but if you stick it out, not wavering in your belief and not concerning yourself with arbitrary deadlines or expectations, that dream will happen.

That's what I mean by a "philosophy of performance"—a guiding principle for what it takes to perform to your complete potential. When you feel yourself slipping back into an old tendency—doubt, overanalysis, letting the feelings of pressure turn into anxiety, for example—you need a philosophy to snap you back into a performer's mindset. When I lecture about philosophies of performance, I often give my students this example:

Everybody puts on his or her pants one leg at a time.

I find this a useful counter to the "false God syndrome." No one is genetically predetermined to be superstar. Even Bill Gates or Lou Gerstner—or any other overachiever you might admire—had to get from nowhere to the top of the mountain. They may *appear* to have it made; but they, too, face the same day-to-day obstacles we all do, at home and with their families, at work and with their colleagues. They, too, put their pants on one leg at a time.

As I was making this point in my performance psychology class at Rice a few years ago, that everyone is this way, a student interrupted me. "That's not right," he said. "I don't put my pants on one leg at a time." I was immediately curious (and checked to see if he even wore pants). "You don't? How do you put your pants on?" "Every morning," he explained, "I stand up on the edge of my bed, holding my pants in front of me, and then try to jump into them both feet at once." The other students howled with laughter. But he was serious. He conceded that he often missed, fell over, and tried again. When I asked him how he picked up this approach, he explained that when he was a little kid, he found getting dressed boring, so his mother created this game of trying to get both legs into his pants at once. He'd continued doing it ever since . . . because "it's fun!"

His classmates thought he was crazy. But I thought his morning ritual was in fact quite brilliant, and right in line with what I was teaching. Here was a guy who started every single day with a party. He turned the otherwise very mindless act of putting on his trousers in the morning into an adventure. With the help of his mother, he had created a habit of thinking that even the most tedious necessities of life should be fun. His morning ritual easily could be turned into a philosophy of performance:

No matter what you are doing, there is a fun way to do it.

The very next morning, I was up on the edge of my bed, trying it myself. I missed on my first try, a classic candidate for *America's Funniest Home Videos*. I laughed out loud, and I had an awesome mindset for the rest of the day.

A few major corporations actually have made having fun their philosophy. "I can honestly say that I have never gone into any business purely to make money," says Richard Branson, the Virgin magnate. "If that is the sole motive, then I believe you are better off not doing it. A business has to be involving, it has to be fun." Branson has proved that his adventuresome, fun-at-all-cost philosophy can make a corporation a massive profit. So has George Zimmer, who opened his first Men's Wearhouse in Houston in the early 1970s and now sits on top of the largest men's retailer in the nation—a $1 billion company with 507 locations. "You know, at some point, we can't pay you enough money," Zimmer told an audience of assistant managers of all his stores in 2003. "That's why we have a different feeling at Men's Wearhouse, and the word fun is always connected. We take fun seriously. You gotta take *fun* seriously in business, because God knows everybody could use some lightening up." In 2003, *Time* magazine published a major feature on how this "unorthodox business philosophy" of profiting from fun had pushed Zimmer, and other entrepreneurs with a similar upside-down management strategy, past their competition.

Life, of course, cannot always be fun. The best performers, however, always will have strategies on hand to help them cope with tough times, even with tragedy. My mother works in hospice care, helping families deal with Alzheimer's disease, drawn-out, uncomfortable terminal illnesses, or the loss of a child. There is no fun way to do such a job, but there always are ways to get people to think about what is happening without being mired in misery, to focus on hope, love, and joy of the moment. In her seminars on bereavement, my mother explains that while we cannot control death or disease, we can control what we do about them. We can weep and tear our hair out in grief, or we can honor a passed relative and carry their memory forward, we can come together as a closer community. Death is often perceived as a waste, but it need not be. And thus another useful philosophy of performance:

You cannot control events, but you can control your reaction to them.

Everyone needs these kinds of principles to hone the habit of exceptional thinking. But just as I cannot tell you what your dream should be, I cannot hand out ready-to-wear philosophies. That's part of the fun of being an exceptional thinker—to figure out *your* corner-stone principles, the guiding thoughts you need as a foundation for consistency in your approach and execution.

Building an Effective Philosophy

Most people already have a philosophy of performance, or at least a piece of one. Over the years, they have adopted certain attitudes to-ward life and work. Unfortunately, such guidelines do not tend to be products of deliberate consideration but accidental (and usually mis-guided) strategies that they pick up from superiors, the media, and the general process of socialization that encourages everyone to "fit in" and be "normal." The result is a lot of people walking around with philosophies that inhibit their chances for success rather than en-hancing them. *Practice makes perfect* is a textbook example; striving for perfection is a sure way to choke under pressure. *Be realistic* is an-other commonly held philosophy, also touted as *Stay within yourself* or *Know your limits*. Phrased either way, it's a restricting belief, and another high performance inhibitor. *Haste makes waste* is a favorite prescription from parents and teachers. But more often than not, to succeed in a big way, you have to take a risk and go for it—now. So is your philosophy of performance helping you or hurting you? You must answer that question as honestly as you can.

Some people already have an effective philosophy. They really do believe, for instance, that *Everyone is human and will make mistakes.* But when the going gets tough, their philosophy is MIA. They go for a job interview, thinking, "I've gotta really be at my best because this is a sweet job and everyone will want it." In other words, "I can't be hu-man now." Their guiding principle is really nothing more than a slo-gan lodged in the back of their mind, or emblazoned on a fancy paperweight that collects dust on their desk. It's based on neither practice nor application. In effect, they really have no philosophy of performance. While they might believe much of what I discussed in Part I about the role of confidence and commitment in high level performance, about the importance of having a motivating dream, their beliefs actually are not guiding what they do in the real world, or how they do it.

Ask yourself, "Is there a disconnect between what I say my philosophy is and the thoughts I entertain all day long, particularly what I focus on in the face of adversity?" If I asked you to write down your thinking cornerstones, would you proceed to file the paper or note card in safe storage, or would you tack it up on your bathroom mirror or computer monitor and thoughtfully digest it every day? A philosophy is only as good as how much you exercise it.

To find the right philosophy for you and use it consistently, it is important to keep two things in mind:

(1) An effective philosophy of performance should be simple and unambiguous.

I coach my clients to have just one, maybe two guiding principles as they enter every performance situation. Otherwise they will be forced to concentrate more on their philosophy than on performing. The key is to figure what the biggest obstacle might be to thinking exceptionally, and then design a philosophy that will counter that roadblock from affecting your attitude and approach. If your problem is dealing with pressure—for instance, if you don't like your hands shaking or stomach churning when you step into the limelight—a useful strategy for you might be to remember:

The human body is hardwired to perform better *under stress.*

Those physical feelings of fight-or-flight are a signal that the stakes are high and you're ready to roll, which raises another possible guiding principle:

Pressure moments are an opportunity to show how good you are.

I concede that these kinds of axioms might appear in fortune cookies. Some will even strike you as clichés, and you will be right. But being exceptional is not an act of snobbery or elitism; it has nothing to do with being skilled at complex thinking. On the contrary, exceptional thinking is about making things simple. Clichés, after all, are truths, albeit familiar ones. So pick out the one most germane to your situation and rely on it. Don't try to create a laundry list of all the philosophies you like.

(2) A performance philosophy must be specific to you.

One-size-fits-all programs will not work. The philosophy of your favorite role model will not necessarily fall in line with your dream. What you need to perform well is likely to be very different from what I need. Frankly, confidence is not a problem for me. My biggest hurdle as a performer is patience. I have so many great projects on my plate that I want to do them all right now! But each requires my focused excitement independently. Therefore, I've built my own personal philosophy around the notion:

The game—life—happens one pitch at a time.

Each of us needs a philosophy that is a set of *personalized* guiding principles for how we want to think. To improve as a performer, you must level with yourself about *your* bad habits of thinking and start developing their converse. You know what impediments stand between you and your dream. After getting this far in this book, you know the elements of exceptional thinking and where you fall short. Base your construction on those rather than wasting time considering what philosophy works for anyone else, no matter how much you admire their way of living and working. Don't adopt any "expert's" prescribed philosophy; rely on yourself to figure it out. Only then will your strategy have a chance to enhance your performance.

From Obstacles to a Philosophy

In Spring 2002, the Cox School of Business at Southern Methodist University in Dallas asked me to do a workshop with new MBA students who were entering SMU's graduate program after significant stints in the working world. My message: You will need a guiding principle for applying all the information and techniques received in business school to your on-the-job experience. To generate such a performance philosophy, I advised them to imagine themselves going to work every morning and sitting down at their desks. "What is the first thought you have every day?" I asked, warning that it had better not be, "Should I have a bagel, or a doughnut?"

Most people do not have a deliberately crafted overriding set of thoughts to use as they go about executing their daily strategies and plans. They definitely have their goals, "success formulas," business plans. But those are the Xs and Os of a career. When they get to the office, they pull up their calendar of meetings on their computers and jump right into work. They immediately start thinking about *what* they have to do. To perform exceptionally, at some point you have to pay attention to *how* you're going to do it. MBA students, like law students and medical students, easily get caught up in the technical aspects of their education.

And the same thing happens for the rest of us in the midst of our working world: Putting out all the fires we encounter can make us feel that having a philosophy is just being idealistic. In fact, a great philosophy of performance is a practical way of looking at the very obstacles most frequently keeping you from being an exceptional thinker. I require executives taking a continuing education course with me to consider the hurdles between them and doing a good job. If you get nervous picking up the phone to make a sales call or heading into a meeting with your supervisor or the board, you have to come up with an axiom that gets you to think effectively about the fight-or-flight responses that inevitably will emerge during your day. Here are some suggestions for performance philosophies to deal with pressure:

- The human body functions at a higher level when stimulated by pressure.
- Pressure moments are opportunities to use all of your training.
- Pressure is an opportunity for success.
- The absence of feeling pressure would be a sure sign of boredom, disinterest, and a lack of importance in what you do.

If your problem is not pressure, but overthinking your performances or spending too much time preparing for things rather than actually doing them—if, in short, you're prone to being an over-motivated underachiever—then you might try your own variations of these axioms:

- You will never win a competition in practice.
- You cannot be successful in a job by staying in school or continually attending training seminars.
- Effort is like entering a long-division competition with only pencil and paper—you tend to make mistakes and you will get whooped by someone with a calculator.

Another fruitful source of performance philosophies is to imagine yourself at the end of your career, attending your own retirement party. What will be the distinctive trait that speakers point to? I suspect you do not want to be that person described as: "She always gave 110 percent." "Whenever I left the office late at night, there was only one light still on." "He had his nose to the grindstone." Or a slight variation: What will be the running joke about you, the phrase you always used, the imitation that office wags did of you? Is it your tendency to say, "Things rarely turn out the way you want," or "I'm prepared for the worst"? Or will people be able to mime your confident strut? Will they imitate your wink and high-five, or your habit of not looking people in the eye?

The answers to such imaginary retrospective questions will help you figure out the "reputation" you want to have for yourself as a thinker. The exercise also will help you recognize the obstacles that you want to use your philosophy to get past. If you have a well-grounded performance philosophy, hurdles, roadblocks, and failure won't be able to knock you off track.

Positive Thinking vs. Positive Action

Negative thinking is extremely powerful. If you believe catastrophe is one step around the corner, then it will be hard either to be genuinely committed or confident. "Think positively" is generally good advice, but it also can be an obstacle to exceptional thinking. Positive thinking tends to be goal-oriented. It also tends to put performers in the Training Mindset, analyzing their stream of consciousness. Exceptional thinkers learn to trust their consciousness. They teach themselves the power of positive *action*. They don't stop to think about how great the act is going to be. Instead, they act.

This is a big difference. A great surgeon is not carving away at your innards, thinking to himself: "I'm a great surgeon, I'm doing a great operation, yes I am." Such self-talk would strike a surgeon as not just silly but potentially very dangerous. Surgeons do not even think, "First I do X, then I do Y, and what is it that comes after that? Right, I do Z." Good surgeons go to work, cut by cut, stitch by stitch, trusting their training and experience. During surgery, they no more think about what they're doing—positively or negatively—than a good salesman in the middle of a deal thinks about the steps in the company sales manual or a great pianist on stage is thinking about what note comes next. Nor are they thinking about the perfect result; they are just doing what they're good at and enjoying it, and they know if that's all they do, the best result possible for that given moment will be there. They do not have to contemplate the importance of being confident because genuinely confident surgeons, salesmen, and musicians arrive with their confidence already in gear. They perform based on their philosophies, not a set of instructions. They no more have to remind themselves to be confident or committed than truly religious people have to jot down "keep the faith" on their to-do list. Being faithful is just who they are.

A philosophy of performance is not a mantra that you repeat over and over to yourself as you perform. It's a guideline to help you keep thinking exceptionally regardless of the factors pushing you to revert to your old habits or socializing you to think like the masses.

The Philosophy of Engagement

The problem of the recipe or 12-step approach to what you do is that life is dynamic and unpredictable. You need a philosophy that isn't specific to particular outcomes, that will keep you thinking in a consistent manner even when everything at work is as far from consistent as you can imagine.

A couple of years ago, I went stunt flying with my good friend Dave Stirton, a former Top Gun Ace and teacher of several generations of fighter pilots. He took me up in a tiny little two-seat stunt plane. We did barrel rolls, a Slit S, loops; we flew upside down; Dave even intentionally stalled the plane, sending us into a dive. When we landed, he gave me a little friendly ribbing: "How was that seatbelt of yours?" he asked, pointing at my harness. I looked down. The two four-inch-wide shoulder straps were crushed almost into strings, as I had been gripping them so hard. "I couldn't let you think I was bored," I said.

As we chuckled and walked back into the hangar, he told me to wait while he went to fetch an article that he thought would be right up my alley. He was right. He handed me an essay that I now pass out with class readings every semester in my performance psychology course. It was a true story about a pilot who, during a routine flight, suddenly felt his plane pulling hard to the right. His altimeter was going crazy. He could hardly steer. But he did what he was trained to do: He kept the plane from spinning out of control by lowering his airspeed, adjusting the aileron on the right wing, stepping on the rudder to counter the yaw, and radioing the control tower to alert that he was coming in for a risky landing. When he stepped out of the cockpit, he was stunned by the condition of his aircraft: The left wing had been ripped off! People came sprinting out to the plane, incredulous. How had he managed to fly and land a plane with one wing? He had no idea. The plane's instruments did not tell him he was flying on one wing. He simply knew he had a problem, and he tried to solve it. In fact, if he had known that the wing was gone, he also would have known that the odds against keeping a one-winged plane in the air were severely against him, and he might have parachuted right away. His philosophy was akin to the various philosophies I've found common among emergency performers, such as ER docs, EMTs, fire fighters, S.W.A.T. specialists, and other rescue workers:

Do what you do (tenaciously).

When you are in an emergency, you can focus on the things going wrong or the low likelihood that you'll come out okay. Or you can focus on the things you know how to do. In class, I often use the example of the person who jumps out of a plane and pulls the cord on his parachute, and it doesn't open. He tries the backup chute, and that, too, fails. He now has two choices: to die or to try not to die. To be sure, the odds against survival are daunting. Yet we all have heard of cases of people who survived to tell the tale of how their parachute failed and how they walked away (or at least enjoyed the ambulance ride). Their fall was broken by trees or they ended up in a lake—with a lot of pain and broken bones, but still alive. An exceptional thinker plummeting toward the earth will rely on this philosophy:

There's always a chance.

He will start scanning the ground for trees or water, anything that might temper his descent and increase the odds for survival. He will open his arms and legs to increase wind resistance, and he'll decide how he is going to collapse or bend his joints to prevent the force of impact from being concentrated. To be honest, I really have no idea how he will pull it off. Exceptional thinkers, though, will get into the challenge of thinking up a solution that they can be confident about. The prospect of death, to borrow from Samuel L. Johnson again, has a way of focusing one's attention.

*   *   *

To help you get the hang of developing your own performance philosophies, I offer the following list of samples. Adapt these strategies however you like and make them part of your thinking. As you do, keep in mind that a winning philosophy is (1) simple and unambiguous, (2) personalized to your unique situation, (3) aimed at maintaining consistently great thinking in the face of the obstacles that normally would bring out your ineffective habits, and (4) about the process, not a roadmap to a particular outcome.

Thriving Under Pressure

- The human body is designed to peform better under stress.
- Pressure is an opportunity—for showing how good you are.
- The bigger the moment, the more you get to use your training.
- Pressure is what turns coal into diamonds.
- You don't get to succeed without being tested or challenged.
- The absence of feeling pressure would be a sure sign of boredom, disinterest, and a lack of importance in what you do.
- Every day do something that challenges you, scares you a little bit, makes you uneasy, or tests your emotions.
- Life is not worth it unless you *feel* it.

Healthy Commitment

- Giving 110 percent does not always add up.
- Work smarter rather than harder.
- Practice does not make perfect; in fact, there's no such thing as perfect.
- You can't win a competition during practice.
- No matter what you are doing, there is a fun way to do it.
- Would you do this for free?
- The experience is the reward.
- Getting paid is just an added bonus.
- If it's worth doing, it's worth doing well.
- If it's worth doing, it's worth doing badly. (For talented people who let their perfectionism get in the way of their productivity.)
- Success is based on inner—not outer—talent.

Self-Confidence

- Everyone is born human.
- Everyone puts his pants on one leg at a time. (Except for one Rice student, and now, yours truly.)
- You'll win (succeed)—if you're given enough time.
- If you can see it in your head, you can do it.
- Tomorrow you get another shot at it.
- Don't take outcomes seriously.
- Self-worth is not about what you've done; it's about valuing all your quirks, foibles, and mistakes.
- There are no guarantees. If you feel you have to have a guarantee to make something worthwhile, don't bother.

- The thrill of a project comes from the uncertainty of its outcome.
- "The team that makes the most mistakes wins." (John Wooden)
- Look at every obstacle as an opportunity to succeed.
- Look at every obstacle as a potentially funny story.
- All I can do is the best I can do.
- I don't go around judging myself relative to other people.

Chasing Your Dreams

- Your thoughts are your thoughts and valuable to you, regardless of whether they are valuable to others.
- What you are after is the best chance to make something happen.
- Life is about finding as much happiness and fulfillment as possible—not about the title on your door or how much money you make.
- It's about finding out what you are capable of doing, not a checklist of accomplishments.
- Success is using your God-given talents, whatever they might be.
- Maximize your ability; don't try to have somebody else's.
- You are born, you live, and you die. You cannot control birth or death, but you can do something about how you live.
- You can't control events, but you can control your reactions to events.
- You get to write your own autobiography.
- It's "in the cards" if you want it to be.
- For every great idea or innovation, someone had to be the first to do it.

There are hundreds of great philosophies you could use as the foundation for your thinking, and the lists above address only some of the areas of performance psychology that we've been talking about. Don't let that stop you. Perhaps the most rewarding aspect of having a philosophy of performance is designing and building it from scratch. And if you draw a blank at first, remember: One of the quickest routes to the right philosophy, for you, is an honest analysis of your own performances, with a cold eye for the defects in how you think under pressure.

CHAPTER 12

The Next .400 Hitter Will Be . . .

We live in a world of statistics and surveys, where politicians and tastemakers do not seem to be able to believe in anything until they have seen the "polling numbers" on it. Who doesn't want "hard evidence"? In a diverse and competitive world, "objectivity" is the preferred mode for evaluating situations and people. The urge to depend on results for evaluating success is understandable. Increases in sales, earnings, net profits, and other standard measures of "productivity" seem so scientific, they must be right.

But playing the numbers game is not always the most effective measure of performance, or the truest. Based on objective assessments, organizations are showing the door to people who may be the most talented performers in the building. How many times have you heard of an employee who was fired as a loser by one company and rose to the top of a major competitor? Stories of the athlete who just can't seem to do anything right for one team but emerge as an essential variable in the success of another team are legion. Their talent has not changed; the performing environment has. The teammates, the coaching, the management—clearly something is making it easier for that person to perform up to his potential. You have to find it, for your sake and your organization's.

If you are a boss, for example, whom do you fire—the person doing his absolute best, or the person who is going through the motions? Most people would point to the slacker. But what if the slacker is supremely talented, producing a mere fraction of his potential, and that hardworking soul giving it everything he has, day in and day out, will never get any better? Great executives would be inclined to keep the slacker and work on bringing out his talent. They know that there's more to performance than just the numbers and that their challenge is to figure out how to tap into the talents of their under-motivated underachievers. If you are an employee not living up to your talent, or you are your own boss, struggling to take your operation to the next step, what you need is not a "wake-up call" or a pep talk, but a better method of evaluation—one entirely different from the traditional "objective" measures that most companies and individuals usually rely on, and have grown all too dependent on.

I know that I have been on the warpath against "evaluation" since the Introduction, declaring it the enemy of great performance, deriding it as the very essence of the dreaded Training Mindset. But the Training Mindset has its place, and so does evaluation—*outside* of performance. At some point, everybody has to step back and gather information about how they're doing. Most people, no matter how successful, could benefit from some improvement; even superstars can fall into bad habits. The key is to measure performance in a manner that does not impede exceptional thinking or reinforce ineffective thinking patterns. How?

1. Evaluate yourself only during those periods set aside in advance for that purpose.
2. When you do evaluate, look only at those variables that in the long run determine success.

That's the way great performers do it: They never evaluate results, just the process—and never during the performance itself.

And the Next .400 Hitter Will Be . . .

I've found that businesspeople have a tough time understanding the distinction between evaluating the process and evaluating the results, while the light bulb goes on immediately for athletes who know the joy (and pain) of the lucky bounce, the miraculous catch, the bad call by an umpire or judge, and "winning ugly." A golfer with a good head, for example, knows that his tournament standing is not necessarily the best measure of his ability. He could quite possibly shoot a 69 and find himself on the cusp of not making the cut if the majority of the field had great days and fired sub-68s. Or he could grind out a 75 on a brutally tough course like the 2002 U.S. Open at Bethpage Black, or be the beneficiary of competitors' miscues, and take the lead. A golfer's scorecard is not necessarily an accurate reflection of how well he's actually hitting the ball. An inordinate string of shots can kick into the rough, greens can change speeds unexpectedly during a round, and the wind can swirl up in ways that seem to prove that Mother Nature is not a golfer.

Of course, you would never see such a thing on the sports page, where box scores rule. There's never a column ranking great thinking or a special "Sportswriter's Prize for the Best Inner Game." In my experience, sportswriters, who are very rarely former athletes, with no on-field experience at the highest levels of even college sports, tend to have a limited understanding of what goes on in the minds of great athletes. (Perhaps even worse, they seem to make little or no educated effort to inform themselves on the subject).* Sometimes great

---

*The most egregious example is the infamous bitterness of the Boston Red Sox press toward Ted Williams, whose major sin was hardly the way he played the game. No one was more passionate and focused, and no one probably was ever better at hitting a baseball. Williams simply did not think the press knew what they were talking about. He never respected the Boston media, and many of them had trouble respecting the best hitter that they would ever see in their lives, never mind the luck of being able to watch him play every day.

athletes start thinking like sportswriters. It's a mistake that always hurts their game.

During the 1995 baseball season, I had the opportunity to discuss self-evaluation with Carney Lansford, a former major league batting champion who was then the hitting coach for the Oakland A's. Despite his talent for hitting a baseball, Carney often found himself making the mistake of thinking like a sports analyst. Sitting in the visitors' dugout in Camden Yards in Baltimore, we talked about the mental aspects of hitting. As he generously shared stories from his career and my colleague David Striegel and I explained what we do as a psychological consultants, Carney suddenly realized something about his career that had never dawned on him before. "You know, we're chatting about how to think and I keep giving you mechanics. Here I am talking about situational statistics and making sure to drive the ball to the right side. Sorry," he said. "I'm just conditioned to approach hitting like a hitter. I was a student of the game."

He paused—and then snapped his fingers. "You know, that's really what we're talking about." He took off the dark, wraparound, sun-reflecting Oakleys that were hiding his eyes, revealing a serious expression. I assumed he was going to espouse the virtues of studying one's craft. Carney, however, went in the opposite direction. "Hitters always think about two things: their swing and their batting average. They're obsessed with them. Heck, we coach guys by the stuff." Lansford then conceded with an ironic chuckle, "You wanna know where to find a struggling hitter? Reading the stat page of the sports section or in the cage in front of a mirror. But that's why so few hitters are great in the brain department. They've got this same bad habit I had of looking at their performance from a physical or statistical standpoint. I bet you could ask any guy out here what his average is and he'd know it down to the last digit. Being a student isn't always such a good thing."

No performance psychologist could have said it better, or with more authority. Carney went on to lament that if he had understood more about the psychology of performance at the time he was playing, he was certain he could have hit .400, something only Ted Williams has done since a guy named Bill Terry hit .401 in 1930. This was hardly idle talk; Lansford was among the leaders of the American League in average, hits, fewest strikeouts, and total bases in seven of his fourteen full seasons. He only won the batting crown once, in 1981, but was in the hunt until the final weeks of the season four other years, against some of the game's legendary contact hitters. "[Wade] Boggs and [Kirby] Puckett and [Don] Mattingly kept beating me out," he recalled with an exasperated smile. "I kept hitting these skids. I couldn't ever quite keep it going like they could. Now I know why."

During his best seasons, Carney Lansford had been close enough to the mountaintop to see .400 within his reach. Looking back on his best seasons at the plate, Lansford noted that he always had a "slump"—twenty or so at-bats when he didn't get a hit. And the culprit, according to Lansford, was constantly evaluating himself in the form of his daily batting average. Lansford clearly had given the matter thought; he was, after all, a self-professed evaluationaholic.

He even had figured out exactly when the worst slump of his career began. It was one of those days that anyone who has played baseball has experienced. Every time up, Lansford had seen the ball clearly and hit it solidly. He felt good in the box. He was stinging the ball. He just had no hits to show for it. After each disappointing at-bat, during which he had either lined the ball directly to a fielder or been the victim of leather robbery, with someone making a spectacular play to get him out, Lansford wondered what a guy had to do to get a break. In the back of his mind, he knew his average was dropping. Yet he managed to shrug off his frustration, until his fourth trip to the plate. He laced one straight up the middle, and to the day I talked with him, he still was not sure how the pitcher got out of the way without getting killed. "I mean, I really hit it on the screws," he said in full animation. Instead of whistling into center field, though, the ball struck the second base bag, ricocheting to the right, all the way to the feet of the first baseman. It had happened so fast—Lansford remembered it as the hardest ball he had hit in his entire career—that he was barely three steps out of the batter's box when he was astonished to see the first baseman pick up the ball and step on first base. He was out; worse, he was now 0 for 4! And then it began to *really* bother him. Walking back to the dugout stunned, he thought, "If I hit the ball as well as I did today and don't get on base, then there's no way I will ever hit .400." Carney Lansford proceeded to go hitless for two weeks.

Days like that turn hitters into amateur mathematicians, figuring out averages in their heads every time through the lineup. It's a rampant trend in the minor leagues, where some coaches actually teach young players to think in terms of a series of ten plate appearances. If you want to be a .300 hitter, all it takes is getting three hits for every ten turns at bat. This approach is supposed to remind players that baseball is not a game of perfect—merely three hits for every ten at-bats will make you a superstar; percentage-wise you only need *half* the success rate that earns a D minus in school! Unfortunately, encouraging such constant counting backfires most of the time. It ensures that naturally talented trusters will spend their entire season mired in steady outcome evaluation, thus honing the *Training* Mindset and keeping themselves *out* of the present by thinking continually about past and future at-bats. Go 0 for 5 and they start pressing, trying to do too much (3 for 5 instead of 3 for 10); go 5 for 5 and they let up on their approach, ensuring an 0-for streak. Either approach breeds a down-spiraling cycle of poor thinking.

What is the take-home message? By thinking about his average, Lansford was evaluating his success based on the outcome of each at-bat rather than how effectively he had prepared for the pitcher, how clearly he picked up the release point, how loose and trusting he was, or how well he made contact. Since outcomes often give inaccurate feedback, Carney was not learning the right things about himself. His confidence and attitude took needless dips. He was not arming himself with knowledge about the parts of his game that he needed to work on and parts he should leave as they were. He tried too hard to compensate for bad breaks. He put his energy into the wrong type of pregame practice.

Years later, Carney Lansford realized that his worst day at the plate—the day when he convinced himself that he could never hit

.400—should have been one of his best. He had hit the ball consistently on the mark, and if he had strolled out to admire the dent in second base, he might have gotten himself thinking about how great it felt to swing so smoothly, to hit the ball effortlessly, harder than ever before. That might have encouraged him to keep trusting his eyes and hands. He might have focused more on the cues that helped him get such a good look at the pitches. And he might have continued swinging a hot bat, picking up an extra twenty hits rather than outs. The difference over a season of 550 at-bats would have made him the next .400 hitter.

Whoever reaches that milestone will have to be as good a natural hitter as Carney Lansford. He also will have to design a self-evaluation strategy based on the hitting process and the other elements of performance that are personally controllable, and not on the statistics of various outcomes.

Evaluate Only the Things You Can Control

All careers are filled with ricochets like Lansford's, the people, things, and events we cannot do anything about. To help you identify the uncontrollable in your work, draw the following chart:

	CONTROLLABLE	UNCONTROLLABLE
INTERNAL		
EXTERNAL		

List as many aspects of your work you can think of that are (1) inside you or individual (internal), (2) interpersonal or group-oriented (external), (3) within your control, or (4) outside your control. Grab a pencil and fill in this chart, or make your own.

I've had the Rice baseball pitching staff complete this very same drill. In fact, we go over their lists many times throughout the season. Probably the most important occasion was the afternoon of Game 3 of the 2003 NCAA College World Series Championship. We were squared off with Stanford, arguably the country's best program, tied at one game apiece. It was one o'clock—eight hours before the national champion would be crowned. Despite a number-one ranking and the nation's most dominant pitching staff, Rice still was considered the underdog. A perennial powerhouse, Stanford had won the College World Series twice and played for the championship in three out of the past four years. No team in Rice's history had ever played for a national championship in any sport.

Supporters were pouring in for the final game by bus, by plane, by any mode of transportation available. A dozen or so Rice football players packed into a single car and drove all night long, showing up in full owl-blue body paint! Needless to say, there was pressure. To help players prepare mentally for the big game, I did what I had done before every game in Omaha: I walked into Omaha's Old Market district with a group of players for lunch.

The team's three top hitters—Craig Stansberry, Vincent Sinisi, and Jose Enrique Cruz—had already been drafted by major league teams, but during the World Series they all had been disappointing at the plate. I asked each to describe where his mind needed to be for that day's big game, and then to think of how to handle obstacles that might get in the way. We'd been playing a lot of stickball out in the park by our hotel so their loose, playful mentality was honed, and all three of them were getting locked into what they would do before and during pitches, rather than the outcome. I had worked with each of them for long hours during the regular season and I could see they were ready to play free of evaluation, in spite of the pressure from the press and the Rice fans to break out of their doldrums. So when the waitress arrived with our lunch (the classic baseball superstition of ordering chicken before every game wasn't the point), I turned to Philip Humber, scheduled to pitch the final game. "Okay, big dog, when you get on the mound, what can you control?"

The team had a running joke that they weren't allowed to score runs when Philip was throwing. He had been Rice's ace pitcher the year before, but in 2003 he'd been struggling to compensate for that lack of run support by trying too hard to get every batter out, and his pitching record had suffered. So when I asked Philip to give a list of the things he could control as a pitcher, he was inclined to spit out, "Getting ahead in the count, not walking batters, keeping runners off base and out of scoring position." I cut him off. "No, what can you *really* control?"

Philip is a bright guy; he'd just been listening to his teammates and picked right up on how they were preparing. "I guess I can't really control anything," he conceded, "except how decisive I am about the pitch selected, where I put my eyes, and releasing the ball." A huge grin came over my face. This kid was going to win big. We continued to talk about being an "Ice Man" on the mound—not having any care whatsoever for what Stanford's hitters, the umpires, or even his own fielders did. Run support or no run support, ahead or behind in the count, getting hit hard or keeping hitters off balance—none of those things are within the control of any pitcher. Philip's job was to find the targets he wanted to hit, and throw the ball. The only point of evaluation is whether or not he was doing that—and *nothing* else.

Philip Humber threw a five-hitter and became the first College World Series pitcher to complete a game in a decade. His icy attitude toward evaluation rubbed off on his teammates, who gave him fourteen runs of support and a national championship. Stansberry went 3 for 4, Cruz went 3 for 4, and Sinisi, one of the nation's best hitters in 2003 but struggling mightily at the plate since the first game of the Series, went 4 for 4. But the best reward of all for me was when I went onto the field to congratulate the team, and Philip hugged me right off the ground, exclaiming, "Doc, it was working!"

In turning clients loose with the performance control chart, I've discovered three interesting trends. The first is the tendency to put too many items in the "controllable" boxes—the same bad habit that Philip had to change. Typically people will mistake certain aspects of their lives as being within their control. Their salary is a classic example. You do the job, you get paid for it. You do the job better, and you should get a raise. But it doesn't always work that way. Your boss is the one who manipulates the purse strings, and he may not have noticed your great work; he may be cheap or looking for ways to cut costs. The company's stock price may be in free fall; perhaps management has decided to freeze all raises or even ask employees to take a cut in salary so that others won't have to be let go. You may be doing a great job, but you were the last hired, and now you will have to be the first fired. Over such decisions, you have no control. Look closely at the controllable boxes and don't fool yourself; can you *really* control all of those things?

The second tendency I've found is to assume that there are internal reasons for most of the external factors of success. Go back to your chart and separate the internal from the external. If you do this honestly and critically, you'll find that you need to move several items to spaces in the external grid.

The third thing I've noticed is that many people tend to confuse the process of success with its by-products. Go through all four boxes and cross out each item that can be classified as a result or conclusion of a performance (or circle the ones that are in play long before a performance outcome is known). A lot of elements get eliminated. When you are finished with this, and when you've been entirely honest, you'll discover that the only things you should be evaluating are the noncrossed (or circled) entries in the controllable column, with the majority of your attention to the internal square. That's where you should be putting all your effort. Your self-assessments should follow one simple question: "Am I putting my energy into the controllable boxes or someplace else?"

Most of my clients are astonished to realize how much time they waste on things they cannot control: the preferences and prejudices of bosses, the personalities and skills of coworkers, the craziness of clients, the genius of competitors, the economic variables of the industry, the ups and downs of the national (or international) economy. If you, too, are brooding over issues you will never be able to change, cross those things out of your life and begin counting the time you could free up for working on the kind of thinking that actually will make you a better performer.

Gauging the Quality of Your Work: When and How

It is difficult to find a mathematical description of attitude. While we have a sense of what it means to be passionate or fully committed, how do you score an emotion? To gauge the process of a performance requires a *qualitative* evaluation, not a quantitative one. Still, the urge to play the numbers game in self-evaluation is strong. Most performers in most professions are conditioned to judge themselves on the basis of their rate of acceptance—approval from their bosses, coworkers, the media, shareholders, and market analysts. It's a well-entrenched habit. So rather than go cold turkey, I let people make the transition from quantitative to qualitative evaluations by putting a number on the psychological aspects of their performances. Go ahead and give a score to your attitude at work, your confidence level, your focus, how well you handle arousal. Make up your own set of statistics. Be sure, though, to appraise your performances by leaning heavily on the *qualitative* tallies.

Ideally, you want to build an evaluation strategy that helps you interview yourself about the quality of your work and the quality of your thinking. As you get comfortable with evaluating effectively, move from digital information to analog, from stat sheets to language. After all, the operating data of the mind is comprised not of numbers but of images and words. Decide what factors you want to keep an eye on over time—commitment, the Trusting Mindset, playing in the present, for example—and then design your own log or feedback system. I advise keeping a journal that includes charts—a couple of columns for the variables you think you need to work on and a couple of columns for those that you think you've mastered. *Maintenance* of exceptional thinking is equally as important as improving or adding components to your mental game. Further, you want to keep track of *all* the qualitative variables that make you, specifically, a psychologically well-conditioned performer. Instead of putting numbers on aspects of your performance, use words and images to describe each factor before and during the performance. If, for example, you are evaluating the level of your commitment to a project or job, don't count the hours you've put in. That's quantitative thinking. Analyze where you put your eyes, how sustained your vision and enthusiasm were, how well you kept track of the real reason you were performing, and what obstacles or setbacks affected your effort, and how.

Set up your journal according to a given day or specific performances, breaking down each in as much detail as you can. In baseball, I like hitters to break it down according to each pitch—what was their confidence, did they correctly make note of the situation, did they see the ball well and trust their hands, and so on. Someone in sales would break down their day according to sales calls. For an engineer, it might be project task to project task. If you were the head of benefits in a corporation, overseeing corporate fitness versus health insurance claims, you would evaluate your performance per employee or per meeting. Try to be as organized and intentional as possible about such written evaluations.

Most important, since it's crucial to separate evaluation from performance and to keep yourself from being an assessment junkie, preset a time block or day, at regular intervals, when you will look back on your performance—every Friday after lunch for two hours, for example. If you are working on different projects, you should be interviewing yourself on how you think you did on each. As head of benefits, you might be extremely intrigued by the upside of switching insurance carriers, while the topic of corporate fitness seems dull, and that may explain why you choked in your presentation to the executive committee on the cost/reward viability of installing a workout room.

At the end of the quarter, you can compile your periodic evaluations. Look for patterns. You might see stretches when you put in a lot of time but your evaluation continually said, "My mind wanders to how the marketing department will perceive this new product." Your boss might have been impressed with your late nights at the office, but you noted, "I was just grinding away, banging my head into the wall over and over." When you described yourself as "focused" or "on fire," what was it about those days or projects that caused that feeling? The log should tell you. Maybe you were working on a project that you had initiated; perhaps your boss set a special deadline that forced you to crank at high speed; or maybe that project was particularly gratifying and reminded you why you got into this line of work in the first place. Such evaluations will give you some insight into what improves your performance and what bogs it down.

Notice that you are not just filling in a chart or checking boxes on the typical self-improvement questionnaire. A qualitative evaluation is not another thing on your to-do list. You don't want to find yourself saying, "I must be performing well because I checked all the boxes on my evaluation sheet." An effective assessment provides working feedback rather than scores. It is really part of the work execution process, serving as a starting point for how you set up your mind for the *next* performance. It should never be an end in itself.* Like performance philosophies and preperformance routines, qualitative evaluations are another tool to help you get into exceptional thinking—and stay there.

---

*This is the problem I find with most self-help books; they are replete with inventories and scales. Jim Loehr's current book, *The Power of Full Engagement*, written with Tony Schwartz, includes hundreds of questionnaires that readers are required to fill out at the beginning of the day, at the end of the day, at the end of the week, constantly. His disciples spend their time filling out forms rather than changing the way they think. The danger is that the performer begins to identify "engagement" with completing the paperwork.

Tracking Trends

Trends and patterns in your performances will emerge over time, but please do not be looking for them every day. You wouldn't run through your preperformance routine after you finish work; nor should you be evaluating yourself before and during go-time. A violinist in mid-concerto would never drop her bow to question her commitment to music; a surgeon is not likely to wake up a heart patient before the operation is complete to ask whether he's feeling better. But how often in the middle of a job or a deal or a presentation or golf game have you gauged how you were doing? I see students reading books and flipping ahead all the time to see how many pages are left in the chapter. Clearly, they are not connected with what they are reading, and the chances of it sinking in are slim. During a performance, the only kind of "feedback" you need is that sense of delight you will get when you are fully absorbed. The worst thing an athlete can do when he's in the groove is to start thinking to himself, "This is incredible. I'm unstoppable. I need to figure out why so I can keep it going." To think about the Trusting Mindset is to make it go away or make it harder for it to appear. As we have seen, that's not just the way the psychology of performance works; it's also the way human biology operates.

So save the evaluating—the Training Mindset—for intervals that don't conflict with performance. Set up specific times during the week, month, or year when you will review your performance logs. If your company has regular corporate retreats, that can be a perfect time to check for patterns in your work and consider ways of redesigning your approach or mindset for the months ahead. Or, reserve blocks of time on your own calendar when you will take a break from executing your skills, when you will instead walk through your self-assessments. Whenever you do decide to evaluate, make sure it is predetermined and systematically planned.

Kinesiologists—scientists who study human motion and motor

memory—tell us that near error-free hand-eye coordination in a complex activity, such as hitting a baseball or golf ball, takes about 1.2 million repetitions. That's hitting a lot of balls. We also know that to become extremely confident you need to practice confident thinking, although fortunately nowhere near 1.2 million times. (Then again, if you managed to practice your confidence 1.2 million times, you'd be as good as Tiger Woods, at least in the game of confidence.) Your self-evaluations will give you the opportunity to see how you've been practicing and where you've been slacking off. For example, "There is a reason why I am not any more confident than before; I talked about working on my confidence, but I never really followed through on putting myself into more situations to test my ability to be confident again and again."

It is useful to have someone to work with during evaluation periods, to ask for advice and suggestions, or to serve as a "training partner," facilitating the assessment of each other's performance patterns. You will almost definitely benefit from a written log, something that athletes in most sports resist, surprisingly. Marathon runners, however, are fanatics about keeping track not only of how many miles they run each week and what their heart rates are, but also how they feel qualitatively each morning and evening. They monitor their sleep, fuel intake, and perceptions of fatigue so as to know whether they should devote the day to a sprint workout or an easy run. Except for extreme endurance competitors, such as cyclists, triathletes, cross-country skiers, and swimmers, most athletes rarely even think of keeping track of such intangible things as mood, restlessness, or well-being. But those factors are no less important to the quality of their performances than for marathon runners. It's just that in team and ballistic sports, quantitative statistics dominate, getting in the way of the more accurate performance measures. (*Coincidently, preparing to be an overachiever in business and most careers is far more like training for triathlons than for fifty-yard dashes.*)

You can keep the same kind of training log whether you are a musician, a doctor, or are in business; anyone who performs under pressure should be looking back at the quality of their performances over time if they're serious about doing their best and improving. After all, you cannot physically see whether your concentration is up or down; there is no confidence meter you can wear. Without a personal performance coach or psychologist like me dogging your every move, self-evaluation is your only effective alternative.

Your journal will tell you things about yourself you would never have thought of. You might, for example, discover that your concentration levels decrease after an hour of steady work or that your focus is down when you don't eat enough protein for breakfast. If you check your log under the heading "confidence" against the overall quality of your performance, you might notice that your confidence is up on your best days and down on your worst—a classic case of what psychologists call "dependent confidence." As we have seen, the best performers tend to be extremely confident even during their worst performances. ("I'm 0 for 10 from the floor this quarter," says a great shooter in basketball. "Give me the ball. I'm due.") Or you might be surprised to find that you experience a lot of anxiety when performing in front of coworkers, but thrive on pressure when the stakes are extremely high—making a presentation to your superiors, for instance. (It is not unusual for people to be more concerned about what their coworkers think of them than the boss.)

This is the kind of information that you can work with. Get a log, get a training partner, and then deliberately schedule evaluation sessions. You'll find your performance greatly improves when you record and attend to the right measures. Just be prepared to take an honest look at yourself.

The Ultimate Judge—Is You

In some jobs, self-evaluation can seem immaterial in relation to the evaluations of others. The success of writers, actors, musicians, and other entertainers often depends on what the critics say. In such intensely competitive careers, a good review can mean the difference between fame and finding a new occupation. The opinion of talent scouts, analysts, recruiters, and reviewers, however, is something that you cannot control. A review from a critic is a classic "outcome"—and the most accomplished artists ignore them. They know how much harder it is to do what they do than to break it down and comment on it. (Is there an arts and entertainment editor who wouldn't give it all up to star in the next Martin Scorcese feature? I have never met an actor whose ambition was to be a drama or movie critic.) Part of being an artist is taking your subjective lumps, and then continuing to perform, instinctually, in your own reality. The greatest artists never perform for the purpose of making money or appearing on Billboard charts. They're successful because of their irreverence for those kinds of evaluations, not the other way around.

I have one writer friend who, when introduced with a glowing introduction about his accomplishments, begins his speeches with some excerpts from his most corrosive reviews in an effort to underline not just the subjectivity of all censure but its irrelevance to his work. If you are in a profession in which criticism cripples you, I would recommend one of those collections of "worst reviews" of books by great writers. If Dostoevsky, Marcel Proust, Mark Twain, James Joyce, Samuel Beckett, Henry James, and so many more of the legends that you yourself might love have been savaged by literary critics (all forgotten, I might add) perhaps a knock or two—or a rave review or two, for that matter—are not the best variables to include in your evaluation strategy.

And the more famous you become as a performer, the greater the odds are that you will lose control of your evaluations. One of the most frustrating aspects of being a top professional athlete is that the media will do all they can to evaluate you . . . the wrong way. What furthers their careers (and puts money in the coffers of the newspapers, TV, and radio organizations, not to mention the advertisers that all media outlets depend on for their revenues and profits) is dramatizing or sensationalizing performance. "Has Bill Russell Lost It?" "Is Tiger in a Slump?" In 2003, Tiger Woods won five tournaments for a total of $4,530,000 and was named Player of the Year. Yet for most of the year, the golf media was blathering on about "Tiger's slump." To be sure, he did not win the money title for the first time in six years; for only the second time in his career, he did not win one of the major tournaments (the Masters, the PGA, the U.S. Open, the British Open). But the idea that the man was in a slump? Tiger knew it was ridiculous, and fellow players kept coming up to him to say, "I wish I were in a slump like you."

If you pressed the sportswriters, they probably would say, "Look at the numbers—no major, no money title. For Tiger, that's a slump." Does Tiger care about the numbers? Nope, not the way average performers do. Tiger Woods has his annual aims, but in terms of evaluating how well he's playing, he couldn't care less about outcomes. Like every great performer, his concern is about his confidence, his commitment, his concentration, and how he's responding under pressure, which is, as even golf writers would concede, astonishing.

But whoever evaluates you—your boss, your board, your partners, maybe even the industry newsletter—they, too, will be looking at the bottom line. And even if you or your company has had a quarter that's better than Tiger Woods's numbers, a reporter from *The Wall Street Journal* or *Fortune* is bound to call you up and wonder, "Do you really think you can keep up that pace?" In the same story, your competitors will be quoted saying that the entire sector was up, that high tide lifted your boat, that your success was due to a lucky product that hit, not the quality of your business plan or your leadership. And before you know it, you will be thinking, "Maybe I can't keep this up."

The real fact is, you did well because you were evaluating yourself properly, checking on the quality of your performance, the process. Start wondering if the critics might be right, and you'll join them in playing the numbers game that this entire chapter seeks to debunk. Thinking exceptionally is about what goes on in *your* head. The great thing about evaluating the quality of your performance and not the results is that you can be the best judge of what you are doing. Your boss, your competitors, the media do not have a clue how well you're thinking. They can't see what you picked for targets or how well you stuck with your philosophy or why you do what you do; they have no idea if you were performing in the present. Such mental states are, by definition, intangible, at least to anyone not armed with a CAT Scan machine. And even if industry critics have accidentally experienced the Trusting Mindset, believe me, they wouldn't have a clue about how to find it again.

You, my friend, on the other hand, now know exactly what it takes to find your groove. You know how to think exceptionally. You know that overconfidence is a good thing. You are also the only person on the planet who knows your true potential. That should be a wonderful revelation because it means that you can do the kind of self-evaluation that is performance enhancing—if you are honest with yourself and if you schedule your evaluations rather than doing them reactively or on the fly. You are now in position to reach your best as a performer so consistently that you sometimes will be able to take it to an even higher level at which what you do becomes a genuine work of art.

CHAPTER 13

The Art of High Performance— Michelangelo, Michael, and You

Michael Jordan was not a very gifted basketball player. That may seem an outrageous (even stupid) thing to say, but it is true—at least by many objective measures. Grab your record book and follow along. Jordan ranked ninth in field goals made, eighteenth in total points, sixth in field goal attempts per forty-eight minutes. Jordan does not rank first in any major NBA statistic. Even in his prime, Jordan was not the fastest or most accurate shooter; he certainly was not a rebounder or brilliant at defense.

So I repeat: Michael Jordan was not a very gifted basketball player. But let me now quickly add: MJ was the greatest player of his era, and maybe the best ever. How did a poor defender and average shooter get to be a five-time NBA MVP—not to mention earn the reputation as the best hoops player and most famous bald head on the planet? Hard work? Yes, the passionately intense, in-the-present, put-all-your-eggs-in-one-basket kind. And genuine, supreme self-confidence. He definitely thrived on pressure. But Jordan had something else going for him that I think is also characteristic of exceptional performers in every field:

He was an artist.

And I am not using the term metaphorically. The amazing things that Michael Jordan and other great athletes do under pressure and in front of millions of fans is, in my opinion, a kind of "performance art" that is comparable to the glories of music, literature, fine art, and architecture.

- Cervantes set Don Quixote and his loyal sidekick Sancho Panza off to tilt at windmills and invented a new way to tell a story in prose form—the novel.
- The early drawings of Michelangelo Buonarotti show the influence of Giotto and Massacio. But within a few years he was the incomparable "Michelangelo," the creator of the *Pietá* and *David,* two of the supreme sculptures of art history. In his future were the Sistine Chapel ceiling and his famous sculptures of *Moses* and the slaves, not to mention some of the most beautiful buildings in Florence and Rome.
- At age twelve he was declared "the second Mozart," but Ludwig van Beethoven set out to become the one and only Beethoven. By the force of his personality, an unusual style at the piano (he pounded his pianos into smithereens), and the unbridled emotion of his compositions, he pulled music from the Classical into the Romantic Era. Critics and intellectuals of his day were shocked by the emotional punch of his Fifth Symphony. By the time of his final and famous Ninth Symphony and its rousing choral rendition of Schiller's "Ode to Joy," Beethoven still was revolutionizing music—even though he was almost stone deaf.
- The Spanish architect Antonio Gaudi's odd and colorful geometric shapes seemed more appropriate to sculpture and painting, and his many critics doubted that his designs could make serviceable buildings. But Gaudi proceeded to remake large areas of Barcelona, turning the Spanish city into one of the most beautiful in the world.

He even designed a building without a single straight edge in the entire structure!

- The painter Vincent van Gogh painted a familiar world, and even himself, in shocking, brightly colored, thick oil paints. No one had ever painted that way before, and the results were unsettling. But now when we see a real stack of hay in a field or an expanse of sunflowers, we say, "It looks like a van Gogh." The painter had re-created reality.

- Samuel Beckett wrote essays, novels, and plays in English *and* French for thirty years in obscurity, and then a play he had written in French—*Waiting for Godot*—was produced in Paris in 1952 and even critics who claimed they did not quite understand what the playwright was up to recognized the play as a modern masterpiece. Beckett kept writing his complex dramas: One featured an aging couple living in separate garbage cans; another blacked out the actress to focus only on her mouth. Beckett's work was filled with anguish and loss, never designed to be popular successes. As he pursued his theme of expressing the inexpressible, Beckett seemed to be a writer whose art was moving toward an inevitable silence—except he won the Nobel Prize for Literature in 1969.

All of the above were indisputably great artists. They also were artists before they were accepted as such, and certainly before they became famous. I am sure you can add your own favorites to the list, from the past and present: writers, poets, painters, sculptors, and musicians who with their own hands have created divine things out of nothing but their imaginations and the urge to make something new. Often, the results appalled contemporary critics, victims of what the art critic Robert Hughes has called "the shock of the new." Inevitably, however, their work influenced the way others practiced their own art and revolutionized the way the rest of us look at the world. As the playwright

Bertold Brecht once said, "Art is not a mirror to reflect reality, but a hammer with which to shape it."

Like any great artist, Michael Jordan created something that didn't exist before, a piece of work that amazed basketball aficionados and experts and inspired other members of his field. Jordan, too, captured fame outside of regular NBA games. "His Airness" was born during slam-dunk contests—a venue for displaying physical artistry. It was only after Michael was crowned slam-dunk champion that he started letting his art into his daily game. The history of sport is filled with similar artistic achievements from genuine artists who never claimed to be.

- In the late 1950s, the two-handed set shot was still in vogue, but Bob Cousy was dazzling his opponents and Boston Celtics basketball fans with his running one hander. One night in 1930 when a taller defender stuck his hand in the face of Kenny Sailor, he stopped—and then sprung into the air, over the reach of his opponent, for the first jump shot in basketball history. Today, it's hard to imagine shooting any other way—always the mark of a work of art.
- Julius Erving seemed able to defy gravity with his leaping dunks; Magic Johnson's moves were, well, magic; and even when his body was slowing down with age, Michael Jordan shocked his opponents with a new shot, a fade-away jumper that they had trouble stopping.
- When you watch highlight films of Bobby Orr playing hockey, you can see the shock in the eyes of his opponents as Orr flashes stick handling that they've never seen before. It's been written numerous times that Orr could kill a two-minute penalty single-handedly by controlling the puck and refusing to relinquish it despite being outnumbered. And hockey fans all have seen photographs or videos of Orr flying through the air, four feet off the ice, his arms outstretched like Superman in

flight, scoring the winning goal to capture the 1970 Stanley Cup.

- In the '80s, Saint Louis Cardinal shortstop Ozzie Smith earned the name "the Wizard of Oz" by making plays while spinning, jumping, and falling off balance—moves that baseball fans had never seen before (at least outside a ballet studio). To this day, if the Oz visits a ballpark, fans roar in unison for him to do a standing back flip on the turf. The Cleveland Indians' Omar Vizquel has picked up where Ozzie left off, patenting his own special move on balls hit deep in the hole at shortstop, the hardest play in baseball: Moving fast to his right, he suddenly slides on his knees toward the ball, stopping his momentum, picks up the ball, and as he stands, turns to his left side to throw the runner out at first. Other shortstops are now practicing Vizquel's invention.

- On September 5, 1906, in a college football game between St. Louis University and Carroll College, Brad Robinson threw a forward lateral to Jack Schneider. It was the first pass in the history of football. It also was an incompletion—and according to the rules at the time, a penalty and an automatic turnover. Not until ten years afterward was the art form accepted into the rulebook.

- And, of course, let's not forget the Harlem Globetrotters, who proved that you could turn the art of basketball into pure (and lucrative) entertainment. The score of the game never matters to the crowd—in fact, it's a point of satire, just the display of physical artistry by a group of supremely talented players.

Using experience and skill, each of these players shocked their audiences with their new ways of performing, and in the process they boosted their métiers to a new level. If reshaping reality by fertile imaginations for new ways to perform customary skills is what art is, if artists do what they do from a personal desire or urge or even a sense of obligation to make art long before anyone recognizes their talents, and if there's also a kind of excitement and special feeling while doing it, then in my book—this book—that makes the greatest athletes true artists.*

Business as Art?

While many might concede that what great athletes do is a kind of art, business always has been perceived as the very contradiction of art. Business, by definition, is about profits and losses, conservative financial projections, the bottom line and "risk management," and thus is the enemy of art. In business, being "creative" is likely to mean cheating, as in "creative bookkeeping." How can business be art?

That inner urge that motivates artists is the dream and commitment that I have been arguing propels all great performers, including people in business, as well as lawyers, surgeons, and the top performers in every field. Like writers, painters, architects, and musicians, the best athletes, scientists, entrepreneurs, salespeople, and others in the business world get into a special mindset when they perform.

---

*I have been making this analogy between art and sports for years, but only recently have I been alerted to some confirmation from a renowned art historian. In *A Fine Disregard: What Makes Modern Art Modern*, Kirk Varnedoe, the former Museum of Modern Art curator, who also has taught at New York University and Columbia, uses the invention of rugby—created with, according to the plaque at England's Rugby School, "a fine disregard for the rules" of English football (a.k.a. soccer)—as the presiding metaphor for artistic innovation. The inventor of rugby, in the midst of a football game, picked up the ball and ran with it, just as every real artist must. For Varnedoe, not surprisingly a rugby player who also played and coached soccer at Williams College, art does not progress; it is rather the result of inspired inventions by imaginative people. Equally important for Varnedoe (and my purposes), making art is a visceral experience (no wonder I myself so much enjoyed playing for national championships in rugby in college). Varnedoe, considered the most articulate art historian of his generation and a member of the Institute of Advanced Studies at Princeton, died in 2003 at fifty-seven of cancer, just a few months after delivering the prestigious Mellon Lectures at the National Gallery of Art in Washington.

They get their kicks from sending new products into the marketplace, creating the next new trend. What could be more fun than imagining revolutionizing the entire world of business?

Art happens by exploring the limits of your abilities and experience, no matter what your field. You probably were hired because of your education, employment background, and/or core skills. But if you go to work every day with the mission of just executing your skills, you never will get any better. If you want to be great at what you do, if you want to impress your colleagues and superiors, you have to *explore* your talent. That means depending on your training and being committed to achieving your potential. It also means experimenting with your talent, trying things that even you yourself do not think are possible. An artist who churns out the same paintings is either a bad artist or a good one who is very bored. If an architect is successful only at converting blueprints into buildings, he is not likely to gain the reputation of being a brilliant architect, a reputation reserved for architects who dream up new kinds of buildings, like Gaudi or Frank Lloyd Wright.

You do have to pass on the notion that there are limits. Breakthroughs require, as we have seen in the previous chapters, an emotional commitment that is cultivated within us. Breakthroughs also require the ability to live with uncertainty—to thrive on it, in fact. Artists are most truly engaged when they do not know how things will turn out. Novelists talk about "following the characters where they take me." Potters wonder what their hands might do today. If winning was all Michael Jordan cared about, he could tour the nation's schoolyard basketball courts and spend his days defeating high school kids. Instead, he retired from basketball for a while to play *baseball*, against pros. Great athletes are eager to test themselves against the best in their game—and sometimes in the games of others. Look at how some of the best athletes are now also recording music.

The very idea of a "great shot" or "amazing move" is its novelty or rarity. Successful salesmen, deal-makers, entrepreneurs, even surgeons enjoy the challenge of performing under the gun, surmounting obstacles, succeeding in situations where failure seems to be the only alternative. Sure, coming out on top is a thrill, but for the best players, the real fun is in the performance, the innovation, airing out something new and letting 'er rip, win or lose. Famed coaches Jimmy Johnson and Barry Switzer went head to head as college coaches in 1987. With Oklahoma trailing 20–7 late in the fourth quarter of the Orange Bowl, Switzer called for a trick play on the goal line. His quarterback executed a "Fumblerooski" . . . and scored! The Sooners eventually lost the game, but when Switzer crossed the field to shake Johnson's hand, he spent the next ten minutes bragging about the Fumblerooski: "Did you see that play!? Man, we got you guys good. Now *that's* football." Switzer had just lost a national championship game, but like some kid on the playground, all he cared about was the art of that one play.

For CEOs of major companies and the most successful entrepreneurs, it's in those same fine, little touches where the art and fun of what they do lies. When you're playing the game with billions on the table, who makes the most is rarely the measure of success. Donald Trump, the New York real estate tycoon with a flare for self-promotion, wrote a book called *The Art of the Deal*. Even "The Donald"'s critics would concede that the title was more than metaphorical. If you are negotiating with New York City to rebuild the West Side of Manhattan, or with Atlantic City to create a new casino, or with NBC for a hit television series starring your astonishing self, will have to be imaginative and creative.

After Lou Gerstner transformed a dying IBM into a darling of Wall Street during a bear market, the press called him a "turnaround artist." And so it has always been in the world of commerce: Some are worker bees, while a few are absolute maestros. When Mayer Rothschild, a coin dealer in Frankfurt's Jewish ghetto, put one of his five sons in charge of a bank he founded in 1798 and then dispatched the other four to set up branches in Paris, Vienna, Naples, and London, he was thinking about making money, not art. But then Rothschild started thinking exceptionally and pulled off deals with a genius, scale, and improbability of Michelangelean proportions: They financed the Duke of Wellington's victory over Napoleon and the Crimean war, helped bankroll the infant State of Israel, and supported the British move for control over the Suez Canal, to name just a few of their most famous deals. The Rothschild international banking group is still one of the most prominent financiers in the world and one of the few independent bankers that has resisted being swallowed up by such global giants as UBS, Salomon Brothers, and Citigroup. When business historians look at Henry Ford's adaptation of the assembly line to sell 15 million Model Ts over twenty years, or Thomas Edison's creation of the first central electric power plant in New York City, they see more than just dollar signs.

All these people, and their no less brilliant and creative successors who have sparked the Internet revolution, took their considerable skills, talent, and experience into various situations and literally changed the game. Solving problems, meeting challenges, and overcoming obstacles with imagination and passion, they created new moves, new ways to do business, new kinds of companies, even a new way to view life itself.

The Ability to "Mess Around"

I learned very early in life about the art of performing, or what my father used to call "building a better mousetrap." My father, Rick Eliot, spent most of his athletic career experimenting with ways to make skiers—and their skis—go faster. At the edge of every race course, he'd set up a tent with benches for ironing and waxing, and experiment with literally two dozen pair of skis—in effect, his own glide test laboratory. If someone came up with a better ski wax or better trail grooming equipment, my father would try to go him one better. And it didn't matter what was going on around him. He'd draw blueprints on his napkin at the dinner table, take scraps and samples to mess around with on vacation. "You've always got to look for a better mousetrap," he would tell me, and we'd head down to the basement of our family house in Vermont, turn on some tunes, and spend the whole night waxing skis.

Dad put this notion of finding a better way at the center of his life. When there was a plumbing problem, he'd try to find a better way to fix it. One time he got so annoyed with the sheets getting tangled in his bed, he sewed a wooden dowel to the comforter so it would stay straight and he could tuck and untuck it with a quick flip of the wrist. When I was a schoolboy baseball player, he built a batting cage for me in the basement with Whiffle balls that could be fired up to 80 m.p.h. so that I could get in plenty of batting practice during the long New England winters. Today he's turned the same space into a gym with equipment he's scientifically engineered for developing rowing-specific muscles. At the age of seventy-three and after a complete ankle replacement—itself a work of art as one of the first one hundred procedures of its kind to rebuild a joint that orthopedists had considered too intricate to be artificially constructed—Dad can no longer run or even walk very comfortably. But with his own home-modified ski boots, he still competes in ski marathons, and three years ago he discovered kayaking. He now races regularly in Master's events, winning trophies over rowers twenty and thirty years his junior. And, of course, he keeps busy in the basement—now his own human performance laboratory—searching for ways to make his kayaks, and himself, go faster.

The best performers tend to do the same—treat what they do as if it were a hobby, or as if they were mad scientists. They have fun exploring the limits of their potential. This is a crucial point to recognize. Many people may have the urge to make masterpieces or to play in the major league or to run major corporations, but may never get there. There are no guarantees, and the greater your strivings, the tougher the competition. But that's why it's so critical to think like an artist. You never will be able to explore the limits of your potential without learning your trade, polishing your skills, and mastering your craft. That's the part that takes time. But you'll also fall short of your potential and fail to find your true calling if all you do is work on your game without devoting significant time to changing your attitude toward work and how you think while doing it. No matter what

level player you are, you can learn how to perform at your utmost—
and like an artist.

One of the first things I advise my clients to do is to spend more
time "messing around." By "messing around," I do not mean disap-
pearing for a few beers. What I want people to do is discover the fun
of engaging themselves in a difficult task and trying to figure it out,
trying to innovate. I want them to forget about the results, whether
the outcome is successful or not. The goal is to make your job seem
like your hobby, to make work more like play. How often have you
heard successful people say, "I can't believe someone is paying me to
do this!" That's the reason some engineers go into the lab on weekends to test out new ideas; why a CEO may have his assistant hold all
calls during the morning so he can read a new book that might spark
an idea, returning later to grapple with a tough problem, his mind refreshed.

Try to remember how loose you were in the early days when not so
much was riding on every game or decision. You might even want to
visit a school yard or playground to watch kids at play, taking note not
only of the children's joy but of their focus and concentration. It may
be "child's play," but those kids are serious. They are paying attention,
and any kid who is not is likely to be ejected from the game (a game,
not incidentally, that is usually completely made up). Many artists
have pointed to their ability to remain "childlike" as the secret to their
success. Just messing around with paints, they are able to re-create the
very world right before their eyes. Isn't that what most of science is—
messing around with different ways of seeing how the world works?
Einstein often pointed to his own childlike ability to ask simple questions about things that everyone else took for granted (like time and
space) as the only route toward scientific breakthroughs.

The first time Omar Vizquel went to his knees at shortstop was an
accident: Going for a ball to his right, he stumbled while trying to put
on the brakes, but still managed to grab the ball. After he threw out the
base runner, Omar had one of those "eureka!" moments more common
in stories about science than in baseball (where I suspect "eureka"

moments actually are more common than in science). His stumble actually made it easier to make the play by stopping his momentum from continuing in the opposite direction from where he had to throw. He began taking pregame fungoes, falling to his knees on purpose, perfecting the move; other "serious" shortstops at first considered his infield practice to be "goofing off." But they soon followed suit.

Art often depends on mistakes and serendipity. The British artist Francis Bacon said that his own best art was always a product of "accident":

> When I begin a new canvas I have a certain idea of what I want to do, but while I'm painting, suddenly, out of the painting itself, these forms and directions that I hadn't anticipated just appear. It is these that I call accidents.

Bacon was unwilling to ascribe such "accidents" to his unconscious, in some classically Freudian way. For him, the art came from a mixture of what he had in mind and what just happened as he brushed paint on the canvas. "There's always an element of control," he explained, "and an element of surprise." Most good athletes would nod their heads in agreement. They know what they are doing, but in the heat of the moment of performance, special things—surprises—can happen. They not only embrace these surprises; they go looking for them. When the best professional golfers hit a wildly errant shot into the woods, they don't berate themselves for an error; they stop to contemplate their "new" shot—a stroke that might come in handy for getting out of some future jam. A few days later when you see them on the practice range, are they working on their swing to prevent that bad shot? No, they're actually practicing making it happen again, perfecting their invention.

But what about a surgeon? Neither you nor I want a surgeon "messing around" during our operation. When you're undergoing heart bypass surgery you want someone very experienced at the kind of surgery you need, and definitely not someone experimenting with new techniques. If that doctor, however, only does the same procedures week after week, year after year, she is bound to get bored and fall into a "going through the motions" mindset—and that's when the biggest mistakes get made. Locked into doing things the "proper" way for so long, she'll also lack the capacity to handle unexpected problems that arise during surgery. The best surgeons, on the other hand, will limit the number of operations they do in a month or a quarter so that they can spend some time learning new techniques or devising their own—in the lab, of course, or with well-informed patients who are out of options and need experimental care. These are the surgeons who get up in the morning eager to get to work. The plodder will wake up one day, wondering why she isn't happy and wondering if there is any difference between her and an assembly-line drone.

A friend of a friend, Dr. Bruce McLucas, is a Los Angeles–based gynecologic surgeon who also is an avid runner. Running in a marathon several years ago, he began talking to a fellow marathoner, who happened to be a urologist, about an electronic cutting probe that surgeons in urology were using. "During the rest of the race," recalls Dr. McLucas, "I began thinking how I might adapt that cutting probe to the kind of surgery I was doing." He eventually came up with a redesign that he had tooled for gynecologic surgery, particularly removing fibroid tumors. Several years earlier, McLucas had put his practice on hold to study endoscopic techniques in which the surgeon makes a tiny incision in the abdomen and inserts a device with a small camera on it that peers inside the patient; the physician then makes a smaller hole through which he inserts his miniscule instruments and proceeds with the surgery, watching what he is doing on a video montior. In the 1990s, McLucas helped pioneer such techniques that have turned much of gynecologic surgery into outpatient procedures, avoiding the dangers of a major incision, not to mention saving patients, employers, and insurance companies the costs of long hospital stays. More recently, McLucas has worked with radiologists to devise an embolization process that blocks the blood supply to fibroids and shrinks them, avoiding fibroid surgery altogether.

That's artistic surgery. For McLucas, it's also fun on the job. "The hours that doctors put in with patients and research can be crushing," he notes. "But when you can actually get inside a human body that is malfunctioning and do something to fix it that no one has ever done before—that kind of thrill keeps you coming back for more and more." I suspect that everyone has had the same experience, whether in a hobby or a sport. One of the keys to becoming a top performer is to bring that kind of focus, delight, and creativity to your work.

"But messing around could get me fired," clients often say to me. It could. But it also could get you a promotion. And it certainly will save you from unhappiness, frustration, work-life angst, staleness, and burnout. You are unlikely to get better at what you do without pushing yourself, without taking some risks, and without making a *lot* of mistakes. And you are highly unlikely to become an overachiever by stubbornly staying at a job that prevents you from thinking artistically. In business, sales and deals get spun out in ways as unpredictable as a mark on one of Francis Bacon's canvases. And how many of the great scientific breakthroughs and revolutionary commercial products, not to mention leading corporations, evolved from serendipity? Penicillin was first discovered in mold. The Post-it was the result of a failed experiment to create a new "super" glue that bonded faster than anything on the market. Picasso was punished for being a poor student, so he started drawing when he was sent to solitary isolation in "the cell." Velcro was discovered when George de Mestral returned home from a stroll in the fields of his native Switzerland covered in cockleburs and couldn't get them off. Silly Putty was a product of World War II efforts to manufacture rubber: Senior GE staff chemist James Wright accidentally mixed boric acid into a silicone test tube. When he tossed out the disgusting result, it bounced back. Unable to find a practical use for the substance, GE chemists continued to play with it for the entire duration of the war, "because bouncing putty is a lot of fun."

The world is full of products and companies that produce them. But someone had to dream up those products and create those companies out of nothing, from a time when they *didn't* work or were unaccepted. Even money itself had to be invented—from the coinage of Ancient Greece to paper money some three hundred years ago, to credit cards of today, as well as more recent creative financial instruments such as the junk bond and mortgage-based securities. Does it take more imagination to create paper money or a junk bond than the coat hanger or paper clip or Mickey Mouse—or the jump shot? I'm not sure. But the one thing they all have in common is someone behind the process, an exceptional thinker enjoying all the failures as if they were works of art.

Conclusion: "Fallor Ergo Sum"

When I talk to students and clients about going after their dreams and the joys of being an exceptional thinker, inevitably somebody will say, "Okay, but what if I fail?" One of the assignments I enjoy giving most is to tell my students to find a videotape of a great game by Michael Jordan, or their favorite superstar. I recommend the NBA title game in 1993 against the Phoenix Suns, when Michael drained the winning basket in the final seconds to win the Bulls' third straight title. I advise my students to watch the game with a sheet of paper that they've divided into two columns—the first for noting every mistake Jordan makes, and the second for how he reacts to it. During this experiment, two revelations inevitably ensue:

1. "I never realized Michael Jordan made so many mistakes!" Virtually everyone says this, and that's because fans watch their superheroes with an eye on the things they're doing so well. Jordan did so many things so artistically that his fans never noticed the mistakes he made, and he made his share of bad passes and poor shots. When my students perform, conversely, they're only keying in on the ways they're performing poorly, or only the aspects of the game that are most difficult.

2. Jordan never reacted to his mistakes as if they were a problem. He would make a foolish play, and as soon as it was over, there he was with the ball again, his tongue hanging out, winking at somebody, looking to make a move toward the basket—classic Michael Jordan, as if he had just made the best play of the game. Students are amazed by this. Michael doesn't even seem to notice his mistake; he certainly doesn't look like someone who cares that he's done something wrong.

It comes as a shock to my students, most of whom have been raised on the idea that to perform well you need to be conscientious. They've just watched one of the great basketball players of all time play a great game—hitting a shot at the buzzer to win the NBA Championship—and the man does not appear to be anywhere near the most conscientious of souls.

If you really want to perform well, you can't be conscientious—it sends you into the Training Mindset; it prevents you from thinking like an artist. Indeed, to make a mistake and then worry about it or sit down and figure out what went wrong or spend the rest of the game—or your life—apologizing for it is the definition of the Training Mindset (and lack of confidence). You need to cultivate a Trusting Mindset, that is free of doubt, worry, or concern for mistakes; you need to cultivate MJ's tongue-hanging-out kind of response to errors.

Many of the performers I have worked with come to me concerned with perfection. Their business is so competitive and cutthroat that they feel any flaws or dips in performance could be career-enders. They pour their attention into trying to maintain spotless track records. Conservative business executives are particularly quick to calculate risks, and the prospect of pushing for a dream that might take ten years and jeopardize their financial future terrifies them. I usually reply, "What's wrong with going broke?" They look at me like I'm a madman. "If I waste all my time and money, I won't be able to support my family," they point out. "Seems like a pretty big problem to me." They aren't looking for all the potentially exciting solutions;

they're entrenched in a mythical philosophy, believing that financial security can't be regained if it is lost, or worse, that money buys freedom, happiness, a better life, etc. Abraham Lincoln went bankrupt. So did Rembrandt. Thomas Jefferson blew all his money and *then* created the University of Virginia. Harry Truman's two efforts to start a business both went bust, and the failure of the young George W. Bush's oil company indicated that he, too, needed a new dream.

Why do we look at failure, disappointment, and loss as the unthinkable, instead of regarding them as among life's most fundamental experiences? No one wants to go through life without feeling love or the thrill of accomplishment. Why go through life without feeling *all* of its emotions, including the downers? As psychologists are quick to point out, you can't enjoy bright days without the frame of reference of darker ones; success is meaningless without failure.

If you've never been discouraged in your life, I know one thing for sure about you—you're not a very big dreamer. For those of us who study high performance and success, the saddest thing we run into is the person whose ambitions are so low that they are never challenged. If you walk around making your decisions based on what will reduce your chance of feeling heartache, you won't do much at all in your life. Such people do not only deprive themselves of the chance for a more fulfilled life, they spend their days stepping out of the way of the very emotions that make us human.

What most people overlook about celebrity is that the more famous you are, the more glaring your mistakes are bound to be. Yet to achieve big things, you have to put yourself in the way of possible disaster; when catastrophe strikes, great performers stand back and enjoy it. When my students and clients express skepticism in the face of such a thought, I present them with one of my favorite horror stories in sports: the final game of the Final Four, Michigan vs. North Carolina for the 1993 NCAA basketball championship.

It was a great game, close from the start, and the lead changed back and forth, coming down to the wire. With eleven seconds remaining on the clock and his team down by only two, Chris Webber got the ball with a chance to win it. A mainstay of Michigan's "Fab

Five," a team that was on everyone's preseason list for winning the national championship, Webber was bound to be a top pick in the NBA Draft. Trouble was, he was now trapped in the corner, surrounded by UNC players, with no chance for a shot. Webber called time out, in a moment that stunned millions of viewers. Michigan had used up all its time outs; Webber's dumb decision cost his team a technical foul and the national championship.

Chris Webber had committed the cardinal sin of sports: He didn't trip or take a bad shot; he made a *mental mistake* that handed over the NCAA title to the Tar Heels of North Carolina. Webber was contrite after the game, but evidently not that contrite because the next day he was in line with his dad at the Department of Motor Vehicles to put in a request for a new license plate. The plates read NO TOS ("no time outs"). Webber had turned the biggest embarrassment of his life into a public announcement. When the press asked him what the deal was, Webber shrugged it off and explained that until the championship game, he had been just a good college player on a good team; but his screwup had turned him into a world-famous basketball player, and he was certain he would cash in on the notoriety.

Webber soon announced that he would leave college to enter the NBA draft. As the number-one pick of the Orlando Magic, Webber received a multimillion dollar professional contract, all thanks to the way he looked at failure. Most basketball fans today probably do not even know that Webber blew the NCAA Championship game, or if they do, it didn't cross their mind as they watched Webber finish fourth in 2001 NBA MVP voting, or start in the 2003 NBA All-Star game, or hit his ten thousandth career point.

Professional athletes must deal with losing more than most, and businesspeople can learn a lot from them about how to deal with failure. The best athletes understand that the pleasure of what they do—and often the glory—rests in the moments when they could fall flat on their faces. The risk of losing, even losing itself, can be an exhilarating experience. Do we remember World Series champions that cruised to easy five-run victories, or the goats of the game or surprise stars? Bill Buckner cost the Red Sox their first world championship in sixty-eight years when a weak hit bounced through his legs instead of into his glove; and Kirk Gibson hit one out of the park to win Game 2 of the '88 Series as a pinch hitter, despite an injury that made it difficult for him to even walk—two of the most unforgettable moments in sports, replete with life. Football fans still have a vivid memory of how the underdog New England Patriots won Super Bowl XXXVI in 2002. Even legendary football coach and commentator John Madden thought it was crazy to risk a turnover with under one minute to play and the entire length of field to drive; his advice was to take a time out and prepare for overtime. The Patriots went for it, charging into the St. Louis Rams defense, and as the clock clicked to 0:00, Adam Vinatieri launched a forty-eight-yard field goal for a 20–17 win.

Dazzling moves and performers taking a shot in the face of the toughest challenges is what thrills us—it's how records are broken and legends are born. There are hundreds of millions of people who choose the safe and easy path. Their work is not recorded in the pages of history.

You also must realize that great careers are not about one game, one deal, or one event of any kind, good or bad. High performance— it bears repeating—is not about results; it's about meeting pressure-packed challenges, doing your best, and enjoying it so much you do it again and again. Here, in the final chapter of the book, I also want to remind you that this is only the beginning of your career as a clutch player. Learning how to perform consistently at your best, picking up the habits of exceptional thinking, and switching into the Trusting Mindset routinely, are not going to happen from just reading a book. The self-improvement industry has much to answer for, but the thing that bothers me the most is the preposterous notion that by finishing a book or listening to some audiocassette, personal fulfillment or a successful career is yours. I believe that anyone can improve their performances and gain more satisfaction from what they do in life. But I also know it is a process that requires changing a lot of old thinking patterns and picking up the new ones that I have laid out in this book—and then practicing them a lot.

Becoming a routine overachiever—as awesome as the experience is—is not nirvana. High performance has nothing to do with the *perfect* performance. Studies have shown that successful entrepreneurs are likely to fall short at least six times before scoring big with one of their ideas. And even when you master high performance thinking, you will backslide and continue to make lots of mistakes. I don't care what line of work you are in, check out your heroes—read their memoirs, dig up magazine and TV profiles, Google them. I guarantee that in every one of their high-flying careers, you will find many low points.

In business, Lee Iacocca had to get fired from running the Ford Motor Company in order to be in a position to be hired to boost Chrysler from near oblivion (and then to write one of the bestselling books of all time to tell the story of this resurrection). The cofounder of Apple Computers, Steve Jobs, got squeezed out of the CEO's spot in 1985, only to be invited back to "Think Different" and save the company more than a decade later. "At Dell," Michael Dell has declared, "innovation is about taking risks and learning from failure." No one understands the role of failure in success better than engineers and research scientists. "The design of any device, machine, or system is fraught with failure," explains Henry Petroski, professor of civil engineering and history at Duke University. "Indeed, the way engineers achieve success in their designs is by imagining how they might fail." Petroski points out that most design is "defensive engineering," adding that "the perfect system is the stuff of science fiction, not of engineering." Once you realize that perfection is impossible, making a mistake is bound to seem nothing more than a slight detour to your objective, a kind of occupational "right of passage," but one that is essential for stretching your potential and reaching the top.

I am not suggesting that anyone take risks for the sake of taking risks, or be creative only for the sake of creativity. In business, however, the ability to "mess around" and the way you view failure are as valuable tools as any other you could possess. "I try to encourage creative solutions to real problems," says Esther Dyson, the famous IT consultant and early prophet of the computer age. "Innovation is good only if it's useful." She does not fear mistakes. "Everything I've learned, I've learned by making mistakes," says Dyson.

I wonder if Dyson is a basketball fan; her motto echoes one of John Wooden's guiding principles: *The team that makes the most mistakes wins*.

Samuel Beckett once declared that "to be an artist is to fail, as no other dare fail, and failure is his world." In a play written some thirty years before *Godot*, a character echoes Descartes's famous line *Cogito ergo sum* ("I think therefore I am") with what seems to be Beckett's own take on the reality of human existence (and art): *Fallor ergo sum* ("I fail therefore I am"). Or to borrow a line from another great artist, Michael Jordan: "I am successful because I fail."*

I mentioned earlier that Jordan does not rank number one in any NBA career statistic. I lied; Michael Jordan does hold one record: *He has missed more shots than any other player in basketball history*. And, as Jordan knows full well, it is because of that statistic that he is the greatest. It's the ultimate in exceptional thinking, to permit not even outright failure to get in the way of—in fact have it add to—the thrill of chasing after your dream.

*   *   *

So get out there and start practicing the performer's mindset. Get that dream clearly in sight, start thinking as weirdly as Yogi, be as committed and confident as Deion, Richard Branson, or Donald Trump, use pressure as your energy bar, and practice laserlike focus, like Tiger and Michael. And like all great performers in every field, learn how to get into the Trusting Mindset routinely. Above all, be an artist. You have nothing to lose but your mediocrity.

---

*A friend who knows Beckett's work better than I pointed to another remark by Beckett in an essay he wrote in French about two painters, the van Velde brothers: "L'art adore les sauts." ("Art adores leaps.") I suspect Beckett and Michael Jordan could have had an interesting discussion about success. I know they would have had a lot in common—more than most literary critics or sports writers would ever imagine.

A Call for Stories

I want to hear from you!

This book gives you the resource you need to become a consistent overachiever. But that's not actually the pinnacle of performance. The most exceptional thinker is the person who goes beyond self-application of the principles in these pages to helping others achieve a great mindset, day in and day out. Michael Jordan often commented that brimming with desire, confidence, and focus was a small accomplishment compared to generating the same level of thinking in his teammates and those around him.

So . . . share your story. Real-world illustrations, as you've seen throughout this book, make the best teaching tools. *Your* real-world example could be invaluable to others.

I'm in the process of compiling stories about people from all walks of life who've used this book to make a difference for themselves. I'm planning on pulling these stories together for a new book, and I invite you to be a part of it, to offer your experiences as an educational tool for future readers.

Here's how:

Step 1: Put this book to work. Take an assessment of your mental game, make some changes, and enjoy the results.

Step 2: Log on to the Web site I created especially for readers: www.overachievement.com
Use the supplementary tools, participate in live Q&A sessions, submit a question for me personally or contact me directly, or interact with other readers to swap tales and ideas.

Step 3: Follow the instructions online to submit your story for inclusion in a future work. You can opt for personal fame, or you can choose to remain anonymous—it's up to you. And best of all, it's a way to take your game to the next level that's totally FREE.

Index